Children's Atlas
of the Universe

Children's Atlas of the Universe

Conceived and produced by Weldon Owen Pty Limited
59–61 Victoria Street, McMahons Point, NSW 2060, Australia

WELDON OWEN GROUP
Chairman: John Owen

WELDON OWEN PTY LTD.
Chief Executive Officer: Sheena Coupe
Creative Director: Sue Burk
Senior Vice President, International Sales: Stuart Laurence
Vice President, Sales and New Business Development: Amy Kaneko
Vice President Sales: Asia and Latin America: Dawn Low
Administration Manager, International Sales: Kristine Ravn

Managing Editor: Jenni Bruce
Art Director: Clare Forte
Design Concept: John Bull
Jacket Design: John Bull
Picture Research: Jenny Mills

Production Manager: Todd Rechner
Production Coordinators: Lisa Conroy, Mike Crowton

Illustrators: Wildlife Art Ltd: David A. Hardy, Tom Connell, Luigi Gallant, Lee Gibbons, Sandra Pond
Star Charts: Wil Tirion

A catalog record for this book is available from the Library of Congress, Washington, DC.

ISBN: 978-1-74089-615-3

Color Reproduction by Chroma Graphics Pte Ltd, Singapore
Printed by Tien Wah Press Pte Ltd

Manufactured in Singapore

A WELDON OWEN PRODUCTION

Children's Atlas
of the Universe

Robert Burnham

WELDON OWEN

CONTENTS

How to Use This Atlas 6

Our Planetary Neighborhood 8

The Home Galaxy 10

The Cosmos 12

The First Observers 14

Models of the Universe 16

Great Leaps Forward 18

Astronomy from the Ground 20

Astronomy from Orbit 22

Visiting Space 24

Probing Space 26

OUR SOLAR SYSTEM

Our Solar System 28

The Planets 30

The Sun 32

Mercury 34

Venus 36

Earth 38

Earth and the Sun 40

The Moon 42

Earth and the Moon 44

Meteors and Meteorites 46

Mars 48

Asteroids 50

Jupiter 52

Saturn 54

Uranus 56

Neptune 58

Pluto 60

Comets 62

DEEP SPACE

Deep Space 64

Nebulas 66

Stars 68

Variable Stars 70

Supernovas 72

Other Solar Systems 74

Star Clusters 76

The Milky Way 78

Galaxies 80

The Local Group 82

Black Holes 84

The Universe 86

STARGAZING

Stargazing 88

Constellations 90

Using a Star Map 92

Winter Stars of the Northern Skies 94

Spring Stars of the Northern Skies 96

Summer Stars of the Northern Skies 98

Autumn Stars of the Northern Skies 100

Winter Stars of the Southern Skies 102

Spring Stars of the Southern Skies 104

Summer Stars of the Southern Skies 106

Autumn Stars of the Southern Skies 108

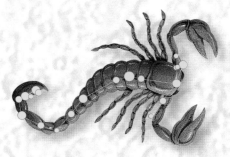

Universe Fact File 110

Glossary 122

Index 126

Acknowledgments 128

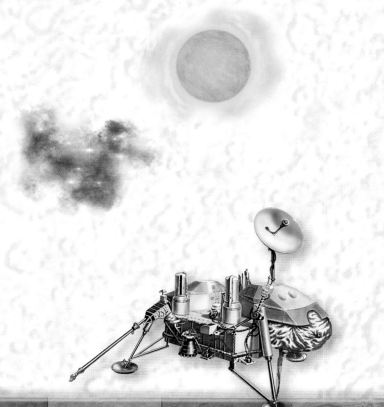

How to Use This Atlas

THE CHILDREN'S ATLAS OF THE UNIVERSE takes you on an exhilarating journey through space. You can prepare yourself for the tour by reading the introductory section (pages 8 to 27). This section begins by explaining how Earth fits into the universe and how the universe fits together. It then guides you through the history of astronomy, from prehistoric times to the present day, with all the latest information on satellite telescopes and space probes.

Visit Earth's neighbors in the Solar System section (pages 28 to 63). Featuring detailed maps and spectacular photographs, these pages describe the Sun and all the objects that orbit it—the eight planets, 143 moons, and many asteroids and comets.

The Deep Space section (pages 64 to 87) takes you beyond the Solar System to the realm of stars and galaxies. Here you will learn about dazzling star clusters, exploding supernovas, amazing black holes, and the mind-boggling birth of the universe.

Now it's time to explore space for yourself. The Stargazing section (pages 88 to 109) shows you how. It has 16 star maps to help you find the most rewarding sights in the night sky, whether you are using the naked eye, binoculars, or a telescope.

At the back of the atlas, the Universe Fact File (pages 110 to 121) includes an astronomy timeline and lists a wealth of data about planets, moons, asteroids, comets, meteors, eclipses, stars, and galaxies. Finally, the Glossary (pages 122 to 125) explains all the main terms used in this book, and the Index (pages 126 to 128) helps you to find any topics that especially interest you.

Stargazing Pages (88–109)

Seasonal Maps The heading tells you what time of year and what part of the world the star maps are for.

Amazing Fact This illustrated box contains a fascinating fact about an aspect of the topic.

Star Maps Each map shows half of the sky you will see, depending on whether you are looking north or south.

Our Solar System Pages (28–63)

Section Symbol This tells you which section of the book you are in.

Photographs The pages feature the latest photographs from space probes.

The Moon

THE MOON IS EARTH'S only natural satellite. It formed soon after Earth did, from the debris that flew out when another body slammed into Earth. As the Moon formed, it was constantly bombarded by meteorites. These punched countless craters into its surface, and big impacts dug broad basins. The scars can still be seen today. The youngest craters have rays, bright streaks of shattered rock flung across the landscape.

Dark lava (molten rock) flowed from under the surface to fill the lowlands and basins. Early astronomers thought these dark areas were the dried-up beds of oceans, so they called them maria, which means "seas" in Latin. In 1959, an early Soviet probe photographed the unseen farside of the Moon and found that nearly all the maria lie on the side facing Earth.

The Moon's gravity is one-sixth of Earth's. This is too weak to hold onto an atmosphere, so the lunar sky always looks black, even in daytime. The lack of an atmosphere also means that the Moon's surface becomes very hot (243°F or 117°C) when it is facing the Sun, and very cold (–243°F or –153°C) when it turns away.

In 1998, the Lunar Prospector spacecraft found ice at the Moon's poles. Since then, that finding has been debated, and several future missions to the Moon are planned to further explore its craters.

MAP OF THE MOON The nearside hemisphere is the side of the Moon that always faces Earth. The farside hemisphere was revealed only when probes first visited. The Moon has a small, hot core, a thick mantle, and a heavily cratered crust.

ON THE SURFACE From 1968 to 1972, six Apollo missions landed astronauts on the Moon and brought back rock samples. Here, astronaut James Irwin stands near the Apollo 15 lunar module and rover in 1971.

Key Facts List This provides the main facts about the object, such as its size, its distance from the Sun, and its length of day.

ORIGIN OF NAME
MONA, THE ANGLO-SAXON WORD FOR "MOON"
DISTANCE FROM EARTH
238,856 MILES (384,401 KM)
DIAMETER
2,160 MILES (3,476 KM)
MASS
1.2% × EARTH'S MASS
ATMOSPHERE
NONE
LENGTH OF DAY (in Earth days)
ROTATION TIME AND SOLAR DAY: BOTH 27.3

LUNAR ICE The Lunar Prospector spacecraft found ice (white) in craters at the Moon's south pole.

Project By trying out these activities and experiments, you can learn more about the topic.

· PROJECT: Drawing Moonlight ·

For this project, you need a piece of paper and a pencil.

① Draw 31 circles, arranged in lines, on a piece of paper. You can make them big or small, but all 31 should fit on the paper, neatly drawn to the same size. (Try tracing around a glass or a coin.)

② Write today's date next to the first circle and continue until all 31 circles have dates.

③ Find the Moon in the sky.

④ Draw what the Moon looks like. If clouds hide the Moon, leave the circle blank or mark it "clouds."

⑤ When you have made a week or two of observations, you will see a pattern developing. What you have drawn are the phases of the Moon (see page 44).

MARE MOSCOVIENSE (Sea of Moscow)

MARE INGENII (Sea of Cleverness)

HOW THE MOON FORMED The young Earth was struck by an object the size of Mars. The debris circled around Earth, then clumped together to form the Moon.

Summer Stars of the Southern Skies

LOOKING NORTH To explore the sky this evening, use the tall figure of Orion the Hunter, standing high in the north. Notice how the colors of the stars Betelgeuse (a cool, red star) and Rigel (a hot, blue one) differ. A row of three dimmer stars in the middle of Orion makes up the Hunter's belt. Extending the belt down to the left points to Taurus the Bull, with the ruddy star Aldebaran and the Hyades and Pleiades star clusters. Aldebaran forms the Bull's angry eye and the Hyades form his face. Extend Orion's belt up to the right and it points to Sirius, the sky's brightest star, in Canis Major, the Big Dog. From Sirius, a line down to the northeast horizon passes Procyon in Canis Minor, the Little Dog, then reaches Regulus in Leo the Lion. Below Orion, the yellow star Capella rises low in the north with Auriga the Charioteer. To its right stands Gemini the Twins, with the two bright stars Castor and Pollux. The highlight of Cancer the Crab is the Beehive star cluster, which can be seen just to the right of Pollux. This beautiful open cluster contains more than 200 stars and looks best through binoculars.

WHERE YOU CAN SEE THIS SKY FROM
SOUTHERN HEMISPHERE AREAS SUCH AS AUSTRALIA, NEW ZEALAND, SOUTH AMERICA, AND SOUTH AFRICA.
WHEN YOU CAN SEE THIS SKY BEST
JANUARY THROUGH MARCH
BEST NAKED-EYE SIGHTS
SIRIUS IN CANIS MAJOR, ORION THE HUNTER
BEST BINOCULAR SIGHTS
BEEHIVE STAR CLUSTER IN CANCER, PLEIADES AND HYADES STAR CLUSTERS IN TAURUS
BEST TELESCOPE SIGHTS
OPEN STAR CLUSTERS M35 IN GEMINI AND M41 IN CANIS MAJOR, CRAB NEBULA (M1) IN TAURUS, ORION NEBULA (M42) IN ORION

GEMINI THE TWINS Castor and Pollux, the two brightest stars in Gemini the Twins, were named after the twins in Greek mythology who hatched from an egg.

PLEIADES The Pleiades are sometimes called "the Seven Sisters," but most people can see only six stars by eye. Those with sharp eyesight may see nine stars.

· AMAZING FACT ·
Legend says the star Canopus was named for a famous navigator for the Greek king Menelaus. The star, used by sailors in the Mediterranean for centuries, is also used by rocket scientists today for guiding spacecraft.

MONOCEROS THE UNICORN The Unicorn was created in the early 1600s, using dim stars. It appears upside down on the star map below.

CRAB NEBULA (M1) The Crab nebula in Taurus is the expanding cloud of hot gas left by a star that was seen exploding in AD 1054.

Argonauts in their quest for the Golden Fleece, a ram's coat of gold kept in a dragon-guarded grove. Other parts of the *Argo* include Vela the Sails, Puppis the Stern, and Pyxis the Compass, all of which lie in the Milky Way. Rising in the southeast below Vela is tiny Crux, the Southern Cross. Centaurus the Centaur partly wraps around it. In the southwestern sky, you'll see a single bright star, Achernar. It marks the end of Eridanus the River, which begins at a point next to Rigel in Orion (see Looking North map, facing page). Look between Achernar and Canopus for a misty patch. This is the Large Magellanic Cloud (LMC), one of two satellite galaxies that orbit our own Milky Way galaxy. The other, the Small Magellanic Cloud (SMC), makes a triangle with Achernar and the Large Cloud.

COLUMBA THE DOVE The Dove, near the top of the map, was invented around 1600. It honors the biblical bird that Noah sent from the ark to look for land.

· LOOK AGAIN ·
• What happened in 1987 in the Large Magellanic Cloud?
• Where is "Octans" in tonight's sky?
• What is the Crab nebula?

BEST NAKED-EYE SIGHTS
CANOPUS IN CARINA, CRUX (THE SOUTHERN CROSS)
BEST BINOCULAR SIGHTS
LARGE MAGELLANIC CLOUD (LMC), SMALL MAGELLANIC CLOUD (SMC)
BEST TELESCOPE SIGHTS
JEWEL BOX STAR CLUSTER IN CRUX, GLOBULAR CLUSTER 47 TUCANAE (47 TUC) IN THE SMALL MAGELLANIC CLOUD (SMC), TARANTULA NEBULA IN THE LARGE MAGELLANIC CLOUD (LMC)

ETA CARINAE NEBULA ...stream once believed to circle the ancient world.

LARGE MAGELLANIC CLOUD (LMC) In 1987, astronomers saw a star explode in this small irregular galaxy. It was the first bright supernova seen since the telescope was invented about 400 years ago.

*D*EEP SPACE PAGES (64–87)

Main Image A powerful main image brings the topic alive. On the Star Clusters pages, the main image details the stars in a beautiful open cluster.

Cross-section A cross-section cone reveals the interior of the object.

Space Probe A space probe that has visited the object is featured in the top right-hand corner.

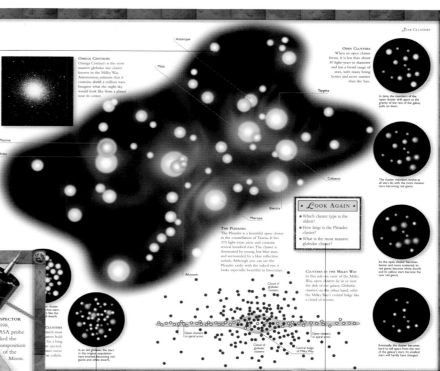

*S*tar Clusters

MOST STARS OCCUR IN GROUPS, which astronomers call associations or clusters. The group with the smallest number of stars is the stellar association. An association has up to a hundred young stars scattered across hundreds of light-years. The brightest members are hot, blue-white stars, each more massive than the Sun. Some associations, however, contain mostly smaller stars that are still forming. The bright stars of the constellation Perseus belong to three associations. No association is more than a few million years old.

Open clusters have many more stars than an association—several hundred to a thousand. They cluster in a much smaller space than an association—only tens of light-years instead of hundreds. Two open clusters near our Solar System are the Pleiades and Hyades. The Sun is also part of an open cluster, but the cluster is hard to identify because it is all around us. Some of our fellow cluster members are stars in the Big Dipper. Open clusters can be as much as 500 million years old.

The giants of the star-cluster kingdom are the globular clusters. They can have up to a million stars concentrated in a region smaller than that taken up by a hundred stars in an association. Stars in a globular cluster are old and well evolved, and include many red giants and white dwarfs. Because the red giants are so much brighter than white dwarfs, they are the most visible stars in a globular cluster.

STELLAR ASSOCIATIONS IN MILKY WAY	ABOUT 150 ARE KNOWN
SIZE OF THE LARGEST ASSOCIATION IN PERSEUS	LESS THAN 100 STARS, ABOUT 800 LIGHT-YEARS IN DIAMETER
OPEN CLUSTERS IN MILKY WAY	OVER 1,000 ARE KNOWN
SIZE OF PLEIADES OPEN CLUSTER	ABOUT 500 STARS, ABOUT 12 LIGHT-YEARS IN DIAMETER
GLOBULAR CLUSTERS IN MILKY WAY	ABOUT 150 ARE KNOWN

OMEGA CENTAURI
Omega Centauri is the most massive globular star cluster known in the Milky Way. Astronomers estimate that it contains about a million stars. Imagine what the night sky would look like from a planet near its center.

OPEN CLUSTERS
When an open cluster forms, it is less than about 30 light-years in diameter and has a broad range of stars, with many being hotter and more massive than the Sun.

In time, the members of the open cluster drift apart as the gravity of the rest of the galaxy pulls on them.

*L*OOK AGAIN
- Which cluster type is the oldest?
- How large is the Pleiades cluster?
- What is the most massive globular cluster?

As the open cluster becomes fainter and more scattered, its red giants become white dwarfs and its yellow stars become the new red giants.

THE PLEIADES
The Pleiades is a beautiful open cluster in the constellation of Taurus. It lies 375 light-years away and contains several hundred stars. The cluster is dominated by young, hot blue stars, and surrounded by a blue reflection nebula. Although you can see the Pleiades easily with the naked eye, it looks especially beautiful in binoculars.

CLUSTERS IN THE MILKY WAY
In this side-on view of the Milky Way, open clusters lie in or near the disk of the galaxy. Globular clusters, on the other hand, orbit the Milky Way's central bulge like a cloud of insects.

Diagram labels: Open clusters in spiral arms, Open clusters in spiral arms, Cloud of globular clusters, Central bulge of Milky Way

In an old globular, the stars in the original population have evolved, becoming red giants and white dwarfs.

Diagrams Clear, colorful diagrams help you to understand complex ideas about objects in deep space.

Look Again To answer these questions, you need to take a close look at the information on the pages.

MARE FRIGORIS (Sea of Cold)

Montes Jura · Plato · Aristoteles
SINUS IRIDUM (Bay of Rainbows)
Eudoxus · Hercules · Atlas
MARE IMBRIUM (Sea of Showers)
Cassini
Aristillus
Euler · Archimedes · Montes Caucasus
Timocharis · MARE SERENITATIS (Sea of Serenity)
APOLLO 15 LANDING SITE
Posidonius
Montes Apenninus · Montes Haemus · Cleomedes
Eratosthenes · MARE CRISIUM (Sea of Crises)
Macrobius
APOLLO 17 LANDING SITE
Kepler · Copernicus
OCEANUS PROCELLARUM (Ocean of Storms)
MARE TRANQUILLITATIS (Sea of Tranquility)
MARE FECUNDITATIS (Sea of Fertility)
APOLLO 11 LANDING SITE
APOLLO 12 LANDING SITE · APOLLO 14 LANDING SITE
Letronne · Ptolemaeus
MARE COGNITUM (Sea of Knowledge)
Gassendi · Alphonsus
APOLLO 16 LANDING SITE
Theophilus
MARE HUMORUM (Sea of Moisture) · MARE NUBIUM (Sea of Clouds)
Arzachel · Catharina
MARE NECTARIS (Sea of Nectar)
Purbach · Fracastorius
Pitatus · Deslandres · Piccolomini
Tycho
LOCATION
Nearside hemisphere

LUNAR PROSPECTOR
During 1998, this NASA probe studied the composition of the Moon.

Rocky crust
Rocky mantle
Molten zone
Core

LUNA 16
The Soviet Union's Luna 16 was the first spacecraft to collect Moon rocks automatically.

43

Map The surface features of the object are shown and labelled on the map.

Locator The object is colored to show its position in the Solar System.

*U*NIVERSE FACT FILE AND GLOSSARY (110–125)

Constellation Figures These show you how to see mythological figures in the stars of the major constellations.

Additional Illustrations These give you more information about the featured object.

Colored Border Each section of the atlas has a different colored border.

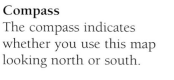

Compass The compass indicates whether you use this map looking north or south.

*K*EY TO SECTION SYMBOLS

| Introduction | Our Solar System | Deep Space | Stargazing | Fact File and Glossary |

Our Planetary Neighborhood

FOR MOST PEOPLE, Earth seems enormous, and life centers on nearby family and friends. Many live and work in an area only a dozen miles across. So it has been for thousands of years. The study of the stars and planets—astronomy—looks far beyond this familiar world and gives a very different view. Astronomy seeks to know where our Earth fits into the universe.

Like scouts standing on a high hill to survey the country ahead, astronomers have turned their telescopes on other worlds beyond Earth and have begun to study them. They have learned that the Sun is a star roughly 330,000 times more massive than Earth. They have concluded that Earth and other planets travel in orbits around the Sun, making part of a family called the Solar System. Most of the planets have "families" of their own. Earth has one moon that travels around it. Mars has two moons, and Saturn has at least 48 together with spectacular rings. Smaller bodies, including asteroids and comets, also travel in the Solar System. Asteroids are rocky or metallic mini-planets, some more than 300 miles (500 km) across. Comets, made of ice and dust, may be only a few miles in diameter, but they can have spectacular tails that stretch for millions of miles.

Until the mid-1900s, astronomers used physics and telescope observations to estimate the size of the Sun and the planets and their distance from each other. They learned, for example, that Earth is about 93 million miles (150 million km) from the Sun. They called that distance the astronomical unit (or AU) and used it to describe other Solar System distances. Today, radar and spacecraft visits provide much more precise figures. But all the figures show that the Solar System is vast.

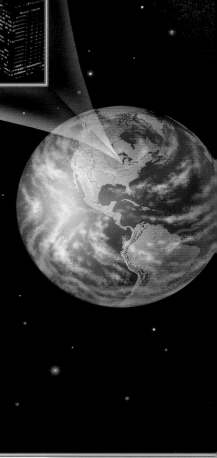

FROM CITIES TO THE SOLAR SYSTEM
A city can seem like a big place when you're walking along its streets, but it is tiny compared to the distances in the Solar System. Driving at 60 miles per hour (100 km/h), it would take you an hour or so to drive across Chicago, about 5½ months to drive to the Moon, and about 175 years to drive all the way to the Sun.

SCOPING OUT SPACE
Invented 400 years ago, the telescope magnifies our view of Earth's neighbors. Even with a small telescope, you can see the Moon's craters or Saturn's rings.

BRIGHT VISITORS
Comets spend most of their time in far parts of the Solar System, but they sometimes pass close to Earth and display spectacular tails. Comet Hyakutake was a beautiful sight in 1996.

✦ AMAZING FACT ✦

Earth travels around the Sun once every 365¼ days, covering a distance of about 584 million miles (940 million km) per year. This means that at this very moment Earth is speeding through space at more than 66,000 miles per hour (107,000 km/h).

OUR CRATERED NEIGHBOR
The Moon is the only one of Earth's neighbors that humans have visited in person. People had studied its surface with telescopes, but many questions about the Moon could be answered only when astronauts brought back lunar rock samples.

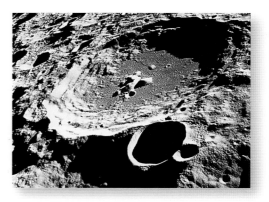

LANDING ON MARS
Spacecraft have told us much about the surface of Mars. In 1972, the Viking 2 revealed a rocky red desert, and in 2004, Spirit and Opportunity rovers landed to study water activity.

A CLEARER VIEW OF SATURN
Currently exploring Saturn, the Cassini-Huygens spacecraft will orbit the planet over 70 times to get a better picture of its rings, moons, and magnetic field.

3 Solar System
Earth is the third of eight planets that orbit the Sun. It travels at an average distance of 93 million miles (150 million km), or 1 AU. Mercury orbits at 0.4 AU, Mars at 1.5 AU, Jupiter at 5.2 AU, and Neptune at 30.1 AU.

2 Earth and Moon
The Moon is Earth's nearest celestial neighbor, but it is still far away by human standards. It orbits Earth at an average distance of 30 Earth diameters, or 238,856 miles (384,401 km).

The Home Galaxy

THE SUN IS ONE of 200 billion stars in the galaxy we call the Milky Way, and the whole Solar System is a tiny dot in the galaxy. Beyond the Solar System, astronomers measure distances in light-years—the distance light can travel in a year. At a rate of 186,000 miles per second (300,000 km/s), light travels about 6 trillion miles (10 trillion km) in a year. The main part of the Milky Way is a disk-shaped spiral of stars that orbits its center. The disk is about 100,000 light-years across and about 1,000 light-years thick.

Just as Earth is not in the center of the Solar System, the Sun is not at the center of the galaxy. It orbits about 33,000 light-years from the center, roughly two-thirds of the way to the Milky Way's edge. One trip of the Sun around the center takes about 226 million years.

Because light takes time to travel, when we see faraway things, we are looking back in time. For things close to us, our "now" is the same as the object's. But the farther away we look, the greater the difference between our present time and the time when the light left a distant body. The Moon is 1.3 light-seconds away, so we see it as it was 1.3 seconds ago. The nearest star system, Alpha Centauri, is 4.3 light-years away. We see this star system as it was 4.3 years ago. When we look at the far edge of the galaxy, we see it as it was about 80,000 years ago. An observer looking back at Earth would see our planet as it was 80,000 years ago, too!

1 Solar System
The Sun and its family of planets and moons seem vast to us, but the Solar System is a tiny speck in the millions of stars in the galaxy.

BEYOND THE SOLAR SYSTEM
When we step outside the Solar System, the vista grows much larger. While planets, moons, asteroids, and comets are the most common objects inside the Solar System, for the Milky Way and other galaxies, the major component is stars.

MEASURING DISTANCES
Astronomers can work out how far away a star is by measuring its parallax—the slight shift in the star's apparent position when it is viewed from opposite sides of Earth's orbit. The greater the shift, the closer the star is to Earth.

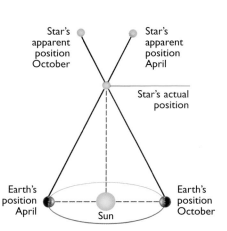

Star's apparent position October

Star's apparent position April

Star's actual position

Earth's position April

Sun

Earth's position October

◆ PROJECT: *Parallax* ◆

1 Hold up a pencil at arm's length in front of a bookcase or window. Close your left eye (or cover it with your free hand) and note where the pencil stands in front of the background.

2 Without moving the pencil or your head, close (or cover) your right eye and open your left. The pencil's apparent change in position is its parallax.

Astronomers determine the distance to nearby stars by measuring their parallax six months apart, when Earth has moved from one side of the Sun to the other (see diagram, above).

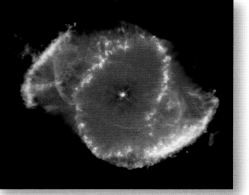

STAR BIRTH AND DEATH
The Milky Way galaxy contains many clouds of gas, which are known as nebulas. In some of these, such as the Rosette nebula (above), stars are being born. Other nebulas, such as NGC 6543 (right), formed when a star shed its outer layers at the end of its life.

STAR CLUSTER

The star cluster known as M22 is one of more than 100 globular star clusters that orbit the Milky Way like moons. Each cluster contains 100,000 to a million stars.

INTO THE HEART

The Very Large Array in New Mexico is a collection of 27 radio telescopes. It uses radio waves to peer through the Milky Way's dust and gas into its heart.

❸ Milky Way

The Milky Way's nearest neighbors are two small galaxies called the Large and Small Magellanic Clouds. The Large Cloud (upper right) lies about 180,000 light-years away, while the Small Cloud (lower right) is 210,000 light-years away. Astronomers believe that someday these galaxies will merge with the Milky Way.

❷ Spiral Arm of Milky Way

Radio telescopes have mapped the gas and dust in the Milky Way. These maps told astronomers that the Milky Way is a spiral galaxy and that the Sun lies near the edge of one of its spiral arms.

The Cosmos

IF THE SOLAR SYSTEM IS JUST a tiny dot in the crowded Milky Way, the galaxy itself is a mere speck drifting through the universe. Surrounding the Milky Way galaxy is the Local Group of about 35 galaxies, most of them small. The Local Group has a diameter of roughly 8 million light-years, but big as it is, this cluster of galaxies is not the whole universe. It is merely one group among many.

The word *cosmos* is Greek and means "the organization of everything." Astronomers who study the structure of the universe are called cosmologists. They use the largest and most sensitive telescopes because only these can detect the faint light coming from the farthest galaxies. Cosmologists have found that galaxies are the basic building blocks of the universe. Galaxies tend to form in groups, such as the Local Group. And these cluster into groups of groups. (For instance, the Local Group belongs to the Local Supercluster of galaxies.) And these superclusters in turn gather into groups of groups of groups.

Where does it end? No one knows for sure. Using a special space telescope, astronomers have detected the fading echo of the Big Bang, the event in which the universe began. This echo shows that in the very early days of the universe, there were no galaxies, no stars, no structures of any kind. Somehow the cosmos changed from this smooth state into one where groups of galaxies fill the universe. Exactly how that happened is still a mystery. Astronomers estimate that the Big Bang occurred about 13.7 billion years ago, which would make the edge of the universe 12 to 15 billion light-years away.

❶ Milky Way
Galaxies are the building blocks of the cosmos. The Milky Way is a spiral galaxy. Other galaxy types are ellipticals and irregulars.

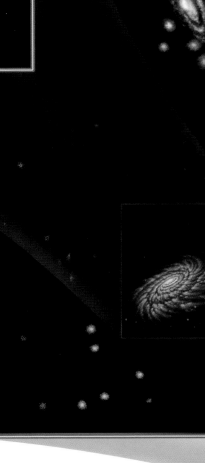

BEYOND THE MILKY WAY
Despite its size, the Milky Way galaxy is tiny compared to the rest of the universe. The distances are so vast that even the speed of light is a very small measuring stick. For example, light from the Andromeda galaxy (M31), a close neighbor, takes more than 2 million light-years to reach us.

◆ PROJECT: *Life in the Cosmos* ◆

Elsewhere in the Milky Way or even in other galaxies, there may be other planets that support life. No one knows for sure whether life exists on other worlds, but the chemistry that governs life appears to be the same all over the universe. Try inventing some alien life forms that could live on the planets listed below. Think about how big they would be, how they would breathe, how they would move around, and what they would eat and drink.

❶ A planet with very weak gravity.

❷ A planet with very strong gravity.

❸ A cold planet much farther from its star than Earth is from the Sun.

❹ A hot planet much closer to its star than Earth is to the Sun.

❺ A gaseous planet with no solid surface.

GALAXIES AND BLACK HOLES
The giant elliptical galaxy M87 sends out powerful radio signals. At its center, there is probably a black hole—an extremely dense object that cannot be seen but is sucking in gas from the galaxy.

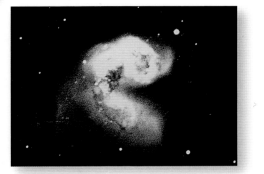

INTERACTING GALAXIES
The galaxies in a cluster of galaxies occasionally pass near one another or even collide. When this happens, few stars hit one another but both galaxies are pulled out of shape.

EDGE-ON GALAXY

The Sombrero galaxy belongs to the Virgo cluster of galaxies. We see the Sombrero almost edge-on. It has a large core and a line of dust running through the middle of its disk.

SATELLITE OBSERVATORY

Astronomers used the Infrared Space Observatory to investigate water clouds in distant galaxies and dust in the Coma cluster of galaxies.

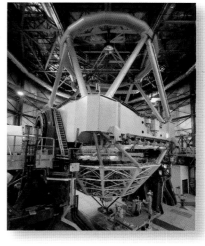

BIG TELESCOPE

The bigger the telescope, the more light it collects. Giant instruments such as the Very Large Telescope in Chile help astronomers study distant, faint galaxies.

❸ Cosmic Structure

Galaxies seem to appear in groups, and groups gather in larger clusters. Cosmologists are studying how such structures form and evolve.

❷ Local Group

With about 35 member galaxies, the Local Group is dominated by the Milky Way and two other large spiral galaxies—the Andromeda galaxy (M31), at upper left, and the Pinwheel galaxy (M33), at right. The rest are small galaxies, some of them resembling the Magellanic Clouds.

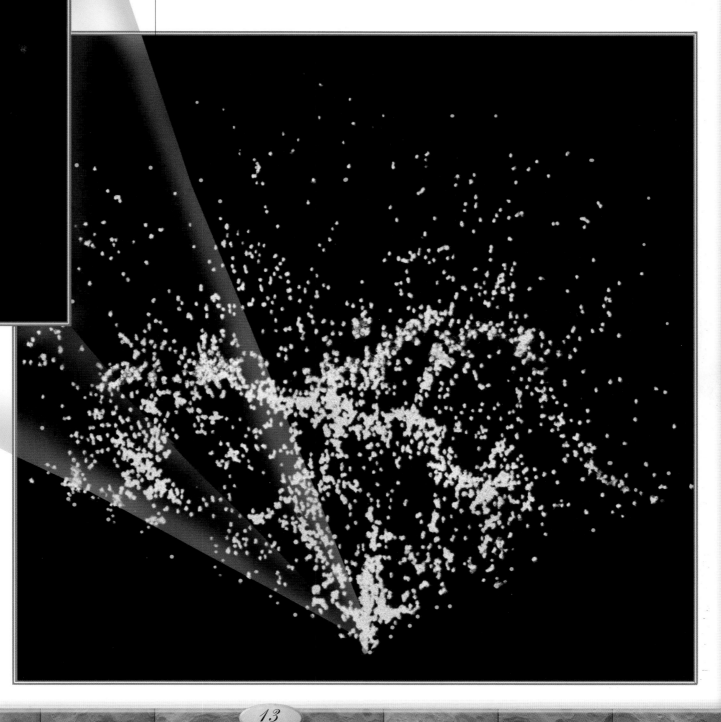

The First Observers

SKYWATCHING IS AS OLD AS HUMANITY itself. Prehistoric people used the heavens as both a clock and a calendar. Sunrise and sunset marked day and night, while the Moon's phases indicated a lunar month. The Sun rose in a slightly different place on the horizon each day, following a cycle that marked a year. People created sky stories to explain how the heavens controlled events on Earth, and saw the outlines of gods and monsters in the arrangement of the stars. They named constellations, the major star formations that appear at different times of year. We use many of these formations today. Some constellations are more than 5,000 years old.

Early astronomers worked without telescopes, relying on their eyes and a few simple instruments. In ancient Sumeria, Babylonia, and Egypt, astronomers recorded when stars rose and set and compiled lists of special events such as lunar and solar eclipses. They developed calendars so they would know when to plant their crops. These keen observers saw that every year the Sun appeared to travel through 12 constellations, which are now known as the zodiac. They also noticed that some stars within the zodiac moved, and they struggled to understand what they were seeing. Today we know that these moving stars are actually planets. The name comes from the Greek word meaning "wanderer."

Ancient Chinese astronomers figured out that the year was 365¼ days long. They also observed comets, eclipses, and exploding stars called supernovas. In the New World, the Maya of southern Mexico built temples that they used for astronomy. They developed a complex calendar based on the movements of the planet Venus. Later on, Venus was also important to the Aztecs of central Mexico. They saw it as a god symbolizing the power of life.

PLANET GODS

The ancient Greeks linked planets with the gods. The Romans adopted this system and gave the planets the Latin names we use today. Because Mercury was the swiftest planet, it was named for the gods' messenger.

BABYLONIAN ASTRONOMY

Astronomers in ancient Babylonia (present–day Iraq) recorded the movements of stars and planets on clay tablets more than 2,500 years ago.

◆ AMAZING FACT ◆

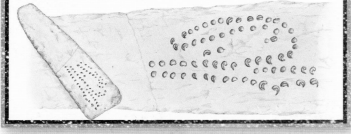

A 32,000-year-old piece of bone could be the oldest astronomical record in existence. Archeologists think markings on the bone might represent the phases of the Moon.

EARTH AT THE CENTER

In early models of the universe such as this, the Sun, Moon, and planets all revolved around Earth. Even today, we say the Sun "rises" and "sets," when in fact it is Earth that is moving. The animals and figures shown here mark the zodiac, the 12 constellations that lie close to the yearly path of the Sun in the sky.

EGYPTIAN CONSTELLATIONS
Constellation figures decorate the tomb of an Egyptian pharaoh. Egyptian astronomers tracked the rising and setting of bright stars like Sirius. They also divided the day and night into 12 periods each.

◆ LOOK AGAIN ◆

● Where do our planet names come from?
● How many constellations does the zodiac contain?
● What was Stonehenge used for?

SUN GOD
This is a Native American Sun god mask. The Sun's importance to life led many early cultures to make it their main god. A Moon goddess usually ruled the night.

STONEHENGE
Begun more than 4,000 years ago, England's Stonehenge helped astronomers observe the Sun and Moon. At the start of summer, they could see the Sun rise between its standing stones.

TAURUS
ARIES
PISCES
AQUARIUS
CAPRICORNUS
SAGITTARIUS

JUNE
MAY
APRIL
MARCH
FEBRUARY
JANUARY

SUN
MERCURY
MOON
JUPITER
THE STARS

◆ PROJECT: *Sun Movements*

For this project, you need a place where you can watch the Sun rising or setting on the horizon.

❶ Find a point facing east or west where a tree or pole lines up with a distant landmark such as a church steeple.

❷ Each clear morning or evening, at dawn or dusk, note where the Sun appears or disappears on the horizon. *Warning: The Sun can permanently damage your eyes, so only ever give the Sun a quick glance at sunrise or sunset and never look at the Sun if it is higher in the sky.*

❸ In about a week you will see changes. The Sun moves in one direction from late June to late December, then moves back again in the following six months.

Early people built monuments to follow the Sun's movements through the year.

Models of the Universe

THE ANCIENT GREEKS STRUGGLED to understand the universe. By the 300s BC, they had established that Earth itself is round. Most Greek astronomers believed that all the heavenly bodies revolved around Earth, but at least one—Aristarchus—thought that Earth revolved around the Sun. In the 100s BC, Hipparchus compiled a star catalog, invented magnitudes to compare star brightness, and calculated the Moon's distance from Earth. The most influential astronomer, Claudius Ptolemy, came along 300 years later. Ptolemy's model built on the work of Hipparchus and explained that all the heavenly bodies moved around Earth. It was accepted for more than a thousand years.

Nicolaus Copernicus (1473–1543) was the first modern astronomer to assert that Earth travels around the Sun. In the next hundred years, other astronomers gathered observations that supported the theory. Tycho Brahe (1546–1601) tried to combine Copernicus's ideas with Ptolemy's. Johannes Kepler (1571–1630), who worked with Tycho, formed the first accurate theory of how the planets move. Then Galileo Galilei (1564–1642) built the first astronomical telescope. He was the first human to see mountains on the Moon, and he discovered the phases of Venus and the four large moons of Jupiter.

Finally, Isaac Newton (1642–1727) proposed a theory that explained the mechanics of both the Solar System and the everyday world. Planets, including Earth, are held in their orbits by the gravity of the Sun. In the same way, the Moon is held by Earth's gravity. Using Newton's theory, astronomers could calculate the size and scale of the Solar System and accurately predict the movements of planets, moons, and comets.

CLAUDIUS PTOLEMY
The Earth-centered universe developed by Ptolemy lasted more than a thousand years. It was replaced by the Sun-centered model of Copernicus.

Ptolemy's model

◆ AMAZING FACT ◆

The great scientist Isaac Newton once saw an apple fall from a tree. This gave him the idea that the gravity that brought the apple to the ground might reach all the way to the Moon and keep it in orbit around Earth.

NICOLAUS COPERNICUS
Aware that his ideas would anger the Catholic Church, Copernicus published his Sun-centered model of the universe only when he was on his deathbed.

SUN AT THE CENTER
In the Copernican model, the Sun lies at the center of the Solar System and all the planets, including Earth, orbit it. When Copernicus published this model, no observations could prove it was right. Astronomical proof that Copernicus was correct didn't come until long after his death.

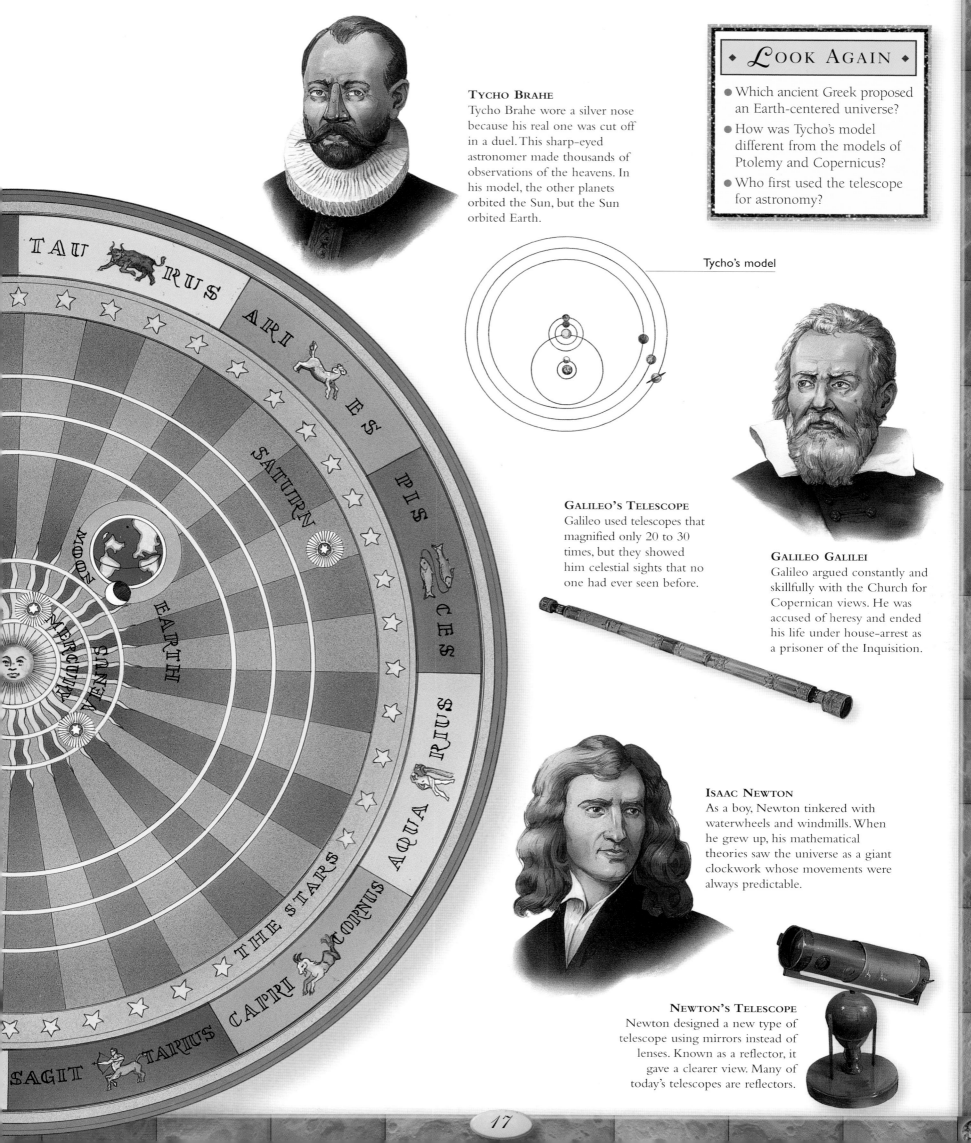

TYCHO BRAHE
Tycho Brahe wore a silver nose because his real one was cut off in a duel. This sharp-eyed astronomer made thousands of observations of the heavens. In his model, the other planets orbited the Sun, but the Sun orbited Earth.

Tycho's model

GALILEO'S TELESCOPE
Galileo used telescopes that magnified only 20 to 30 times, but they showed him celestial sights that no one had ever seen before.

GALILEO GALILEI
Galileo argued constantly and skillfully with the Church for Copernican views. He was accused of heresy and ended his life under house-arrest as a prisoner of the Inquisition.

ISAAC NEWTON
As a boy, Newton tinkered with waterwheels and windmills. When he grew up, his mathematical theories saw the universe as a giant clockwork whose movements were always predictable.

NEWTON'S TELESCOPE
Newton designed a new type of telescope using mirrors instead of lenses. Known as a reflector, it gave a clearer view. Many of today's telescopes are reflectors.

Great Leaps Forward

SINCE THE 1700S, NEW THEORIES and new technology have led to great leaps in our understanding of the universe. With Newton's mathematical tools, astronomers could calculate the orbits of planets, moons, and comets. Edmond Halley (1656–1742) confirmed Newton's "clockworks" by predicting that a particular comet would pass by Earth again. When it did return after Halley's death, it was named for him.

More powerful telescopes also led to discoveries. William Herschel (1738–1822) was a musician and amateur astronomer when he discovered the planet Uranus in 1781. He then became a full-time astronomer, building big telescopes that showed him many faint star clusters and nebulas. His goal was to understand the Milky Way galaxy and discover where the Sun lay within it.

In the 1850s, Robert Kirchoff (1824–87) and Robert Bunsen (1811–99) invented the spectroscope. In the decades that followed, this device showed that stars were balls of hot gases, while planets simply reflected sunlight. Some nebulas were found to be sheets of thin gas. Others were masses of stars. By 1900, the spectroscope had turned astronomers, who mainly studied stars' positions, into astrophysicists, who study what the universe is made of.

The 20th century has seen huge advances. Albert Einstein (1879–1955) became world famous after his theory of relativity was tested at a solar eclipse in 1919. His theories suggested the universe was expanding, a fact that astronomers such as Edwin Hubble (1889–1953) were discovering at about the same time. More recently, spacecraft have revealed details of the planets, while high-tech telescopes have provided clearer views of distant objects and shown us the universe in wavelengths invisible to the eye.

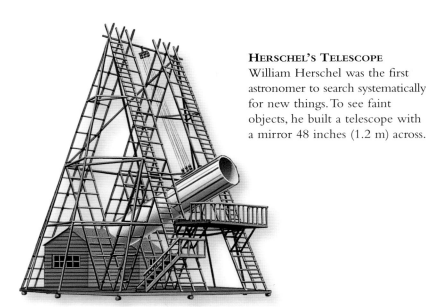

HERSCHEL'S TELESCOPE
William Herschel was the first astronomer to search systematically for new things. To see faint objects, he built a telescope with a mirror 48 inches (1.2 m) across.

ALBERT EINSTEIN
As they investigate the universe, astronomers now use Einstein's work daily. Computers calculate model stars and galaxies based on his theories. The models are then checked against telescope observations.

♦ AMAZING FACT ♦

The idea of black holes—objects whose gravity is so strong that light rays can't escape—was first proposed in the 1700s. But the idea was ignored until the 20th century because no astronomer could imagine how such a strange object could ever exist.

Slit helps the spectrograph to produce a clean spectrum

Lens makes the light entering the prism parallel

Light from star

Telescope

SPECTROSCOPE
A spectroscope can break light into the colors it is made up of. The result is called a spectrum. A spectrograph is a device that records this spectrum. Astronomers study a star's spectrum to learn about the chemical elements that make it shine. A spectrum can also show how fast a star, nebula, or galaxy is moving toward us or away from us.

SPIRAL GALAXY
In the early 1900s, astronomers argued about spiral-shaped objects like this. Some said it was a young Solar System, others that it was a galaxy with millions of stars. The second group was proved right, and it is now known as the Pinwheel galaxy (M33).

EDWIN HUBBLE
Hubble's discoveries revealed that spiral galaxies were immense collections of individual stars. He also showed that the universe was expanding and calculated its rate of expansion.

◆ PROJECT: *Splitting Light* ◆

For this project, you need a piece of cardboard, a straight glass filled with water, and a sheet of paper.

❶ Make a long, narrow slit in the piece of cardboard.

❷ Put the glass of water on the sheet of paper near a sunny window, with the piece of cardboard between the Sun and the glass.

As the Sun shines through the slit into the water, you can see sunlight break into the colors of its spectrum—just as a spectroscope splits the light from stars and planets into its spectral colors.

Prism splits light into its component colors

Photographic plate records spectrum of star

❶ No shift = galaxy at rest

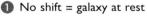
❷ Shift to the red = galaxy moving away from Earth

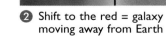
❸ Shift to the blue = galaxy approaching Earth

DOPPLER SHIFT
If a light source stays at about the same distance from Earth, its spectrum has characteristic lines (1). If the source is moving away from Earth, the light waves are longer and the spectrum lines shift toward the red (2). If the object is moving toward Earth, the waves are shorter and the lines shift toward the blue (3). This effect is named for its discoverer, Christian Doppler.

Astronomy from the Ground

MOST OBJECTS IN THE NIGHT SKY are faint and give off only dim beams of light. To make more discoveries, astronomers always need to collect more light. The answer lies in building ever-bigger telescopes. The first telescopes were refractors, but astronomers soon learned how to make much bigger telescopes using mirrors. In the 1700s, William Herschel built one with a mirror 48 inches (1.2 m) across (see page 18). It was a giant for its day and is impressive even now. Larger and larger telescopes followed. Completed in 1948, the 200-inch (5-m) Hale Telescope on Palomar Mountain in California was used to discover distant objects known as quasars. This was long the world's largest telescope, but today more than a dozen bigger telescopes exist.

It is hard for a telescope to get a clear view of the night sky. City lights wash out the stars, and Earth's atmosphere distorts the starlight passing through it, creating an effect like the shifting bright and dark bands on the bottom of a swimming pool. Most big telescopes are on remote mountaintops, far from cities and above the most distorting part of Earth's atmosphere.

Traditional telescopes are optical, which means they collect the kind of light that our eyes can see. Stars, planets, and galaxies also send out invisible radiation (see page 22). This includes radio waves, which are less affected by Earth's atmosphere and so can be studied from the ground. Radio waves are much longer than visible light waves, so radio telescopes must be much larger than optical telescopes. The antenna of the largest single radio telescope, the Arecibo in Puerto Rico, measures 1,000 feet (305 m) across. Astronomers can connect several radio telescopes together and make them work as a single instrument. This technique is called interferometry. It lets radio telescopes capture details more sharply than optical telescopes can.

MOUNTAINTOP VIEWS
An international array of telescopes, including the two Keck telescopes, covers the top of Hawaii's Mauna Kea mountain. With an altitude of 13,800 feet (4,200 m), it is the world's best astronomy site.

GIANT MIRRORS
Big telescope mirrors tend to sag under their own weight, so they need special designs. The mirror of the Vatican Telescope (shown here) has a very thin surface supported by a honeycomb of glass.

Keck II dome

Each Keck Telescope stands eight stories tall and weighs 300 tons (270 tonnes).

KECK TELESCOPES
The two Keck Telescopes on Mauna Kea are among the world's largest. Each dome contains a reflector telescope with a mirror nearly 400 inches (10 m) across. These two giant eyes can work independently or they can work together to provide a sharper view than either telescope could achieve alone.

As Earth turns, stars and galaxies rotate across the sky. The telescope is mounted on a moveable base so it can track their movement.

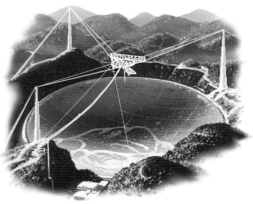

ARECIBO TELESCOPE
The enormous Arecibo Radio Telescope is set in a natural hollow on the island of Puerto Rico. It studies planets and stars, and also listens for radio signals that might come from extraterrestrial life.

Refractor

Reflector

REFLECTORS
Reflector telescopes collect light and produce images with mirrors. They can be built in giant sizes. Today, nearly all professional and most amateur telescopes are reflectors.

REFRACTORS
Refractor telescopes use lenses to collect light and form images. Lenses are expensive to make and cannot be any larger than 40 inches (1 m) in diameter.

The giant mirror that collects the light is not a single sheet of glass. It is made up of 36 individual hexagonal segments, each almost 6 feet (1.8 m) wide.

Keck I dome

Moveable shutter

Moveable shutter

Instrument assembly

Electronics workshop

Control room

Computer room

Mirror cleaning room

Machine workshop

Mirror storage barn

Computer room

In the control room, operators use computers to move and point the telescope. The light collected is sent through a suite of high-tech instruments, producing images and data for astronomers to analyze.

VERY LARGE ARRAY
Astronomers capture radio waves with giant dish antennas. The Very Large Array near Socorro, New Mexico, USA, has 27 antennas that can be linked to act like a single giant dish.

RADIO IMAGE
This radio image of Saturn was made with the Very Large Array. It has been colored according to temperature. The colors show that the planet (reddish orange) is much warmer than the rings around it (blue).

✦ LOOK AGAIN ✦
- Why do astronomers build bigger telescopes?
- What is the difference between a refractor and a reflector?
- Why do radio telescopes use such huge dish antennas?

Astronomy from Orbit

EVEN BEFORE THE FIRST artificial satellites were put into orbit in 1957, astronomers were planning ways to send up space observatories. They knew that they would be able to see deeper into space without the distortion of Earth's atmosphere, and they hoped to detect new kinds of signals that don't reach Earth's surface. The Orbiting Solar Observatory, launched in 1962, was the first of many astronomical satellites that have sent new information to astronomers on Earth.

Some space telescopes capture visible light, but many explore the other kinds of radiation that planets, stars, and galaxies give off. The full range of radiation is known as the electromagnetic spectrum. Radio and infrared radiation travel in longer waves than visible light, while ultraviolet, X-ray, and gamma-ray radiation have shorter waves.

The best known satellite observatory is the Hubble Space Telescope (HST). Launched in 1990, HST was the first of four Great Observatories created by the United States' National Aeronautics and Space Administration (NASA). Each Great Observatory is exploring one part of the electromagnetic spectrum. HST covers the visible part of the spectrum plus the ultraviolet and part of the infrared. On the short-wave side of visible light, the Chandra X-Ray Observatory and the Compton Gamma-Ray Observatory are designed to detect radiation from hot stars, supernova explosions, and colliding black holes. On the long-wave side of visible light, the Spitzer Space Telescope, launched in 2003, is studying the clouds of gas and dust that give birth to stars and other solar systems.

CHANDRA X-RAY OBSERVATORY
The Chandra Observatory is surveying the entire sky. It is looking for X-rays from objects such as distant exploding stars and merging clusters of galaxies.

HUBBLE SPACE TELESCOPE
The Hubble Space Telescope has studied almost everything in the universe, from the most distant known galaxies to minerals found around lunar craters. Astronauts visit from time to time to upgrade instruments and fix failing parts.

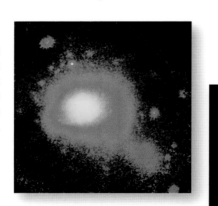

X-RAY GALAXIES
ROSAT, a German-built X-ray satellite, took images showing very hot gases surrounding two galaxies in the Coma galaxy cluster.

HUBBLE HOURGLASS
The Hubble Space Telescope captured this spectacular image of the Hourglass nebula. The nebula is made up of rings of glowing gas around a fading star.

ELECTROMAGNETIC SPECTRUM
The Sun shines most strongly in the visible part of the spectrum, but the universe gives off radiation with both longer and shorter waves. Because our atmosphere blocks most of these other signals, astronomers send telescopes into space to see them.

♦ AMAZING FACT ♦

A doctor's X-ray machine produces X-rays that travel through our skin and tissue but not through our bones. The X-rays that pass through can make a photographic image showing our bones. An X-ray telescope receives natural X-rays from outer space and can tell us about the objects that send out the rays. Some are gas clouds hotter than a million degrees.

RADIO WAVES

Radio telescopes

SPITZER SPACE TELESCOPE
This satellite observatory's mission is to study places where stars and planets are born. Such places give off radiation that falls mostly in the infrared region of the spectrum.

COMPTON GAMMA-RAY OBSERVATORY
This satellite detected radiation from mysterious gamma-ray bursts, which may be caused by the collision of two neutron stars or other violent explosions in the distant reaches of space.

INFRARED		ULTRAVIOLET	X-RAYS	GAMMA RAYS
SIRTF	HST	Ultraviolet satellite	Chandra	Compton
	VISIBLE			
	Ground observatory dome			

Visiting Space

PEOPLE DREAMED OF FLYING INTO SPACE for centuries, but the dream became a reality only in the late 1950s. Using rockets developed from the weapons of World War II, Soviet scientists sent the first satellite into space in 1957. In 1961, Soviet Yuri Gagarin became the first human to orbit Earth. Soon afterward, the United States announced a program called Apollo to send people to the Moon.

A trip to the Moon required a giant booster rocket and a complex mission plan. After several Apollo test flights around Earth, Apollo 8 took three astronauts to orbit the Moon in December 1968. They didn't land because the lander craft had not yet been built. More test flights followed. Then Apollo 11's Neil Armstrong and Buzz Aldrin landed on the lunar Sea of Tranquillity on July 20, 1969. Five more Apollo Moon landings followed, collecting hundreds of lunar rocks.

As Apollo ended in 1972, the United States was designing a new spaceship, the space shuttle. A shuttle can hold seven astronauts and orbit Earth for two weeks or more. Shuttles have been used for launching satellites and planet probes, but their main purpose is building the International Space Station.

A space station orbits Earth and can be occupied by people for long periods of time. The first space stations were launched in the early 1970s, but the most successful was the Russian Mir station, which was almost continuously occupied from 1986 to 1999. The International Space Station will use crews from many nations. They will study how to fly to Mars. Bases on the Moon and Mars are the next steps for humanity in space.

◆ PROJECT: *Moon Base* ◆

Construct a base on the Moon. You can use cardboard, old cartons, craft sticks, dirt, modeling clay, thin plastic sheets, aluminum foil, wire, paints, and glue. There's no particular recipe—use your imagination. But remember that a Moon base must have these things:

❶ Places for people to live, grow food, do scientific studies, and repair equipment.

❷ A radio antenna to communicate with Earth.

❸ Vehicles to carry astronauts on exploration trips.

❹ A rocket to bring astronauts back to Earth.

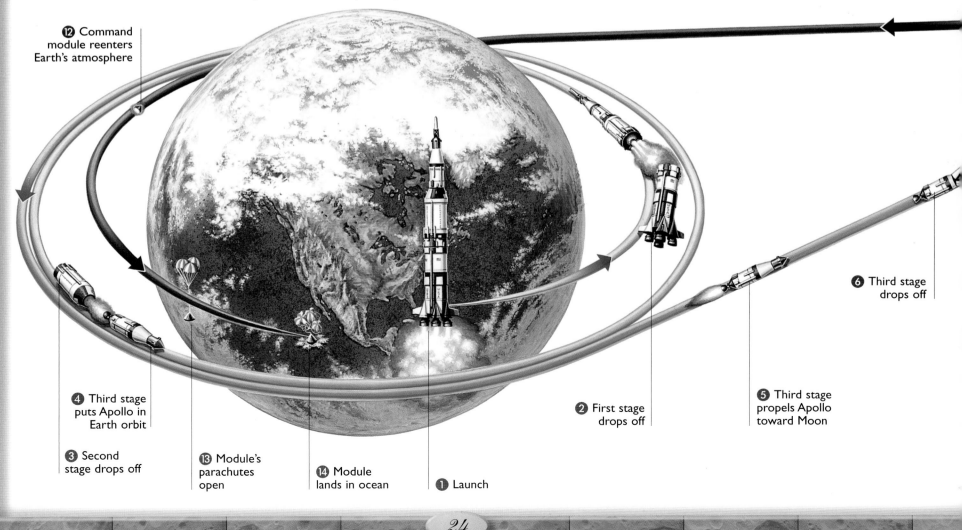

⓬ Command module reenters Earth's atmosphere

❹ Third stage puts Apollo in Earth orbit

❸ Second stage drops off

⓭ Module's parachutes open

⓮ Module lands in ocean

❶ Launch

❷ First stage drops off

❺ Third stage propels Apollo toward Moon

❻ Third stage drops off

ROVING THE MOON
This folding Moon buggy helped astronauts travel farther and collect more rock samples. It had four-wheel drive—and four-wheel steering!

FLOATING INSIDE MIR
The Russian space station Mir was cramped, but it taught crews—Russian, American, and many others—how to live and work in space.

SPACEWALKING
Construction workers in space need to leave their spacecraft to move big things around. Backpacks with small thrusters can turn an astronaut into a mini-spaceship.

INTERNATIONAL SPACE STATION
The station will include more than 100 components from 16 countries. When finished, it will be more than 100 yards (100 m) long and weigh more than 500 tons (450 tonnes).

7 Command and service modules stay in orbit while lunar module separates

11 Service module discarded

10 Lunar module discarded

9 Lunar module meets up with command and service modules

8 Lunar module lands on Moon

JOURNEY TO THE MOON
The Apollo spacecraft was launched by a powerful rocket, the Saturn 5. The rocket had three stages that propelled the craft and then dropped off, leaving the light Apollo craft to travel into space. Once Apollo reached the Moon, two astronauts landed in the lunar module, while a third orbited in the command and service modules.

SPACE SHUTTLE LAUNCH
Designed as "space trucks," the four space shuttles are the workhorses for assembling the International Space Station. The shuttles will need to make several dozen flights to build the station.

◆ AMAZING FACT ◆
It took Apollo astronauts three days to travel to the Moon (and three days to come back). But a trip to Mars would take at least six months each way—and you would have to stay on Mars for almost a year and a half, waiting for the planets to be lined up right for your return.

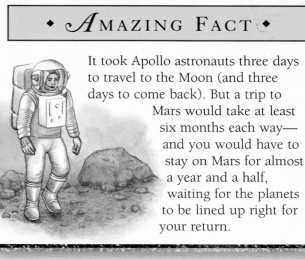

Probing Space

TO EXPLORE BEYOND THE MOON, scientists have relied on robot probes. These are cheaper and safer than manned spacecraft and can go places that people can't. Sending spacecraft to planets follows a time-tested pattern. Flyby spacecraft go first—these take photographs and collect data as they travel past the planet. They are followed by orbiters, which travel around the planet like a moon. And then come the landers, spacecraft that actually touch down on the planets. Each type of mission sends back information via radio waves that tells scientists and engineers about the conditions the next probe will meet.

Several missions have been launched from space shuttles, but most probes now leave Earth on rockets because they are cheaper. Probes often loop around the Solar System, flying past a number of planets before reaching their goal. For example, the Cassini probe goes past Venus (twice), Earth, and Jupiter before arriving at Saturn. The gravity of each planet speeds up the spacecraft and sends it onward—and scientists get a free flyby of three extra planets.

Every planet has been visited by at least one robot probe. Uranus and Neptune have had only a single flyby, but others have had many visits. Mars, for instance, has been visited with flybys, orbiters, landers, and a rover. Dwarf planet Pluto's turn is also being planned. The New Horizons mission is on its way to fly past Pluto and its moon Charon, then continue into the outer reaches of the Solar System to visit a comet.

Other missions either underway or planned include a close flyby of the Sun, rock sample returns from Mars, orbiters for Mercury and Neptune, a lander for Neptune's moon Triton, and an orbiter to look at Europa, a mysterious moon of Jupiter.

◆ PROJECT: *Aiming a Probe* ◆

Launching a spacecraft at a distant planet is extremely difficult. Both Earth and the planet are moving. It's much more difficult than threading a needle from across the room. To get some idea of what it's like, try this project:

1 Cut a ring out of cardboard, making a 10-inch (25-cm) hole in it.

2 Use a piece of string to hang the ring from the branch of a tree.

3 Take several steps back and try to toss wads of paper through the hole. A windy day just makes it more realistic!

1 Pathfinder lander separates from orbiter

2 Parachute opens, slowing the lander's descent

MARS PATHFINDER
The 1997 Mars Pathfinder mission tested a new way to land a spacecraft—airbags. Airbags don't contaminate rock samples with rocket exhaust. The Pathfinder lander carried a rover called Sojourner that spent three months exploring Mars's surface.

3 Airbags around lander inflate

FLYBY

Between 1979 and 1989, a flyby probe known as Voyager 2 visited the four gas-giant planets—Jupiter, Saturn, Uranus, and Neptune. As it flew past, the probe collected lots of data about each planet.

ENTRY PROBE

In 1995, the Galileo orbiter shot an entry probe into Jupiter's dense atmosphere. The probe sampled gases as it fell, radioing data to the orbiter.

LANDER

Between 1970 and 1982, ten Soviet Venera landers reached Venus's surface. The immense heat and pressure made each lander malfunction after a few minutes, but four of the landers managed to photograph their surroundings, showing gritty sand and slabs of volcanic rock.

ORBITER

The Cassini spacecraft arrived at Saturn in 2004 and will orbit the ringed planet for four years. It also dropped a lander probe onto Titan, Saturn's biggest moon.

COMET PROBE

The Stardust probe flew past comet Wild 2 and captured particles from its tail, bringing them back to Earth in 2006.

ROVER

Rover craft let scientists explore beyond the reach of a lander. Here Pathfinder's Sojourner rover examines the Martian boulder Yogi, about a yard (1 m) across.

◆ AMAZING FACT ◆

Voyager 1 is the most distant human-made object, at more than 6.9 billion miles (11 billion km) from Earth. Launched in 1977, it visited Jupiter and Saturn in 1979–80 and is now on the outer edge of the Solar System. Voyager 1 should keep sending back data until at least 2020.

4 Lander cocooned in airbags lands

5 Airbags deflate

6 Airbags retract and petals of lander open

7 Sojourner rover leaves lander and explores nearby

Our Solar System

AT THE CENTER of the Solar System is the enormous Sun, which makes up 99.9 percent of the Solar System's mass. Orbiting the Sun are the eight planets along with smaller bodies called asteroids and comets, all controlled by the Sun's powerful gravity. Just as planets orbit the Sun, most planets have at least one moon orbiting them. The four largest planets also have rings, Saturn's being the biggest and most famous.

The eight planets travel in the same direction almost on the same level, or plane. Their orbits are flattened circles called ellipses. If a planet had a perfectly circular orbit, the distance between the planet and the Sun would always be the same. In an elliptical orbit, the distance varies—Mars, for example, travels as far from the Sun as 155 million miles (249 million km) and as near as 129 million miles (207 million km). But planet orbits are still much more circular than the orbits of comets. Some comets have such elliptical orbits that they travel from the scorching zone around the Sun to an icy darkness halfway to the nearest stars.

Thousands of years ago, people tracked the motions of planets and comets with the unaided eye. When the telescope was invented 400 years ago, astronomers could start to study the details of the planets. Since about 1960, spacecraft have revealed many more features, including the red rocks of Mars, a giant storm on Neptune, and erupting volcanoes on Jupiter's moon Io. We used to think that ours was the only solar system, but scientists have recently found planets circling distant Sun-like stars. There may even be other planets like Earth.

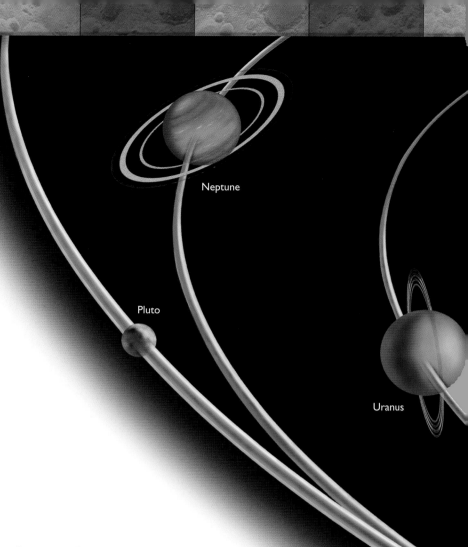

ORBITING PLANETS
Four small planets lie near the Sun, while four large ones orbit farther out. The tiny dwarf planet, Pluto, is usually farther from the Sun than Neptune is, but it has a more elliptical orbit that sometimes takes it closer than Neptune.

SOLAR SYSTEM STARS
JUST 1, WHICH WE CALL THE SUN

SOLAR SYSTEM PLANETS
8: MERCURY, VENUS, EARTH, MARS, JUPITER, SATURN, URANUS, NEPTUNE

SOLAR SYSTEM MOONS
143 MOONS FOUND SO FAR (5 ORBITING ASTEROIDS)

SOLAR SYSTEM ASTEROIDS
MILLIONS, BUT ONLY ABOUT 10,000 HAVE WELL-MAPPED ORBITS

SOLAR SYSTEM COMETS
ASTRONOMERS GUESS TRILLIONS

DISTANCE FROM THE SUN
The diagram shows each planet and dwarf planet Pluto, their average distance from the Sun, and part of the Sun itself, all to scale. Light from the Sun can reach us in only eight minutes, but takes four hours to travel out to Neptune.

◆ PROJECT: *Draw an Orbit* ◆

For this project, you need two push-pins, a pencil, letter-size (A4) paper, cardboard as big as the paper, and a length of light string or strong thread about a foot (30 cm) long.

❶ Tape the paper to the cardboard, then push the two pins into the middle of the paper about 5 inches (12 cm) apart.

❷ Tie the string ends to make a loop and place it over the two pins.

❸ With the pencil holding the loop taut as shown, trace an oval.

❹ Change the spacing of the pins to vary the shape of the oval.

The oval curve is called an ellipse, the path that planets and comets follow. The closer together the two pins are, the more the ellipse will look like a planet's orbit. When you put the pins farther apart, the ellipse becomes more elongated and comet-like.

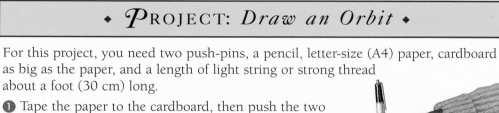

Mercury: 36 million miles (58 million km)

Venus: 67 million miles (108 million km)

Earth: 93 million miles (150 million km)

Mars: 142 million miles (228 million km)

Asteroid belt

Jupiter: 483 million miles (778 million km)

Saturn: 890 million miles (1,432 million km)

Uranus: 1,784 million miles (2,871 million km)

Trojan asteroids

Jupiter

Mars

Venus

Mercury

Asteroid belt

Earth

Saturn

Comet

DAY AND YEAR

The time a planet takes to make one trip around the Sun is called its year. A planet also rotates on its axis—an imaginary line through its center. One full rotation is the planet's time of rotation, or sidereal day. Earth's time of rotation is 23 hours and 56 minutes; its solar day—the time from noon one day to noon the next—is 24 hours.

1 revolution around
Sun = 1 year

1 rotation on
axis =
1 sidereal day

◆ AMAZING FACT ◆

Distances in the Solar System mean long journeys for space probes. It took the Lunar Prospector more than four days to reach the Moon. The Mars Pathfinder (shown at right) took seven months to get to Mars. And Voyager 2 traveled two years on its way to Jupiter, then another ten years to reach Neptune.

Neptune: 2,795 million miles
(4,498 million km)

Pluto: 3,675 million miles
(5,914 million km)

The Planets

THE PLANETS FALL INTO TWO MAIN GROUPS—small rocky worlds and large gas-rich ones. They are like this because of how they formed. About 4.6 billion years ago, the Sun and planets were born from a cloud of dust and gas. The thickest part of the cloud became the core and grew even thicker as it sucked in matter. This core, called the proto-Sun, grew hotter as it collapsed. Eventually nuclear reactions began inside it and it started to shine as a star—our Sun.

Meanwhile, the rest of the cloud settled into a disk called the solar nebula, which was slowly turning. The nebula was hot where it lay near the proto-Sun and icy cold at its edges. Particles in the nebula collided and stuck together, forming small bodies, which attracted more particles and grew larger. The bodies closest to the proto-Sun were too hot to hold much water or ice. They evolved into small, rocky planets—Mercury, Venus, Earth, and Mars. Farther from the Sun's heat, Jupiter, Saturn, Uranus, and Neptune formed. They are called gas giants because of their great size and because they are rich in hydrogen, helium, and other gases.

Between Mars and Jupiter is a band of asteroids—rocky or metallic fragments that never formed a planet. Finally, out where the Sun's heat barely reached, icy bodies took shape. These were small, very cold, and loaded with frozen water and some rocky elements. A few collided to form objects such as Pluto. Others became comets.

PLANETS KNOWN SINCE PREHISTORY
Mercury, Venus, Mars, Jupiter, Saturn

PLANETS RECENTLY DISCOVERED
Uranus   1781 by William Herschel
Neptune   1846 by Urbain Leverrier and J.C. Adams

PLANETS VISITED BY PROBES
All planets have been visited by at least one space probe.

PLANETS WITH MOONS
6 planets are orbited by moons: Earth, Mars, Jupiter, Saturn, Uranus, Neptune

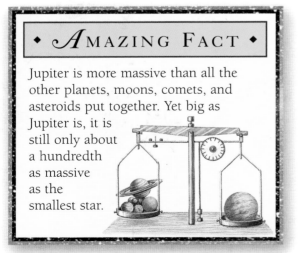

◆ AMAZING FACT ◆

Jupiter is more massive than all the other planets, moons, comets, and asteroids put together. Yet big as Jupiter is, it is still only about a hundredth as massive as the smallest star.

ROCKS AND GAS
Shown here to scale are all of the Sun's planets and Pluto. They divide naturally into two main types—small rocky planets like Earth and big gas-giant planets like Jupiter. (Tiny Pluto is something of a special case all by itself.) Each planet rotates at a particular angle around its axis, an imaginary line through the planet's center (indicated here by the small gray markers).

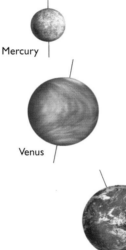

Mercury

Venus

Earth

Mars

THE ROCKY PLANETS
The four inner planets are made mostly of rock and are small compared to the gas-giant planets. Mercury is airless, but Venus, Earth, and Mars have relatively thin atmospheres that were mostly erupted from volcanoes.

Jupiter

❶ SOLAR SYSTEM BIRTH
The Solar System begins when a cloud of dust and gas collapses to form a dense core surrounded by a broad disk called the solar nebula.

❷ Proto-Sun Forms
The nebula's densest part quickly attracts dust and gas. It grows larger and hotter and becomes the proto-Sun.

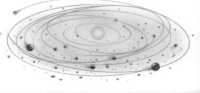

THE GAS GIANTS

The four gas-giant planets formed from icy and gaseous materials, the same sorts of materials that made up the Sun. These planets all have thick, deep atmospheres of hydrogen and helium.

Saturn

PLUTO

The little world of Pluto is unlike either the rocky planets or the gas giants. It probably formed from icy materials beyond Neptune's orbit. The gravity of the gas-giant planets then moved Pluto to its present orbit.

Pluto

Uranus

Neptune

◆ LOOK AGAIN ◆

- What are the two main kinds of planets?
- How many planets have been discovered in recent times?
- Which is the smallest planet? Which is the largest?

❸ Small Bodies Form
Particles stick together into fragments of rock and ice called planetesimals—the building blocks of planets.

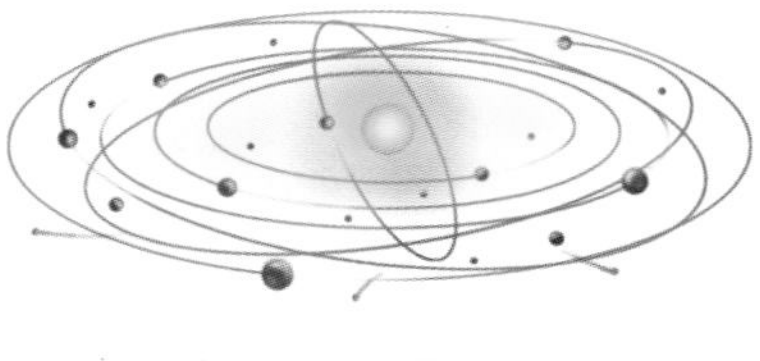

❹ Proto-planets Form
The planetesimals clump together, often in violent collisions, to form larger bodies called proto-planets.

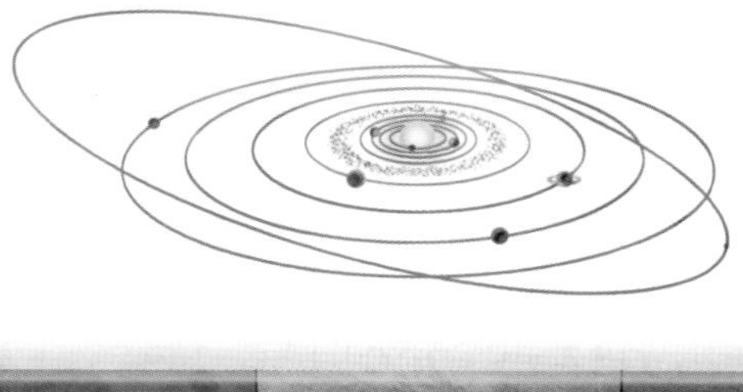

❺ Eight Planets Emerge
The Sun becomes a star, and its radiation blows away any leftover dusty gas, leaving behind eight planets and Pluto.

The Sun

To us, the most important object in our sky is the Sun. Its energy powers Earth's climate and supports life. Yet the Sun is an ordinary star like a billion others in the Milky Way galaxy.

Like other stars, the Sun is a huge ball of hot gas, mostly hydrogen (92.1 percent) and helium (7.8 percent). In its core, extremely high temperatures and pressures fuse hydrogen into helium. This nuclear fusion releases energy that slowly travels to the surface and makes the Sun shine.

The Sun's heat and light make it dangerous to look at, so astronomers use telescopes fitted with special filters to study its surface, which is known as the photosphere. They can see that the photosphere is split into granules, cells formed by currents of gas rising from inside the Sun. Small dark regions known as sunspots come and go, and giant loops of gas called prominences leap from the surface. Occasionally, part of the photosphere erupts in a solar flare, one of nature's most powerful explosions.

The Sun's life is not quite half over, with about 7 billion years to go. Eventually, our star will run out of hydrogen to turn into helium. It will first swell to become a red giant star and then shed its outer layers, leaving behind a tiny hot star called a white dwarf (see page 68).

ORIGIN OF NAME
Sunne, the Anglo-Saxon word for "Sun"

DIAMETER
865,000 miles (1,392,000 km)

MASS
332,946 x Earth's mass

SURFACE TEMPERATURE
9,900°F (5,500°C)

CORE TEMPERATURE
27,900,000°F (15,500,000°C)

TIME OF ROTATION
25 Earth days at equator, 34 Earth days near poles

◆ Look Again ◆

- How much longer does the Sun have to live?
- How long does it take energy from the Sun's core to reach the surface?
- Why are sunspots dark?

MAP OF THE SUN
The photosphere's sunspots and prominences appear and vanish over time. Beneath the photosphere, energy from the core trickles out through the radiative zone, then moves in currents through the convective zone, like water boiling in a pot. The energy takes 200,000 years to travel from core to surface.

CORONA
The Sun's corona is a dim halo of superhot gas. Because it is faint compared to the rest of the Sun, it can be seen clearly only when the Sun is completely hidden by the Moon during a total solar eclipse.

◆ Amazing Fact ◆

The Sun rings like a bell! Sound waves bounce around inside the Sun every several minutes. These waves are too low frequency for humans to hear, but astronomers use special devices to analyze them. This "ringing" helps astronomers study the Sun's structure.

LOOPS OF GAS
The Sun's powerful magnetic fields bend and twist gas near the surface into loops. If the magnetic lines break, gas sprays out into space.

SOLAR FLARE
Solar flares erupt mainly when there are many sunspots on the Sun. The enormous energy a flare releases can disrupt communications and cause electric power blackouts on Earth.

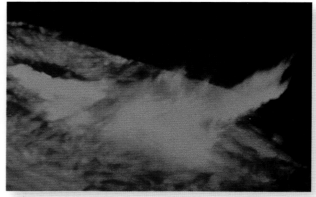

SUNSPOT CYCLE
The number of sunspots waxes and wanes every 11 years. As the spots increase, they occur closer to the solar equator. As the last spots of one cycle fade, the first of a new cycle appear.

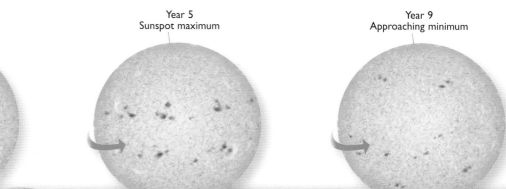

Year 1
Sunspot minimum

Year 5
Sunspot maximum

Year 9
Approaching minimum

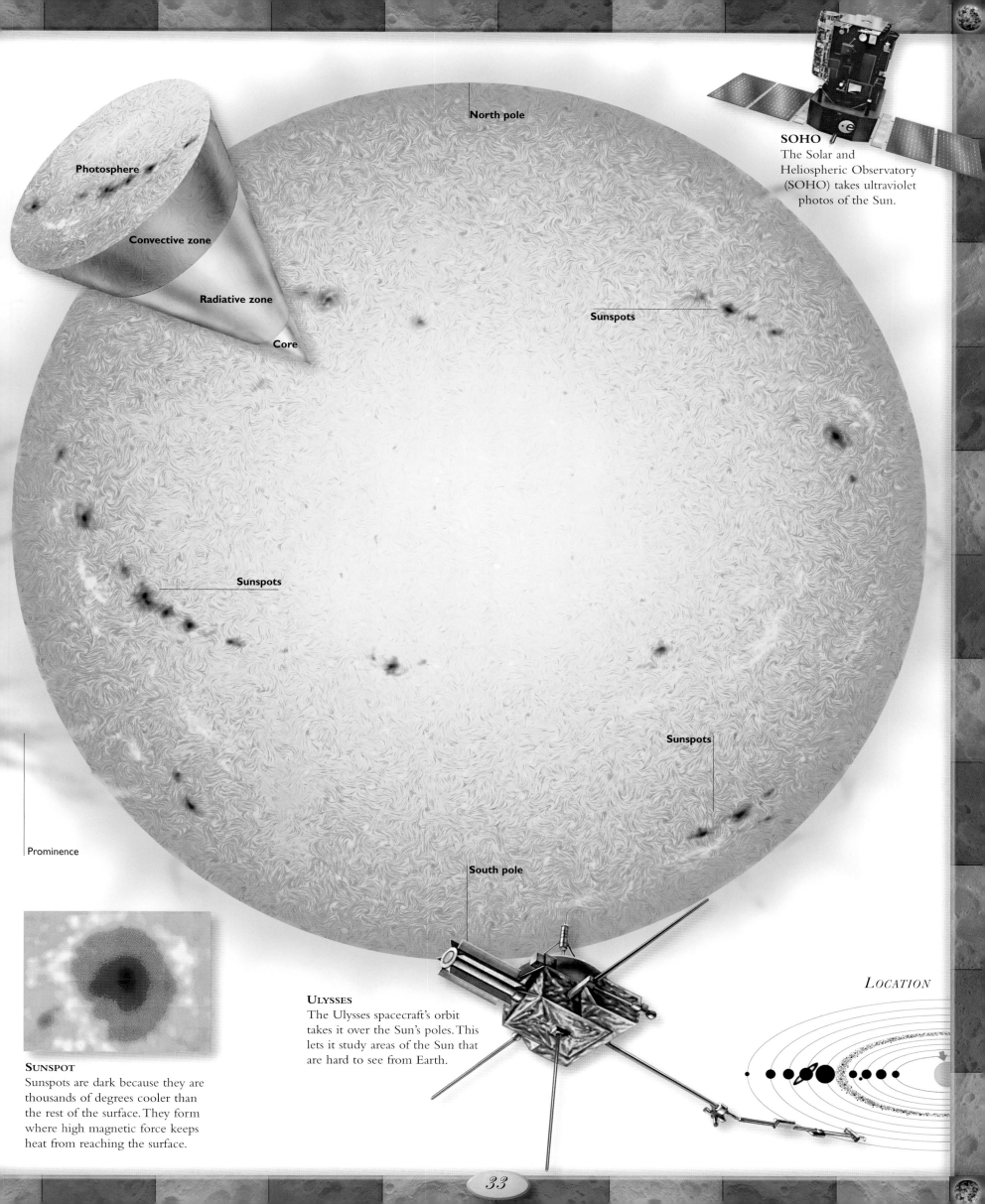

Photosphere

Convective zone

Radiative zone

Core

North pole

Sunspots

Sunspots

Sunspots

Prominence

South pole

SOHO
The Solar and
Heliospheric Observatory
(SOHO) takes ultraviolet
photos of the Sun.

SUNSPOT
Sunspots are dark because they are
thousands of degrees cooler than
the rest of the surface. They form
where high magnetic force keeps
heat from reaching the surface.

ULYSSES
The Ulysses spacecraft's orbit
takes it over the Sun's poles. This
lets it study areas of the Sun that
are hard to see from Earth.

LOCATION

Mercury

MERCURY IS THE CLOSEST planet to the Sun. This makes it hard to see from Earth because it always lies near the Sun's glare. It also makes Mercury's sunny side very hot—temperatures can reach 873°F (467°C), but since there is little atmosphere to trap the Sun's energy, they plunge to −274°F (−170°C) on its night side. At the planet's north and south poles, some craters are always in shadow and may contain patches of underground ice. If so, the water probably came from collisions with icy comets.

In 1974–75, photos from the Mariner 10 spacecraft showed that Mercury's surface looks like the Moon (see page 43). It is covered with craters and basins—the scars of impacts. The biggest basin, Caloris, is 800 miles (1,300 km) across. But Mercury is not just a bigger version of the Moon. It has a huge iron core, which is probably the source of Mercury's magnetic field. Mysteriously, this field is only a hundredth as strong as Earth's.

Mercury's year—one orbit of the Sun—is only 88 Earth days long, but its day—one rotation on its axis—lasts 59 Earth days. This means that an astronaut on the planet's surface would see sunrise occur once every 176 Earth days.

ORIGIN OF NAME
MERCURIUS, THE ROMAN MESSENGER OF THE GODS

DISTANCE FROM THE SUN
36 MILLION MILES (58 MILLION KM)

DIAMETER
3,029 MILES (4,875 KM)

MASS
55% X EARTH'S MASS

ATMOSPHERE
NONE

MOONS
NONE

LENGTH OF DAY (in Earth days)
ROTATION TIME: 59 / SOLAR DAY: 176

LENGTH OF YEAR
88 EARTH DAYS

MAP OF MERCURY
Mercury's cratered surface was mapped by the Mariner 10 spacecraft. Because of its flight path, Mariner mapped only half the planet. The Messenger spacecraft is on its way to Mercury and will begin orbiting the planet in 2011 to further explore its surface.

CRATERS AND LAVA FLOWS
Thousands and thousands of impact craters cover Mercury, but between the craters lies a surface built by flows of lava (molten rock). In this photo, you can see fractures in the surface.

Rocky crust

Rocky mantle

CALORIS BASIN
(behind cross-section cone)

TIR PLANITIA

◄ Fet

LONG DAY, SHORT YEAR
During its year of 88 Earth days, Mercury turns on its axis one and a half times. The marker on its surface shows that it completes only half of a solar day in this time. A full solar day from noon to noon lasts 176 Earth days!

Year begins

Rotation begins

Rotation ends

A GIANT IMPACT
The Caloris Basin formed when a huge object slammed into Mercury. The impact sent such powerful shock waves through the iron core that it created hills 3,000 miles (almost 5,000 km) away on the other side of the planet.

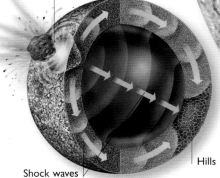

Caloris Basin impact

Hills

Shock waves

• PROJECT: *Making Craters* •

For this project, you need a baking pan, flour and water, and a few round objects of different sizes such as a ball bearing, a marble, and a golf ball. Do this project outdoors—it can get a little messy.

❶ Mix the flour with water until it is soft, but not runny.

❷ Fill a baking pan nearly to the top with the flour mixture.

❸ Put the pan on the ground.

❹ Stand over the pan and drop objects into the mixture from various heights. Remove them carefully after each impact, leaving the crater.

❺ Try dropping a larger object from a low height, then throwing a smaller one from the same height at higher speed. Which makes a bigger crater?

• AMAZING FACT •

Mercury has wrinkles! After the planet formed and cooled, its core shrank. The crust buckled, pushing up giant wrinkles of rock called scarps.

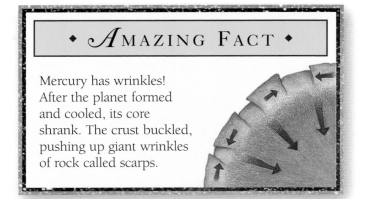

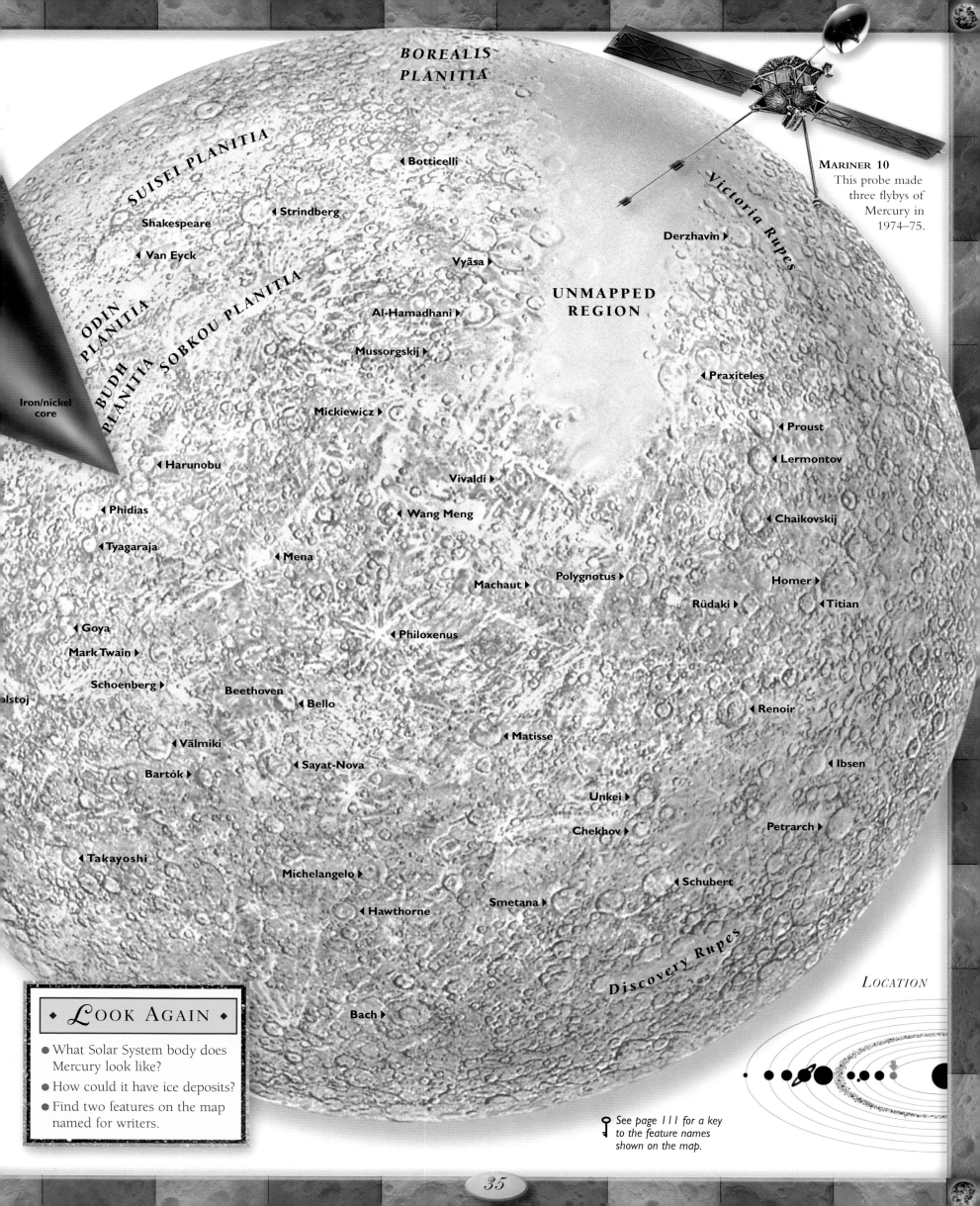

BOREALIS
PLANITIA

SUISEI PLANITIA

◄ Botticelli

Shakespeare

◄ Strindberg

◄ Van Eyck

Vyãsa ►

ODIN
PLANITIA

Al-Hamadhani ►

UNMAPPED
REGION

Victoria Rupes

Derzhavin ►

BUDH
PLANITIA

SOBKOU PLANITIA

Mussorgskij ►

◄ Praxiteles

Iron/nickel
core

Mickiewicz ►

◄ Proust

◄ Harunobu

Vivaldi ►

◄ Lermontov

◄ Phidias

◄ Wang Meng

◄ Chaikovskij

◄ Tyagaraja

◄ Mena

Polygnotus ►

Homer ►

Machaut ►

Rüdaki ►

◄ Titian

◄ Goya

◄ Philoxenus

Mark Twain ►

Schoenberg ►

Beethoven

◄ Renoir

olstoj

◄ Bello

◄ Matisse

◄ Vãlmiki

◄ Ibsen

Bartók ►

◄ Sayat-Nova

Unkei ►

Chekhov ►

Petrarch ►

◄ Takayoshi

◄ Schubert

Michelangelo ►

Smetana ►

◄ Hawthorne

Discovery Rupes

LOCATION

◆ **𝓛OOK AGAIN** ◆

Bach ►

● What Solar System body does
Mercury look like?

● How could it have ice deposits?

● Find two features on the map
named for writers.

MARINER 10
This probe made
three flybys of
Mercury in
1974–75.

⚲ See page 111 for a key
to the feature names
shown on the map.

Venus

VENUS IS THE SECOND PLANET from the Sun, and the one most like Earth in size. We often see Venus looking like a bright star in the morning or evening sky. The brightness comes from sunlight reflected off a layer of white sulfuric acid clouds about 30 to 40 miles (50 to 70 km) above the planet's surface. Venus has a dense atmosphere—it is mostly carbon dioxide and presses down nearly 100 times more heavily than Earth's. The thick gases let sunlight through, but block outgoing heat. This greenhouse effect has given Venus the Solar System's hottest surface, with a temperature of 880°F (470°C).

Between 1978 and 1994, the Pioneer, Venera, and Magellan spacecraft used radar to map Venus's surface. Volcanoes and lava flows dominate the landscape, but there are only about a thousand impact craters, far fewer than on Mercury. Lava flows from volcanoes and cracks in the surface have repaved the planet, covering up early craters. Some scientists think Venus may even have volcanoes that still erupt.

Two unexplained oddities are that Venus takes longer to rotate once on its axis than it does to travel once around the Sun, and that it rotates backward compared to Earth.

ORIGIN OF NAME	VENUS, THE ROMAN GODDESS OF BEAUTY
DISTANCE FROM THE SUN	67 MILLION MILES (108 MILLION KM)
DIAMETER	7,521 MILES (12,104 KM)
MASS	82% x EARTH'S MASS
ATMOSPHERE	CARBON DIOXIDE, 96 TIMES DENSER THAN EARTH'S AIR
MOONS	NONE
LENGTH OF DAY (in Earth days)	ROTATION TIME: 243 / SOLAR DAY: 117
LENGTH OF YEAR	225 EARTH DAYS

BRIGHT CLOUDS
Sulfuric acid clouds show up as swirls in this ultraviolet photo. The clouds race around the planet every four days.

PROJECT: Jam-Jar Greenhouse

For this project, you need an outdoor thermometer, a glass jar with a lid, and a sunny day.

❶ Place the jar outside in the sunshine with its mouth up and the lid off. Put the thermometer inside with the bulb pointing down.

❷ Wait a few minutes for the temperature to stop rising, then make a note of the temperature.

❸ Now put the thermometer inside the jar with the bulb pointing up. Screw on the lid, and place the jar back in the sunshine with the lid down.

❹ Again wait for the temperature to stabilize. Has the temperature changed?

What you have done is to create a mini-greenhouse effect. Trapped by the lid of the jar, sun-warmed air cannot escape and it grows hotter.

MAP OF VENUS
Spacecraft have mapped all of Venus's surface, revealing mountain ranges, volcanoes, and lava flows. Most of these features have been named for women. Venus lacks the moving crustal plates that join and divide Earth's landmasses.

Rocky crust

Rocky mantle

VENUSIAN VOLCANOES
Volcanoes are common on Venus and many impact craters show signs of flooding by lava. This image created from Magellan data shows Maat Mons, a volcano 5 miles (8 km) high.

Ovda Regio

XUDRA PLANITIA

APHRODI

ISHTAR TERRA

Lakshmi Planum

Cleopatra

Tellus Tessera

Beta Regio

GUINEVERE PLANITIA

Maxwell Montes

Devana Chasma

Sappho Patera

Pavlova Corona

Eistla Regio

NAVKA PLANITIA

Heng-o Corona

TINATIN PLANITIA

APHRODITE TERRA

Phoebe Regio

AINO PLANITIA

Dione Regio

Alpha Regio

Hathor Mons

Innini Mons

Eve Corona

Alpha Regio hemisphere

Clouds reflect much of Sun's energy

Some solar energy passes through clouds and heats surface

GREENHOUSE EFFECT
Venus suffers from a runaway greenhouse effect. Strong sunlight filters through the clouds and heats the surface, but the clouds and carbon dioxide in the atmosphere keep the heat from escaping back into space. Venus just cannot cool down.

Carbon dioxide keeps heat from escaping into space

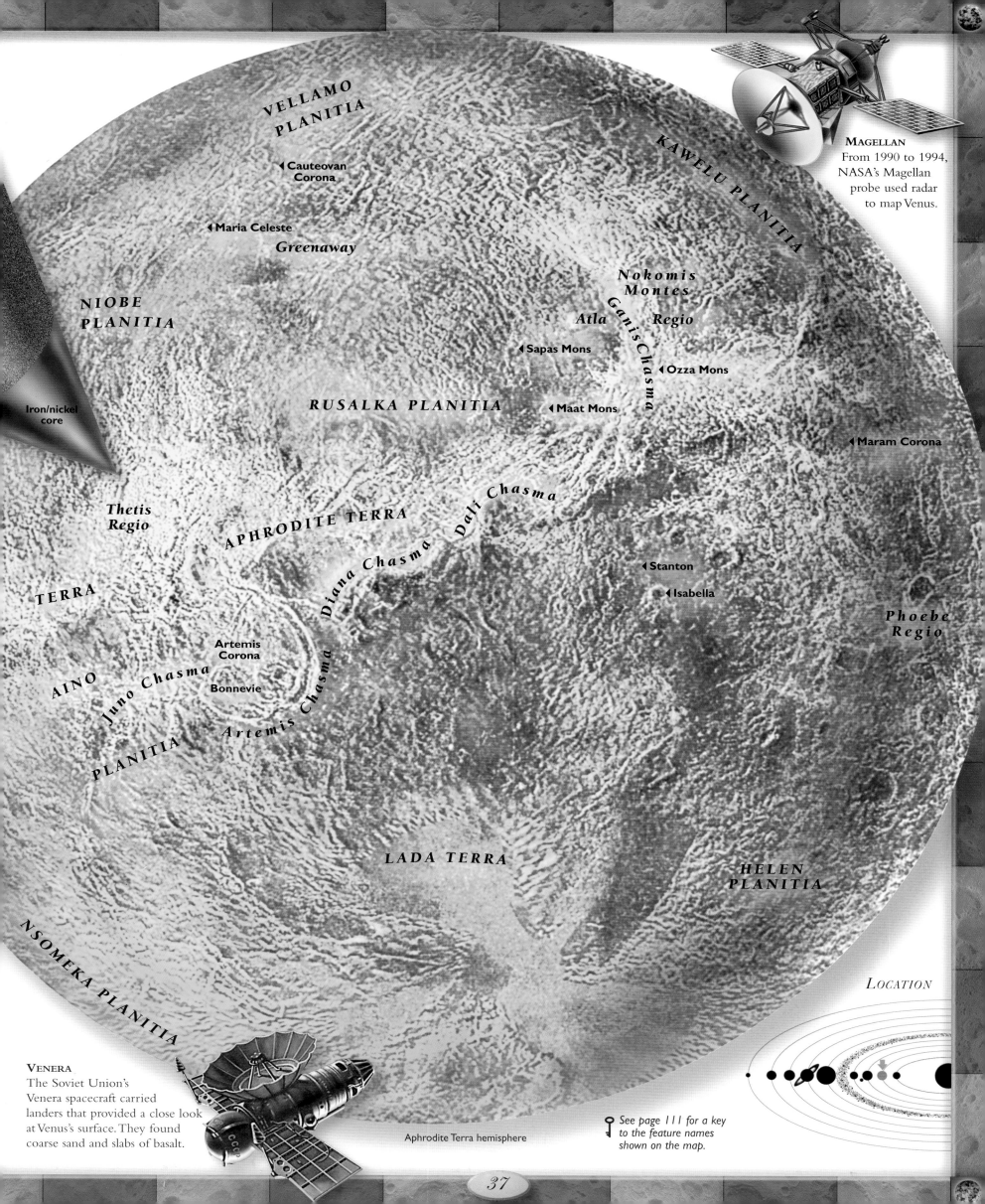

VELLAMO
PLANITIA

◄ Cauteovan
Corona

◄ Maria Celeste
Greenaway

NIOBE
PLANITIA

KAWELU PLANITIA

MAGELLAN
From 1990 to 1994,
NASA's Magellan
probe used radar
to map Venus.

*Nokomis
Montes*

Atla GanisChasma *Regio*

◄ **Sapas Mons**

◄ **Ozza Mons**

Iron/nickel
core

RUSALKA PLANITIA

◄ **Maat Mons**

◄ **Maram Corona**

*Thetis
Regio*

APHRODITE TERRA

Dali Chasma

Diana Chasma

◄ **Stanton**

◄ **Isabella**

TERRA

*Phoebe
Regio*

AINO

*Artemis
Corona*

Juno Chasma

Bonnevie

Artemis Chasma

PLANITIA

LADA TERRA

HELEN
PLANITIA

NSOMEKA PLANITIA

LOCATION

VENERA
The Soviet Union's
Venera spacecraft carried
landers that provided a close look
at Venus's surface. They found
coarse sand and slabs of basalt.

⚲ *See page 111 for a key
to the feature names
shown on the map.*

Aphrodite Terra hemisphere

37

Earth

The third planet from the Sun, Earth is the largest of the small rocky planets. Seen from space, it is the Blue Planet, thanks to the soft blue haze of its atmosphere and the deep blue of the oceans that cover 71 percent of it. Earth is the only planet whose surface has water in all three of its forms—solid, vapor, and liquid—and appears to be the only planet with life. The oceans help reduce the extremes of hot and cold by absorbing solar energy at hot regions around the equator and moving it to cooler regions toward the poles. These differences in heat and cold drive our weather and climate.

When Earth formed, it was hot enough for its rocks to melt. Iron and nickel sank to form a core, while lighter materials separated into a middle layer—the mantle—and an upper layer—the crust. The outer core remained molten, but the crust cooled and became stiff. It broke into pieces called plates, which fit together like the pieces of a jigsaw puzzle. Thin plates lie under the oceans, and thick plates carry continents. Heat from the core drives mantle rocks in slow convection currents that push the plates together and pull them apart. Called plate tectonics, this process has moved continents all over the globe.

ORIGIN OF NAME
Eorthe, the Anglo-Saxon word for "ground"

DISTANCE FROM THE SUN
93 million miles (150 million km)

DIAMETER
7,926 miles (12,756 km)

MASS
1.0 Earth mass = 6 x 10^{24} tons (5.5 x 10^{24} tonnes)

ATMOSPHERE
Nitrogen 78%, oxygen 21%

MOONS
1: the Moon

LENGTH OF DAY (in hours/minutes)
Rotation time: 23 h 56 m / Solar day: 24 h

LENGTH OF YEAR
365.25 days

VOLCANIC ACTIVITY
Molten rock, or magma, rises from Earth's mantle and erupts at weak parts of the crust, building volcanoes in repeated eruptions. This is how the Hawaiian Islands formed—volcanoes are still erupting there now.

SHAPING THE LANDSCAPE
Erosion by waves, wind, and rain shape the landscape. These cliffs, for example, will be slowly pushed back as waves batter them down. Erosion has erased many ancient features and made Earth's surface among the youngest in the Solar System.

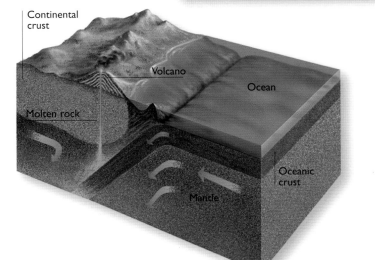

Continental crust

Volcano

Ocean

Molten rock

Oceanic crust

Mantle

COLLIDING PLATES
When a thin plate of oceanic crust and a thick continental plate collide, the oceanic plate dives beneath the continent and melts. Molten rock from deep within Earth rises to create volcanoes. These collisions happen about as fast as a fingernail grows.

EUROPE

Caspian Sea

Hindu Kush

Arabian Peninsula

Arabian Sea

Sahara Desert

AFRICA

Great Rift Valley

Lake Victoria

Madagascar

LIFE ON EARTH
Life flourishes everywhere on Earth and takes almost endless forms. Because of its distance from the Sun, Earth is neither too hot nor too cold and there is plenty of liquid water. Scientists don't know where life came from, but liquid water appears crucial to life.

Birds

Plants

◆ PROJECT: *Erosion in a Tray* ◆

Do this project outdoors. You need a large shallow tray, enough sand to almost fill the tray, and a hose and a supply of water.

❶ Fill the tray with sand and soak it thoroughly with water.

❷ Hold up one end of the tray about an inch (2 or 3 cm).

❸ Hold the hose over the edge of the tray's high end and trickle a thin stream of water into the tray.

❹ Let the water run steadily and observe how it erodes channels in the sand.

❺ To experiment, change the tray's elevation or the amount of flow. Place small rocks in the stream's path and see how it flows around them. Smooth the sand and scratch a straight groove— how long does the stream flow within it?

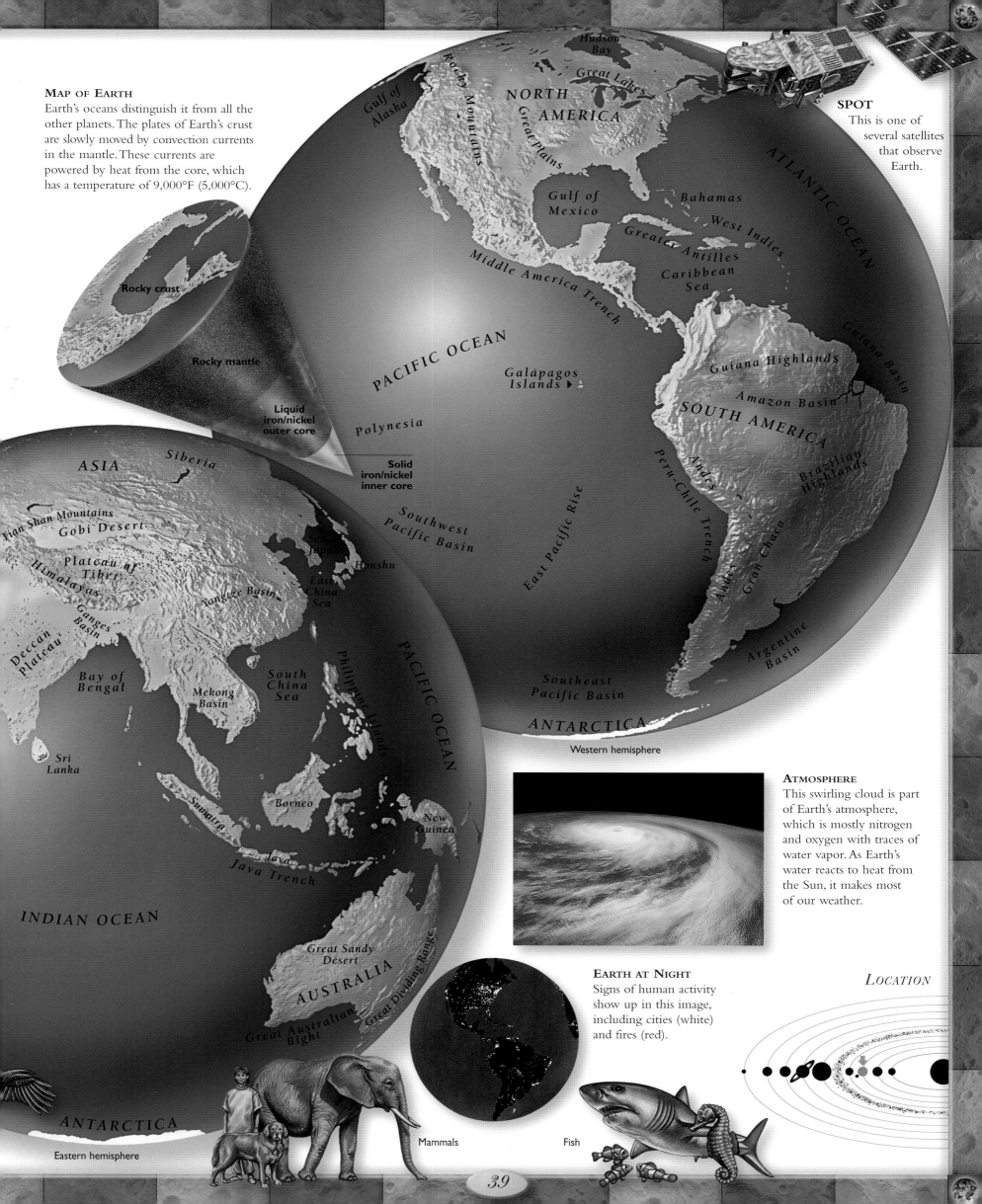

MAP OF EARTH
Earth's oceans distinguish it from all the other planets. The plates of Earth's crust are slowly moved by convection currents in the mantle. These currents are powered by heat from the core, which has a temperature of 9,000°F (5,000°C).

Rocky crust

Rocky mantle

Liquid iron/nickel outer core

Solid iron/nickel inner core

SPOT
This is one of several satellites that observe Earth.

NORTH AMERICA
Hudson Bay
Great Lakes
Gulf of Alaska
Rocky Mountains
Great Plains
Gulf of Mexico
Bahamas
West Indies
Greater Antilles
Caribbean Sea
Middle America Trench
ATLANTIC OCEAN
Guiana Highlands
Guiana Basin
Amazon Basin
SOUTH AMERICA
Brazilian Highlands
Peru-Chile Trench
Andes
Gran Chaco
Argentine Basin

PACIFIC OCEAN
Galápagos Islands ▶
Polynesia
Southwest Pacific Basin
East Pacific Rise
Southeast Pacific Basin
ANTARCTICA

Western hemisphere

ASIA
Siberia
Tian Shan Mountains
Gobi Desert
Himalayas
Plateau of Tibet
Deccan Plateau
Ganges Basin
Yangtze Basin
Sea of Japan
Honshu
East China Sea
Bay of Bengal
Mekong Basin
South China Sea
Philippine Islands
Sri Lanka
Sumatra
Borneo
New Guinea
Java
Java Trench
PACIFIC OCEAN
INDIAN OCEAN
Great Sandy Desert
AUSTRALIA
Great Dividing Range
Great Australian Bight

ANTARCTICA

Eastern hemisphere

ATMOSPHERE
This swirling cloud is part of Earth's atmosphere, which is mostly nitrogen and oxygen with traces of water vapor. As Earth's water reacts to heat from the Sun, it makes most of our weather.

EARTH AT NIGHT
Signs of human activity show up in this image, including cities (white) and fires (red).

LOCATION

Mammals

Fish

Earth and the Sun

As Earth spins on its axis, we get day and night, and as it moves around the Sun, we get changing seasons. The seasons happen because Earth is tilted—its rotation axis tips 23.5 degrees to its orbit. This means that the amount of sunlight and solar energy falling on most parts of Earth varies during the year.

Around June 21 each year, the North Pole tilts most directly toward the Sun. This day is called the solstice. In the Northern Hemisphere, it marks the Sun's highest path across the sky and the start of summer (winter in the Southern Hemisphere). Around December 21, another solstice occurs when the North Pole tilts most directly away from the Sun. This marks the Sun's lowest path across the sky and the start of winter in the Northern Hemisphere (summer in the Southern Hemisphere). In March and September, the Sun passes directly over the equator, and day and night are equally long everywhere on Earth. This is the equinox and the start of spring or autumn in much of the world.

Some parts of the globe do not experience four seasons. The regions around the equator receive the most direct sunlight and stay warm all year round. The polar regions receive the least sunlight—in winter there is no sunlight for several months.

The Sun influences Earth in other ways, too. The solar wind, a flow of charged particles from the Sun, is always flowing past Earth. Earth's magnetic field deflects most of the particles, but some get through. They strike the upper atmosphere near the north and south magnetic poles, making the air glow. From the ground, we see rippling curtains of light called auroras.

EARTH CLOSEST TO THE SUN
EARLY JANUARY—91.5 MILLION MILES (147 MILLION KM)

EARTH FARTHEST FROM THE SUN
EARLY JULY—94.5 MILLION MILES (152 MILLION KM)

DISTANCE EARTH TRAVELS PER YEAR
584 MILLION MILES (940 MILLION KM)

AVERAGE SPEED OF EARTH
66,000 MILES PER HOUR (107,000 KM/H)

HOTTEST TEMPERATURE
HOTTEST TEMPERATURE EVER RECORDED ON EARTH—136°F (58°C) AT AZIZIA, LIBYA, SEPTEMBER 13, 1922

COLDEST TEMPERATURE
COLDEST TEMPERATURE EVER RECORDED ON EARTH—−129°F (−89°C) AT VOSTOK STATION, ANTARCTICA, JULY 21, 1983

◆ AMAZING FACT ◆

The sunlight warming your face right now left the Sun's surface just over 8 minutes ago. (And moonlight is sunlight that bounced off the Moon only 1.3 seconds ago.)

SEASONS
The seasons change as the amount of sunlight falling on your part of Earth changes. Around June 21, the North Pole tilts most directly toward the Sun, making summer in the Northern Hemisphere and winter in the Southern Hemisphere. Six months later, the situation is reversed.

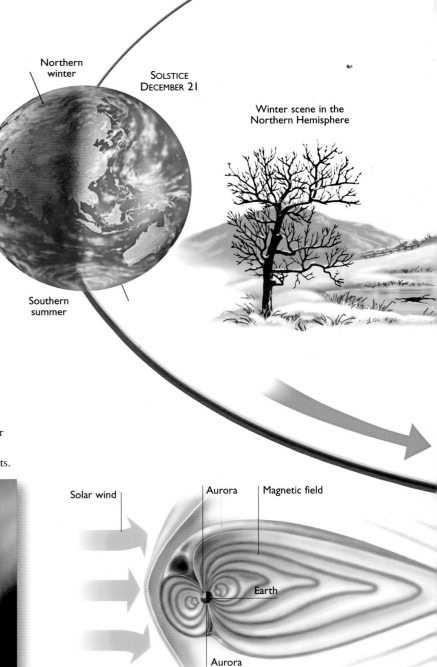

Northern winter

SOLSTICE
DECEMBER 21

Winter scene in the Northern Hemisphere

Southern summer

AURORA
Also known as the Northern or Southern Lights, auroras are stronger and more frequent when the Sun is very active and displays many sunspots.

Solar wind | Aurora | Magnetic field

Earth

Aurora

MAGNETIC FIELD
Generated by the iron in Earth's core, a magnetic field surrounds our planet like a web. It helps to protect Earth from the charged particles of the solar wind. When particles do get through to our atmosphere, they cause auroras.

AURORA FROM SPACE
Astronauts on the space shuttle Discovery photographed this Southern Hemisphere aurora from above.

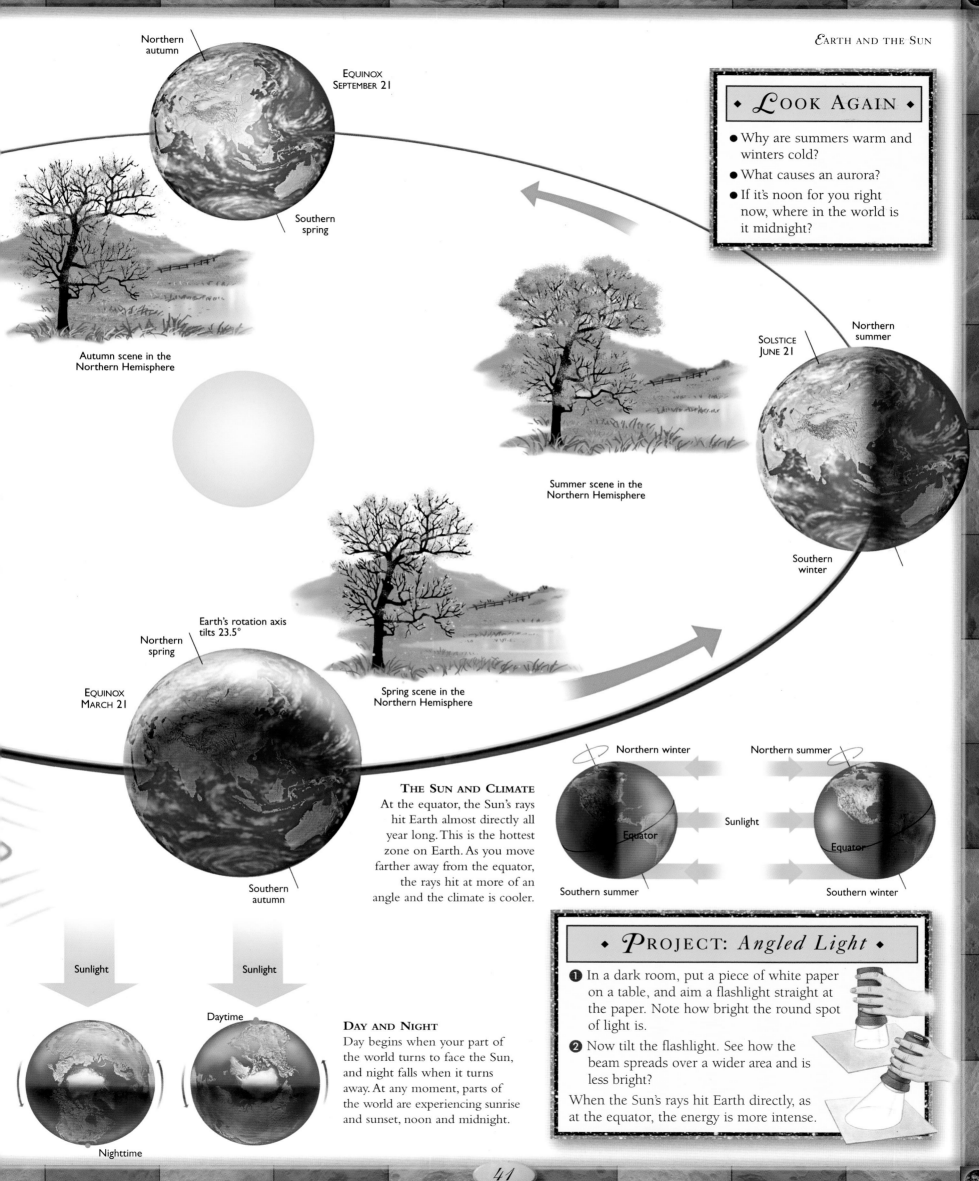

Northern autumn

EQUINOX
SEPTEMBER 21

Southern spring

Autumn scene in the
Northern Hemisphere

SOLSTICE
JUNE 21

Northern summer

Summer scene in the
Northern Hemisphere

Southern winter

Earth's rotation axis
tilts 23.5°

Northern spring

EQUINOX
MARCH 21

Spring scene in the
Northern Hemisphere

Southern autumn

THE SUN AND CLIMATE

At the equator, the Sun's rays hit Earth almost directly all year long. This is the hottest zone on Earth. As you move farther away from the equator, the rays hit at more of an angle and the climate is cooler.

Northern winter

Northern summer

Sunlight

Equator

Equator

Southern summer

Southern winter

Sunlight

Sunlight

Daytime

DAY AND NIGHT

Day begins when your part of the world turns to face the Sun, and night falls when it turns away. At any moment, parts of the world are experiencing sunrise and sunset, noon and midnight.

Nighttime

The Moon

THE MOON IS EARTH'S ONLY natural satellite. It formed soon after Earth did, from the debris that flew out when another body slammed into Earth. As the Moon formed, it was constantly bombarded by meteorites. These punched countless craters into its surface, and big impacts dug broad basins. The scars can still be seen today. The youngest craters have rays, bright streaks of shattered rock flung across the landscape.

Dark lava (molten rock) flowed from under the surface to fill the lowlands and basins. Early astronomers thought these dark areas were the dried-up beds of oceans, so they called them maria, which means "seas" in Latin. In 1959, an early Soviet probe photographed the unseen farside of the Moon and found that nearly all the maria lie on the side facing Earth.

The Moon's gravity is one-sixth of Earth's. This is too weak to hold onto an atmosphere, so the lunar sky always looks black, even in daytime. The lack of an atmosphere also means that the Moon's surface becomes very hot (243°F or 117°C) when it is facing the Sun, and very cold (−243°F or −153°C) when it turns away.

In 1998, the Lunar Prospector spacecraft found ice at the Moon's poles. Since then, that finding has been debated, and several future missions to the Moon are planned to further explore its craters.

ORIGIN OF NAME
MONA, THE ANGLO-SAXON WORD FOR "MOON"

DISTANCE FROM EARTH
238,856 MILES (384,401 KM)

DIAMETER
2,160 MILES (3,476 KM)

MASS
1.2% X EARTH'S MASS

ATMOSPHERE
NONE

LENGTH OF DAY (in Earth days)
ROTATION TIME AND SOLAR DAY: BOTH 27.3

MAP OF THE MOON
The nearside hemisphere is the side of the Moon that always faces Earth. The farside hemisphere was revealed only when probes first visited. The Moon has a small, hot core, a thick mantle, and a heavily cratered crust.

Rocky crust

Rocky mantle

ON THE SURFACE
From 1968 to 1972, six Apollo missions landed astronauts on the Moon and brought back rock samples. Here, astronaut James Irwin stands near the Apollo 15 lunar module and rover in 1971.

OCEANUS PROCELLARUM
(Ocean of Storms)

LUNAR ICE
The Lunar Prospector spacecraft found ice (white) in craters at the Moon's south pole.

◆ PROJECT: *Drawing Moonlight* ◆

For this project, you need a piece of paper and a pencil.

❶ Draw 31 circles, arranged in lines, on a piece of paper. You can make them big or small, but all 31 should fit on the paper, neatly drawn to the same size. (Try tracing around a glass or a coin.)

❷ Write today's date next to the first circle and continue until all 31 circles have dates.

❸ Find the Moon in the sky.

❹ Draw what the Moon looks like. If clouds hide the Moon, leave the circle blank or mark it "clouds."

❺ When you have made a week or two of observations, you will see a pattern developing. What you have drawn are the phases of the Moon (see page 44).

MARE MOSCOVIENSE
(Sea of Moscow)

Birkhoff
D'Alembert
Landau
Kovalevskaya
Fitzgerald
Cockcroft
Mach
Mendeleev
Anderson
Hertzsprung
Schuster
Chaplygin
Korolev
Keeler
Heaviside
Tsiolkovskiy
Galois
Aitken
Gagarin
MARE INGENII
(Sea of Cleverness)
Pavlov
Van de Graaff
Leeuwenhoek
Roche
Leibnitz
Apollo
Oppenheimer
Planck

MARE ORIENTALE
(Eastern Sea)

Farside hemisphere

HOW THE MOON FORMED
The young Earth was struck by an object the size of Mars. The debris circled around Earth, then clumped together to form the Moon.

MARE FRIGORIS
(Sea of Cold)

Montes Jura

SINUS IRIDUM
(Bay of Rainbows)

▸ Plato

◂ Aristoteles

Eudoxus ▸

Hercules ▸   ◂ Atlas

MARE IMBRIUM
(Sea of Showers)

Cassini ▸

Aristillus ▸

Montes Caucasus

MARE SERENITATIS
(Sea of Serenity)

Posidonius ▸

◂ Euler   Archimedes ▸

Timocharis ▸

APOLLO 15
LANDING SITE

Cleomedes ▸

Molten
zone

Montes Apenninus

Montes Haemus

Macrobius ▸

Core

Eratosthenes ▸

◂ APOLLO 17
LANDING SITE

MARE
CRISIUM
(Sea of
Crises)

◂ Kepler

◂ Copernicus

MARE
TRANQUILLITATIS
(Sea of Tranquillity)

APOLLO 12 ▸
LANDING SITE

◂ APOLLO 14
LANDING SITE

APOLLO 11 ▸
LANDING SITE

MARE
FECUNDITATIS
(Sea of Fertility)

◂ Letronne

MARE
COGNITUM
(Sea of Knowledge)

Ptolemaeus ▸

APOLLO 16 ▸
LANDING SITE

◂ Gassendi

Alphonsus ▸

◂ Albategnius   Theophilus ▸

MARE
HUMORUM
(Sea of Moisture)

MARE
NUBIUM
(Sea of Clouds)

Arzachel ▸

Catharina ▸

MARE
NECTARIS
(Sea of Nectar)

Pitatus ▸

◂ Purbach

Fracastorius ▸

◂ Piccolomini

◂ Deslandres

Tycho ▸

LOCATION

Nearside hemisphere

LUNA 16
The Soviet Union's Luna 16
was the first spacecraft to collect
Moon rocks automatically.

Earth and the Moon

ABOUT ONCE EVERY MONTH, the Moon orbits Earth. It always keeps the same side turned toward us, so it appears to us that the Moon does not spin on its axis. But if we watched the Moon from Mars, we would see that it turns once on its axis each month—the same time it takes to revolve once around Earth! For astronauts on the Moon, the lunar day and night last about two weeks each.

The Moon shines only because it is reflecting the light of the Sun. Throughout the month, we see different amounts of the Moon lit up, depending on where it is in its orbit. These changes are called phases. At New Moon, the Sun is shining on the farside of the Moon, so the side that faces us—the nearside—is dark and we cannot see it. At Full Moon, the nearside is fully lit. At other phases, we see only part of the Moon's sunlit surface.

Occasionally, the Moon, Earth, and Sun line up and we see eclipses. During a solar eclipse, the Moon passes directly between Earth and the Sun, and its shadow passes over part of Earth. For people in the narrow path of the shadow, the Sun is blacked out partially or totally. Solar eclipses occur because the Moon is just large enough and close enough to Earth to cover the Sun.

Lunar eclipses are much easier to see. When the Moon passes directly behind Earth, Earth blocks direct sunlight. The Moon darkens but doesn't disappear altogether—instead, it glows a deep copper-orange, colored by sunlight that filters through Earth's atmosphere. A lunar eclipse can last more than an hour. During that time, anyone on the nighttime side of Earth can see the eclipsed Moon.

| **DURATION OF THE MOON'S ORBIT** |
| SEEN FROM EARTH (FROM ONE NEW MOON TO THE NEXT)—29.5 EARTH DAYS |
| RELATIVE TO THE STARS—27.3 EARTH DAYS |
| **MAXIMUM DURATION OF A TOTAL SOLAR ECLIPSE** |
| 7 MINUTES 40 SECONDS |
| **HOW OFTEN TOTAL SOLAR ECLIPSES OCCUR** |
| ABOUT ONCE A YEAR, BUT ONLY ALONG A NARROW PATH |
| **USUAL DURATION OF A TOTAL LUNAR ECLIPSE** |
| ABOUT 1 HOUR TO 1 HOUR 40 MINUTES |
| **HOW OFTEN LUNAR ECLIPSES OCCUR** |
| 1 TO 3 TIMES A YEAR, OVER A WIDE AREA |

✦ AMAZING FACT ✦

Until they understood why solar eclipses occurred, people were often afraid of them. The Chinese, for example, described solar eclipses as a dragon swallowing the Sun. Terrified people would bang on drums, blow horns, and shake noise-makers to scare the dragon away. Of course, it always worked!

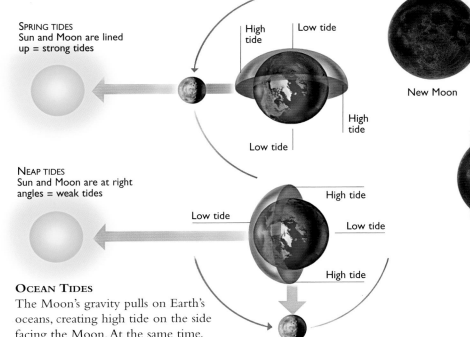

SPRING TIDES
Sun and Moon are lined up = strong tides

High tide   Low tide
High tide
Low tide

New Moon

NEAP TIDES
Sun and Moon are at right angles = weak tides

High tide
Low tide   Low tide
High tide

OCEAN TIDES
The Moon's gravity pulls on Earth's oceans, creating high tide on the side facing the Moon. At the same time, the Moon's gravity also pulls on Earth, so another high tide occurs on the opposite side. Tides are strongest when the Sun and Moon line up.

EARTHSHINE
A pale, ghostly light can sometimes be seen inside the Moon's bright crescent. This is earthshine—sunlight reflecting from Earth's clouds, land, and oceans.

LUNAR ECLIPSE
When the Moon passes through Earth's shadow it causes a lunar eclipse. The Moon turns dark and often copper-orange in color. The color comes from sunlight filtering through Earth's atmosphere.

Sun

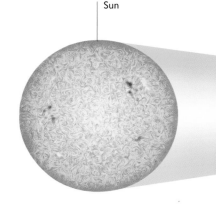

SOLAR ECLIPSE
Moments before the Moon completely covers the Sun in a total solar eclipse, sunlight streams through valleys on the Moon and makes a diamond-ring effect. An edge of the Sun is the diamond, and its corona—or outer atmosphere—is the ring itself.

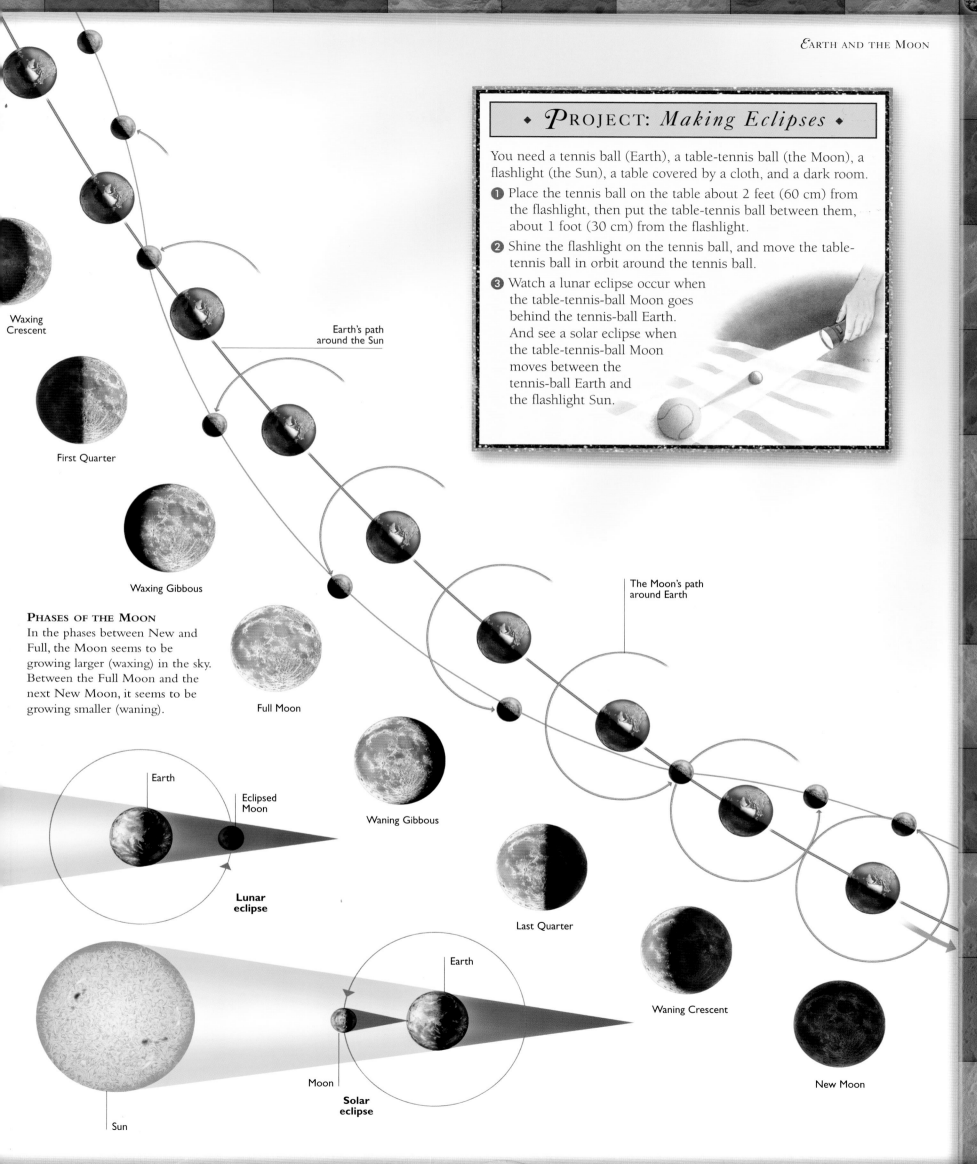

Waxing
Crescent

Earth's path
around the Sun

First Quarter

Waxing Gibbous

PHASES OF THE MOON
In the phases between New and
Full, the Moon seems to be
growing larger (waxing) in the sky.
Between the Full Moon and the
next New Moon, it seems to be
growing smaller (waning).

Full Moon

Earth

Eclipsed
Moon

Waning Gibbous

**Lunar
eclipse**

The Moon's path
around Earth

Last Quarter

Earth

Waning Crescent

Moon

**Solar
eclipse**

Sun

New Moon

◆ PROJECT: *Making Eclipses* ◆

You need a tennis ball (Earth), a table-tennis ball (the Moon), a
flashlight (the Sun), a table covered by a cloth, and a dark room.

1 Place the tennis ball on the table about 2 feet (60 cm) from
the flashlight, then put the table-tennis ball between them,
about 1 foot (30 cm) from the flashlight.

2 Shine the flashlight on the tennis ball, and move the table-
tennis ball in orbit around the tennis ball.

3 Watch a lunar eclipse occur when
the table-tennis-ball Moon goes
behind the tennis-ball Earth.
And see a solar eclipse when
the table-tennis-ball Moon
moves between the
tennis-ball Earth and
the flashlight Sun.

Meteors and Meteorites

MORE THAN 200 TONS (180 tonnes) of space debris enter Earth's atmosphere every day. Fluffy dust grains, bits of cosmic debris the size of peas, and occasional larger pieces of rock or iron continually enter Earth's atmosphere. Because these objects travel at more than 8 miles per second (13 km/s), friction with air molecules causes most of the material to burn up in the atmosphere. The result is a bright streak of light called a meteor, or shooting star. Before it enters the atmosphere, a piece of debris is called a meteoroid. If it survives to hit the ground, the debris is called a meteorite.

Most meteoroids come from asteroids, the bodies that orbit mainly between Mars and Jupiter, or from comets, which travel in huge elliptical orbits through the Solar System. When asteroids collide, pieces break off and become meteoroids drifting through space. Comets shed dust as their ices boil away in sunlight. This dusty debris becomes a swarm of small meteoroids that may eventually enter Earth's atmosphere. Some meteoroids were once part of the Moon or Mars. These pieces were blasted off the surface when it was hit by a large asteroid.

Meteorites are usually small enough to hold in your hand, but they can be bigger than houses. In the past, giant meteorites have created huge craters on Earth. And even small meteorites can do damage. In 1992, one smashed a car in Peekskill, New York. Another killed a dog when it fell in Egypt in 1911.

METEORITE CRATER

When a big meteorite falls, it leaves a crater in the ground. Meteor Crater in Arizona is 4,000 feet (1,220 m) across and 650 feet (200 m) deep. It formed 50,000 years ago when a house-size nickel-iron meteorite struck at 7 miles (11 km) per second.

METEOR

The streak of light in this photo is a meteor. On a clear night, you might see three or four meteors an hour. Very bright meteors are known as fireballs.

ORIGIN OF NAME
METEOR COMES FROM THE GREEK WORD FOR "THINGS IN THE ATMOSPHERE."

ALTITUDE WHERE METEORS BURN OUT
70–50 MILES (110–80 KM)

SIZE OF METEOROIDS
METEOROIDS RANGE FROM TINY SPECKS TO HOUSE-SIZE.

SIZE OF METEORITES
METEORITES ARE USUALLY FIST-SIZE, BUT CAN BE HUGE. THE LARGEST ONE FOUND ON EARTH IS THE HOBA METEORITE IN NAMIBIA, WHICH WEIGHS 65 TONS (60 TONNES).

LARGEST KNOWN CRATER ON EARTH
VREDEFORT, SOUTH AFRICA: 190 MILES (300 KM) ACROSS

STONY METEORITE
Stony meteorites make up 92 percent of all meteorites. They formed early in Solar System history and can tell scientists what the young Solar System was like.

IRON METEORITE
Iron meteorites make up only 7 percent of all meteorites, but are the kind most commonly found because they look extraterrestrial.

• AMAZING FACT •

On November 17, 1833, people on North America's east coast saw a spectacular meteor storm, with up to 200,000 meteors falling per hour. Thousands of meteors lit up the sky every minute.

STONY-IRON METEORITE
A minority (1 percent) of meteorites are a mixture of stony material and iron. Scientists think they come from asteroids that have completely melted.

MARS METEORITE ALH 84001
In 1996, several NASA scientists reported finding evidence for ancient life in this meteorite from Mars called ALH 84001. Most scientists now disagree.

Meteoroids drift among the planets controlled by the gravity of the Sun and planets, and by the pressure of sunlight.

Small meteoroids usually come from comets, which leave behind a trail of dust as their ices boil away in sunlight.

SPACE DEBRIS
If you see a quick streak of light in the night sky, it is probably a meteor. The meteoroid might burn up completely or land on the ground as a meteorite.

On certain dates, many meteors appear to come from one part of the sky. These meteor showers (see page 113) occur when Earth passes through a stream of dust from a comet.

To survive passing through the atmosphere, a meteorite must be large and tough—or else very small and light, so it slows before burning up.

Although no large meteorite impact has happened in human history, scientists expect that the next big impact is just a matter of time and chance.

◆ *L*OOK AGAIN ◆

● What's the difference between a meteor and a meteorite?

● Where do most meteorites come from?

● What happens when a big meteorite falls?

47

Mars

MARS IS THE PLANET MOST like our own. It has four seasons, polar ice caps, channels carved by water, and a rotation time just 41 minutes longer than Earth's. On the young Mars, conditions were probably like those on the early Earth, so life may have begun there as well. But spacecraft have found no signs of life, and scientists think Mars became too hostile for living things long ago.

Mars looks red in the sky, earning it the nickname the Red Planet. The color comes from its rusty-orange rocks and fine red sand. It is a cold desert—the planet's atmosphere of carbon dioxide is too thin to stop heat from the Sun escaping into space. Temperatures can peak at 81°F (27°C) by day but drop to a chilly –190°F (–123°C) at night.

The southern half of the planet is heavily cratered. The northern plains are smoother and flatter, and may once have had large lakes or even an ocean. Giant extinct volcanoes include Olympus Mons, which is 15 miles (24 km) high. The Valles Marineris is a canyon as long as the United States is wide.

Mars is the most studied planet, apart from Earth. More than 20 probes have visited and others are on their way. Scientists are now investigating ways to send astronauts to our red neighbor.

ORIGIN OF NAME
MARS, THE ROMAN GOD OF WAR

DISTANCE FROM THE SUN
142 MILLION MILES (228 MILLION KM)

DIAMETER
4,213 MILES (6,780 KM)

MASS
10.7% X EARTH'S MASS

ATMOSPHERE
CARBON DIOXIDE—0.01% AS DENSE AS EARTH'S AIR

MOONS
2: PHOBOS AND DEIMOS

LENGTH OF DAY (in Earth hours/minutes)
ROTATION TIME: 24 H 37 M / SOLAR DAY: 24 H 40 M

LENGTH OF YEAR
687 EARTH DAYS

MAP OF MARS
Space probes have mapped the surface of Mars in detail, revealing giant volcanoes, deep canyons, and ice. Traces of magnetism suggest that the rocky mantle and crust may once have had moving plates like Earth's.

ON THE SURFACE
The Pathfinder spacecraft landed where streams from the highlands once emptied onto the northern plains. It found many rock types and a landscape unchanged for more than a billion years.

Rocky crust

Rocky mantle

AMAZONIS PLANITIA

THE POLES
The northern polar ice cap is frozen water, covered in winter by a layer of carbon dioxide snow mixed with dust.

THE TWO MOONS OF MARS
Phobos and Deimos, the two Martian moons, are covered in craters and a layer of dusty shattered rock. They have irregular shapes and may be asteroids captured by Mars's gravity.

Deimos

Phobos

RED ROVER
Rovers like Sojourner, carried by Mars Pathfinder (see pages 26–27), move around on a planet's surface and can explore a wider area than a fixed landing craft can.

VASTITAS BOREALIS
Lyot
Moreux UTOPIA PLANITIA
ELYSIUM PLANITIA
Cassini Antoniadi
ARABIA TERRA ISIDIS PLANITIA
Schiaparelli
Terra Sabaea TYRRHENA TERRA
Huygens
Herschel
HELLAS PLANITIA
PROMETHEI TERRA TERRA
PLANUM AUSTRALE

Eastern hemisphere

♦ PROJECT: *Making a Red Planet* ♦

For this project, you need a piece of clean steel wool, tap water, a dish or saucer, and rubber gloves to protect your hands.

❶ Stretch the steel wool to loosen its weave, then put it in the dish and wet it. Leave it for several days.

❷ Pick up the steel wool with rubber gloves, and examine it closely. The rusted wool will be fragile and crumbly, leaving a reddish-orange residue.

As the iron in the steel wool mixes with water and oxygen in the air, it rusts. Many Mars rocks contain iron-bearing minerals. These minerals have slowly rusted, leaving a ruddy dust on the surface and in the atmosphere.

VASTITAS BOREALIS

ARCADIA PLANITIA

ACIDALIA PLANITIA

Iron core

◄ Olympus Mons

Alba Fossae

Alba Patera ▾

Tantalus Fossae

Tempe Fossae

TEMPE TERRA

◄ Uranius Patera

Ceraunius ► Tholus

◄ Fesenkov

LUNAE PLANUM

Ascraeus ► Mons

◄ Tharsis Tholus

Ares Vallis

ONIS TIA

Pavonis ► Mons

Tharsis Montes

VALLES MARINERIS

MARGARITIFER TERRA

DAEDALIA PLANUM

Arsia ► Mons

Ius Chasma

Coprates Chasma

CIMMERIA

TERRA CIMMERIA

Claritas Fossae

SYRIA PLANUM

SINAI PLANUM

◄ Lassell

◄ Holden

◄ Koval'skiy

◄ Pickering

SOLIS PLANUM

◄ Hale

◄ Hecates Tholus
◄ Elysium Mons

ICARIA PLANUM

◄ Slipher

TERRA SIRENUM

Porter ►

◄ Lowell

ARGYRE PLANITIA

Ross ►

Wright ►

Trumpler ► Chamberlin ►

◄ Phillips

Stoney ►

◄ Schmidt

IMMERIA

PLANUM AUSTRALE

Western hemisphere

MARS POLAR LANDER
This probe was sent to Mars's southern polar region to look for water.

LOCATION

See page 111 for a key to the feature names shown on the map.

Asteroids

BETWEEN MARS AND JUPITER, there are millions of asteroids, small irregular bodies made of rock or metal left over from the Solar System's birth. The strong gravity of Jupiter keeps them from clumping together to become a planet like Earth or Mars. Asteroids are sometimes called minor planets.

The biggest asteroid is Ceres, almost 600 miles (1,000 km) across. It was first spotted in 1801, making it the first asteroid discovered. Ceres is round like the rocky planets, but smaller asteroids have odd shapes because their gravity is not strong enough to pull the asteroid material into a sphere. Spacecraft visits to asteroids such as Gaspra and Ida reveal that they have cratered surfaces covered by a dusty layer of shattered rock.

Not all asteroids orbit in the main belt. The Trojan asteroids travel in Jupiter's orbit. They don't collide with Jupiter because they are moving at the same speed as the giant planet. Other asteroids have wide elliptical orbits that cross the orbits of Earth and other large planets. Astronomers watch these near-Earth asteroids carefully. If a large one collided with Earth, the impact could create tidal waves, huge forest fires, and great clouds of dust and ash that would block out sunlight for months.

Our planet was built up by countless collisions of asteroid-like materials, and scientists believe that asteroids today can tell us about the Solar System's early history. The Near-Earth Asteroid Rendezvous (NEAR) visited asteroid Eros in 2000, and Hayabusa may bring back a rock sample from an asteroid.

ORIGIN OF NAME
ASTEROID MEANS "STAR-LIKE," WHICH IS HOW AN ASTEROID LOOKS IN A TELESCOPE.

DISTANCE OF MAIN BELT FROM THE SUN
FROM 204 MILLION MILES (329 MILLION KM) TO 335 MILLION MILES (539 MILLION KM)

SIZE
ASTEROIDS RANGE FROM A FEW FEET (LESS THAN A METER) ACROSS UP TO CERES, THE LARGEST ASTEROID AT 567 MILES (913 KM) IN DIAMETER.

NUMBER OF MAIN BELT ASTEROIDS
UNKNOWN—PROBABLY HUNDREDS OF MILLIONS

NUMBER OF NEAR-EARTH ASTEROIDS
PROBABLY SEVERAL THOUSAND—ABOUT 4,000 KNOWN

IDA
Seen by the Jupiter-bound spacecraft Galileo, Ida is about 37 miles (60 km) long. The speck beside Ida in this photo is its tiny moon Dactyl, which is just 1 mile (1.6 km) wide.

GASPRA
Also photographed by Galileo, Gaspra is about 11 miles (18 km) long. With fewer craters than Ida, Gaspra appears to have a younger surface.

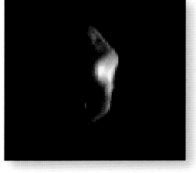

EROS
The NEAR probe took this snapshot of Eros in 1998. Eros is a piece of rock about 21 miles (33 km) long, irregular in shape and pocked with craters. It rotates once every 5¼ hours.

MATHILDE
Before Eros, NEAR visited Mathilde. About 41 miles (66 km) across, Mathilde is as dark as coal and has large craters. Scientists think it may be like a giant pile of rubble.

COLLISION WITH EARTH
Asteroids have struck Earth many times in the past, but the most recent big impact was 65 million years ago. This led to such a change in Earth's climate that dinosaurs became extinct.

◆ PROJECT: *Lighting Up Asteroids* ◆

For this project, you need a bright flashlight, a dark room, and some rocks, balls, and other objects. Some should be rough, others smooth. Try covering one object in silver foil.

❶ Put the objects on the table in front of you. Take a few steps back and shine the flashlight on them.

❷ Notice how different objects reflect different amounts of light.

❸ See how the appearance of each object changes as you shine the flashlight directly or from one side.

Scientists study asteroids as they rotate, showing changing textures and patterns of shadow and light.

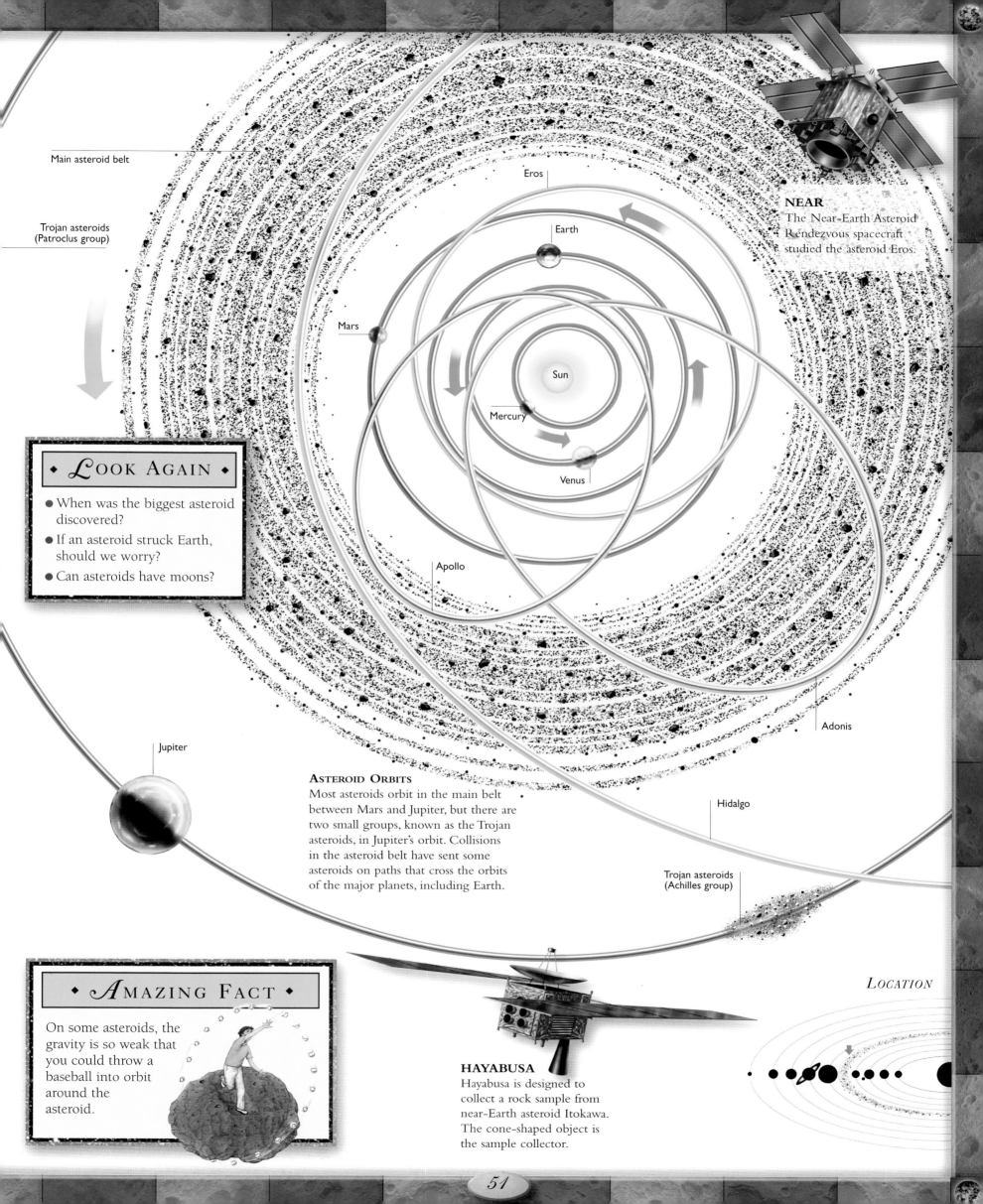

Main asteroid belt

Trojan asteroids
(Patroclus group)

Eros

Earth

Mars

Sun

Mercury

Venus

Apollo

NEAR
The Near-Earth Asteroid
Rendezvous spacecraft
studied the asteroid Eros.

◆ LOOK AGAIN ◆

● When was the biggest asteroid
discovered?

● If an asteroid struck Earth,
should we worry?

● Can asteroids have moons?

Adonis

Jupiter

Hidalgo

ASTEROID ORBITS
Most asteroids orbit in the main belt
between Mars and Jupiter, but there are
two small groups, known as the Trojan
asteroids, in Jupiter's orbit. Collisions
in the asteroid belt have sent some
asteroids on paths that cross the orbits
of the major planets, including Earth.

Trojan asteroids
(Achilles group)

◆ AMAZING FACT ◆

On some asteroids, the
gravity is so weak that
you could throw a
baseball into orbit
around the
asteroid.

HAYABUSA
Hayabusa is designed to
collect a rock sample from
near-Earth asteroid Itokawa.
The cone-shaped object is
the sample collector.

LOCATION

Jupiter

THE MOST MASSIVE of all the planets, Jupiter is an enormous ball of gas—mostly hydrogen and helium, like the Sun, along with small amounts of water, methane, and ammonia. This giant planet lacks a solid surface. The upper layers are gaseous but deeper down, as pressures and temperatures increase, the hydrogen and helium become more like a liquid. Deeper still, pressure makes the hydrogen behave like a liquid metal. At the center is a small, rocky core more than three times hotter than the surface of the Sun.

A day on Jupiter lasts less than 10 hours. This rapid spin creates winds that blow at up to 300 miles per hour (500 km/h) and whip its colorful clouds into long bands. The light bands are called zones. The dark bands, known as belts, show deeper layers. Among the zones and belts are a number of oval spots. These are giant storms that thrive on the energy of the winds and heat from Jupiter's core. They can persist for years or even centuries—the biggest storm, the Great Red Spot, has been visible for at least 300 years.

In 1610, astronomer Galileo Galilei discovered Jupiter's four largest moons—Io, Europa, Ganymede, and Callisto. Today, we know of 49 moons, ranging from Ganymede, at 3,273 miles (5,268 km) across, to Leda, at 10 miles (16 km) across. In 1979, the Voyager 1 probe discovered that Jupiter also has a thin system of rings. These are mostly made of microscopic dust particles.

COMET IMPACTS
In July 1994, more than 20 fragments of comet Shoemaker-Levy 9 struck Jupiter. The impacts left dusty smudges that lasted months.

MAP OF JUPITER
Jupiter's top layer shows light zones and dark belts of fast-moving clouds, as well as storms such as the Great Red Spot. These icy features conceal an extremely hot interior. The giant planet is still cooling off from its formation, which occurred nearly 5 billion years ago.

Rings

ORIGIN OF NAME	
JUPITER, THE MOST POWERFUL OF THE ROMAN GODS	
DISTANCE FROM THE SUN	
483 MILLION MILES (778 MILLION KM)	
DIAMETER	
88,846 MILES (142,984 KM)	
MASS	
317.8 X EARTH'S MASS	
MOONS	
49—LARGEST ARE IO, EUROPA, GANYMEDE, AND CALLISTO	
LENGTH OF DAY (in Earth hours and minutes)	
ROTATION TIME AND SOLAR DAY: BOTH 9 H 55 M	
LENGTH OF YEAR	
11.9 EARTH YEARS	

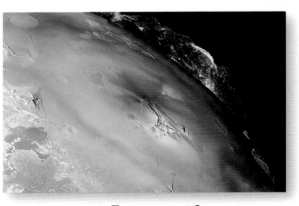

ERUPTION ON IO
In this photo of Jupiter's moon Io, a plume of sulfur shoots from one of its many volcanoes. The gravity of Jupiter and its other moons continually tugs at Io, creating internal heat that escapes through eruptions.

MOON: IO
The innermost Galilean moon has an iron core and a rocky mantle and crust. Unlike Jupiter's other large moons, Io has no ice or water because it formed near the planet, where temperatures were high.

✦ PROJECT: *Jupiter in a Pie-Pan* ✦

You need a glass or aluminum pie-pan, a coin, tap water, and a bottle of liquid food coloring.

❶ Place the coin on a level kitchen counter, under the center of the pie-pan so the pan turns easily.

❷ Pour about half an inch (1 or 2 cm) of tap water into the pan.

❸ Carefully place a large drop of food coloring in the pan at the edge, and spin the pan slowly. Notice how streamers of food coloring take the same shapes as Jupiter's bands of clouds.

ICE ON EUROPA
In this photo of Europa's surface, the red lines are dusty water that has leaked through cracks in the moon's bright icy shell. We do not know whether the water under the shell is still liquid or has frozen.

North pole

North polar region

Gaseous hydrogen

Liquid hydrogen

Metallic hydrogen

Rocky core

North temperate belt

North tropical zone

North equatorial belt

Equatorial zone

Great Red Spot

South equatorial belt

South tropical zone

South temperate zone

GALILEO
The Galileo orbiter arrived at Jupiter in 1995 and shot a probe into the planet's clouds.

MOON: CALLISTO
Callisto is the most heavily cratered object in the Solar System. Scientists think there may be a layer of salt water underneath its crust.

MOON: EUROPA
A crust of ice covers what may be an ocean of water on Europa. Some scientists think that the ocean, if it exists, could be heated by tidal forces or underwater volcanoes and might contain life, much as life exists in Earth's deepest oceans.

MOON: GANYMEDE
Ganymede has a metallic core, a rocky lower mantle, an icy upper mantle and crust, and a weak magnetic field. On the surface, old, dark regions full of craters alternate with young, bright, grooved terrain.

LOCATION

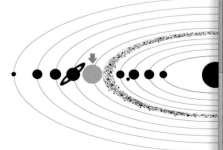

Saturn

SATURN IS KNOWN AS the Ringed Planet. Jupiter, Uranus, and Neptune also have rings, but Saturn's are the most magnificent. From Earth, we can see what look like three broad, smooth rings. The A ring is the outside one. Next comes the Cassini division, a dark gap 2,900 miles (4,670 km) wide. The B ring is the widest and brightest, 16,000 miles (25,750 km) across. The narrower C ring, just inward, appears pale and semi-transparent.

Three spacecraft—Pioneer 11 and Voyagers 1 and 2—have visited Saturn since 1979. They revealed that the rings are made up of thousands of ringlets, each made up of icy chunks. Even the empty-looking Cassini division contains many particles. Scientists think that the rings are the remains of several smashed moons. As time passes, ring particles collide and slowly spiral into Saturn. Millions of years from now, the rings will be gone.

Saturn seems like a pale, cool copy of Jupiter. It has no solid surface and, like Jupiter, is nearly all hydrogen and helium, with traces of other gases such as methane and ammonia. Although Saturn is nearly as big as Jupiter, it has only 30 percent as much mass. A bit like a giant marshmallow, Saturn would float if you could find a large enough ocean.

The winds at Saturn's equator blow at more than 1,000 miles per hour (1,600 km/h)—much faster than Jupiter's winds. Saturn has fewer storms than Jupiter does because it has less internal heat, but large white clouds of ammonia ice crystals break out at its equator about every 30 years.

Outside the main rings orbit at least 48 moons, ranging from Titan, 3,200 miles (5,150 km) in diameter, to Pan, just 12 miles (20 km) across. Titan is the target for the Huygens probe on the Cassini spacecraft, which reached Saturn in 2004.

ORIGIN OF NAME
SATURNUS, THE ROMAN GOD WHO WAS FATHER TO JUPITER

DISTANCE FROM THE SUN
890 MILLION MILES (1,432 MILLION KM)

DIAMETER
74,896 MILES (120,533 KM)

MASS
95.2 X EARTH'S MASS

MOONS
48—LARGEST IS TITAN

LENGTH OF DAY (in Earth hours and minutes)
ROTATION TIME AND SOLAR DAY: BOTH 10 H 39 M

LENGTH OF YEAR
29.4 EARTH YEARS

◆ AMAZING FACT ◆

When Galileo Galilei first discovered the rings of Saturn in 1610, he didn't know what he was looking at because his telescope was not very sharp. He thought the planet had "ears" or "handles."

MAP OF SATURN
Saturn has numerous rings, but only the A, B, and C rings can be easily seen from Earth. Near the surface, Saturn's hydrogen and helium are gaseous, but they become fluid, and then metallic, deeper in. The rocky core has about twice the Sun's surface temperature.

Gaseous hydrogen

Liquid hydrogen

INSIDE THE RINGS
Saturn's rings are made of chunks of ice and rock. The rings are thousands of miles wide but only some 40 to 400 feet (12 to 120 m) thick.

Cassini division

B ring

D ring

A ring

C ring

Encke division

F ring

HUYGENS PROBE
Huygens parachuted through Titan's atmosphere to its surface. Titan might have organic chemicals like those on the early Earth.

CASSINI
The Cassini orbiter took more than six years to reach Saturn.

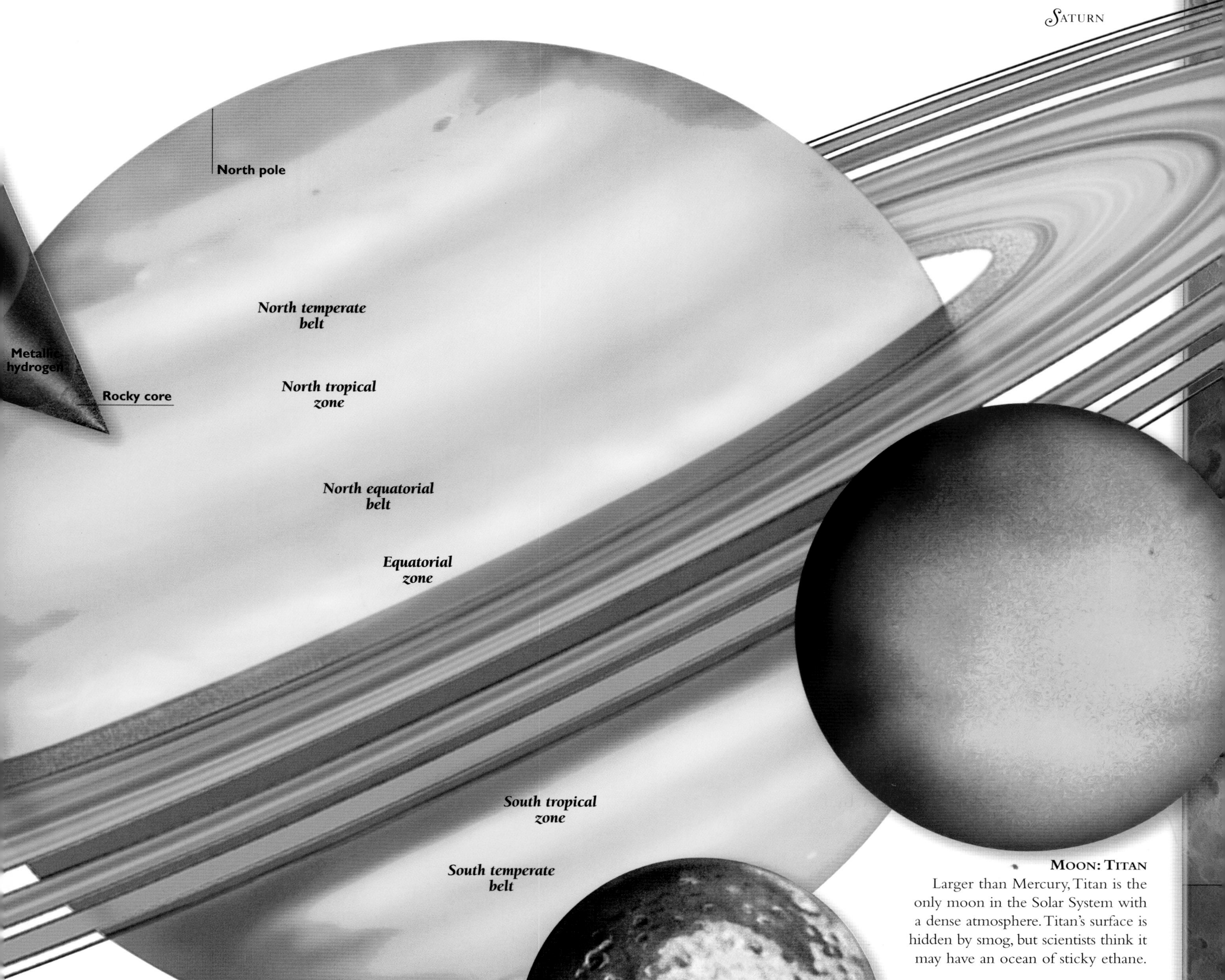

North pole

North temperate
belt

Metallic
hydrogen

Rocky core

North tropical
zone

North equatorial
belt

Equatorial
zone

South tropical
zone

South temperate
belt

MOON: TITAN
Larger than Mercury, Titan is the
only moon in the Solar System with
a dense atmosphere. Titan's surface is
hidden by smog, but scientists think it
may have an ocean of sticky ethane.

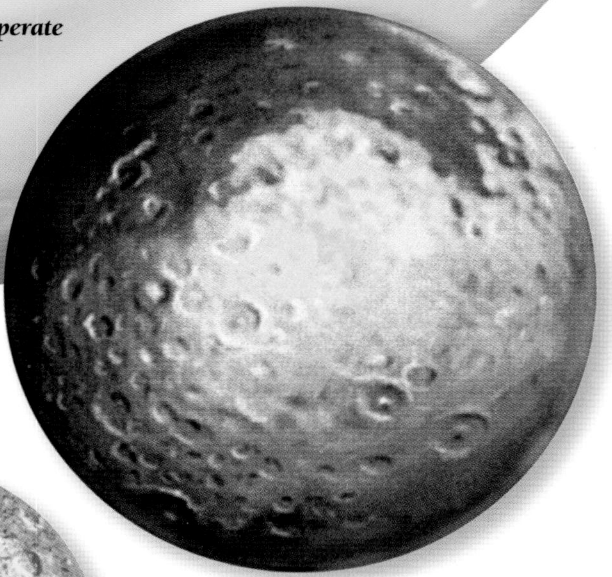

MOON: IAPETUS
The side of Iapetus that faces
forward in its orbit is as black as
tar, while its trailing side is snowy
white. The "tar" may be dust
knocked off another moon by tiny
meteorite impacts.

LOCATION

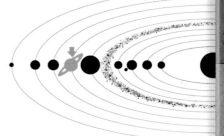

Herschel
crater

MOON: ENCELADUS
Enceladus has a bright surface and
regions almost free of craters. This
hints that the moon may have been
resurfaced by volcanic eruptions. Such
eruptions may still sometimes occur.

MOON: MIMAS
The impact that made the giant
Herschel crater nearly broke Mimas
apart. Today, the gravity of Mimas
helps clear ring particles from the
Cassini division.

Uranus

In 1781, William Herschel looked through his telescope and found Uranus, the first planet discovered in modern times. Uranus has a diameter about four times greater than Earth's, but it orbits so far from the Sun that Herschel and other observers could tell little about the planet. Most of what we now know about Uranus was learned from the Voyager 2 spacecraft flyby in 1986.

Uranus might be called the planet-on-its-side—Earth's axis tilts 23.5 degrees to its orbit, but Uranus's axis tips almost 98 degrees. When Voyager 2 flew past, Uranus's south pole was pointing almost directly at the Sun, and the northern hemisphere was in darkness. Voyager saw a bland, blue-green Uranus without any features. Scientists using the Hubble Space Telescope are now seeing signs of storms in Uranus's northern hemisphere as it emerges from its long, dark winter.

The blue-green color of Uranus comes from traces of methane in its upper atmosphere. The methane reflects the blue wavelengths of sunlight and absorbs the red. Most of Uranus, however, is hydrogen and helium, like the Sun. And like the other gas-giant planets, it has no solid surface.

In 1977, astronomers watched a star wink on and off before disappearing behind Uranus. This revealed that Uranus has a set of narrow, dark rings. Eleven rings are now known. The dark gray ring particles are a few inches to 10 yards (10 cm to 10 m) across.

Uranus has five large moons, including Miranda, which has a surface unlike any other moon in the solar system. In recent years, many smaller moons have been discovered. There are at least 22 of these dark asteroid-like objects.

◆ Look Again ◆

- How were Uranus's rings discovered?
- Why are storms starting to appear on Uranus?
- How did Uranus end up with a large tilt to its axis?

Map of Uranus
So far, the face of Uranus has appeared featureless, but that might change as it continues its orbit. Beneath Uranus's gaseous top layer is a dense liquid layer and a hot rocky core. The planet is circled by 11 rings.

Seasons
Uranus's orbit takes 84 Earth years, so each pole receives a long period of constant sunlight followed by a long period of darkness. The atmosphere is growing more active as Uranus approaches its equinox, when the Sun is over its equator.

2007

2030
Southern winter
S   N

Northern summer

1985
Southern summer
S   N

1966
S   N

Northern winter

Origin of Name
Uranus, the most ancient of the Roman gods

Distance From The Sun
1,784 million miles (2,871 million km)

Diameter
31,763 miles (51,118 km)

Mass
14.5 x Earth's mass

Moons
27—largest is Titania

Length of Day (in Earth hours and minutes)
Rotation time and solar day: both 17 h 14 m

Length of Year
84.1 Earth years

The Sideways Planet
What tilted Uranus's rotation axis? Scientists speculate that as Uranus was forming, a large object struck and knocked it over on its side. The impact may also have created the moons and rings, which orbit in line with Uranus's equator.

❷ Uranus tips on its side, debris from impact circles equator to form rings

Surface of Miranda
Scientists believe Miranda's grooves (seen in the top left and bottom right of this photo) mark where eruptions were starting to resurface the moon. When Miranda's internal heat ran out, the landscape froze in place.

North pole

◆ Amazing Fact ◆

The telescope that William Herschel used to discover Uranus in 1781 was a 6-inch (3.9-cm) Newtonian reflector. This is no bigger than many of the backyard telescopes available today.

North pole

❶ Large object strikes Uranus

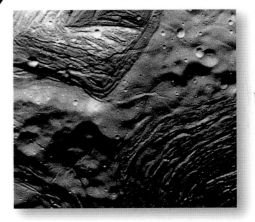

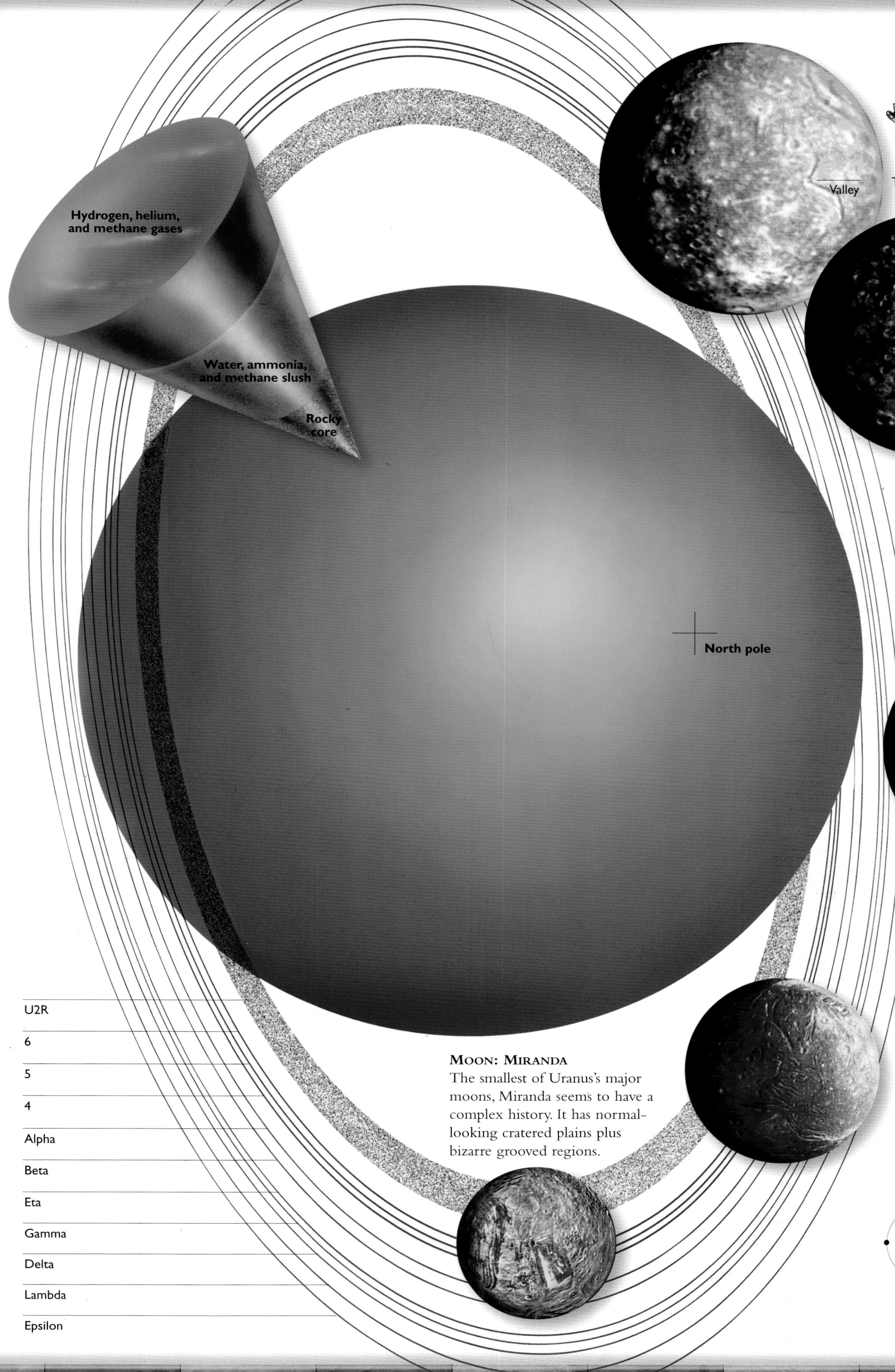

Hydrogen, helium,
and methane gases

Water, ammonia,
and methane slush

Rocky
core

+ **North pole**

U2R

6

5

4

Alpha

Beta

Eta

Gamma

Delta

Lambda

Epsilon

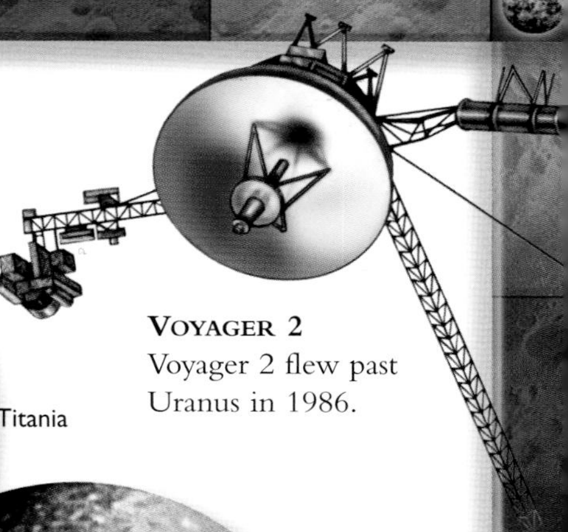

Valley   Titania

VOYAGER 2
Voyager 2 flew past
Uranus in 1986.

Rays

Oberon

**MOONS: TITANIA AND
OBERON**
Titania and Oberon both
display many craters. Some
of Oberon's craters have
bright rays and dark floors.
Titania also has long valleys
caused by geological faults.

MOON: UMBRIEL
Umbriel measures more
than 700 miles (1,150 km)
across. Its heavily cratered
surface probably hasn't
changed in billions of years.

MOON: ARIEL
As well as its craters, Ariel
displays long valleys and
areas that look as if they
have been resurfaced by
volcanic eruptions.

MOON: MIRANDA
The smallest of Uranus's major
moons, Miranda seems to have a
complex history. It has normal-
looking cratered plains plus
bizarre grooved regions.

LOCATION

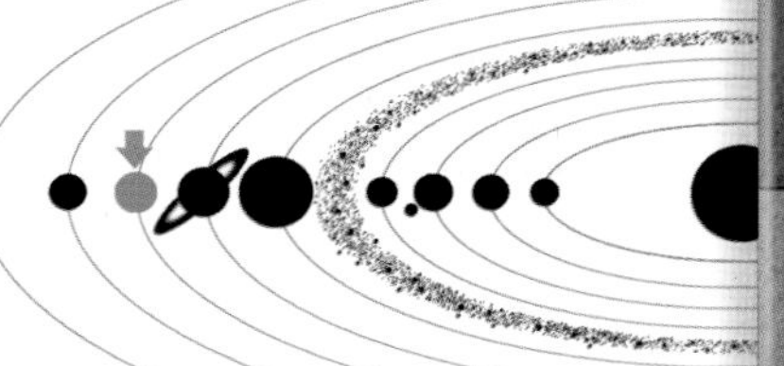

Neptune

Neptune is the Sun's last gas-giant planet. It was first spotted in 1846 after astronomers noticed that Uranus wasn't moving along its orbit exactly as it should. Guessing that an unknown planet was orbiting farther out and influencing Uranus, the astronomers John Couch Adams in England and Urbain Leverrier in France independently calculated where the new planet might be. When observers Johann Galle and Heinrich d'Arrest checked, they found the new planet right where Adams and Leverrier had predicted.

Since Neptune orbits far from Earth, little was known about it until the Voyager 2 spacecraft paid a flyby visit in 1989. The spacecraft showed that Neptune is a cold, blue echo of Uranus, with some important differences. Like Uranus, Neptune is a ball of hydrogen, helium, and methane. The tilt of Neptune's axis (29.6 degrees) is not as extreme as Uranus's, so its seasonal changes are less dramatic. Neptune has raging storms and clouds. Voyager photographed a giant storm known as the Great Dark Spot and a fast-moving cloud of methane ice crystals called the Scooter. Observations from Earth show that storms come and go over the years, probably driven by Neptune's internal heat.

Two Neptunian moons were known before Voyager. Its flyby added six. They range from Triton, with a diameter of 1,681 miles (2,706 km), to Naiad, just 36 miles (58 km) wide. Triton has erupting geysers, but the other moons are inactive worlds.

Astronomers discovered the rings of Neptune in 1984. They found that one of the six rings has clumps in it, caused perhaps by moons that are yet to be discovered.

ORIGIN OF NAME
Neptunus, the Roman god of the ocean

DISTANCE FROM THE SUN
2,795 million miles (4,498 million km)

DIAMETER
30,775 miles (49,528 km)

MASS
17.2 x Earth's mass

MOONS
13—largest is Triton

LENGTH OF DAY (in Earth hours and minutes)
Rotation time and solar day: both 16 h 7 m

LENGTH OF YEAR
164.9 Earth years

GREAT DARK SPOT
This 1989 photo from Voyager 2 shows the Great Dark Spot (upper left), the white Scooter (center), and the Dark Spot 2 (lower right). All the features have vanished since the photo was taken.

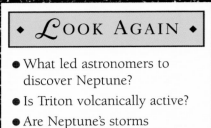

MAP OF NEPTUNE
Neptune is circled by six faint rings. The planet is colored blue by traces of methane in its gaseous surface. Beneath the surface, Neptune probably has a deep "ocean" of water, ammonia, and methane and a hot rocky core.

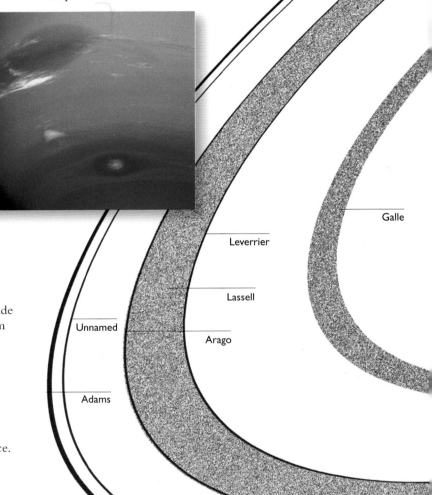

Galle

Leverrier

Lassell

Arago

Unnamed

Adams

NEPTUNE'S RINGS
The rings of Neptune are made up of particles that range from microscopic to the size of a house. The ring particles contain ice darkened by dust and scientists think they are fragments of moonlets that broke up in collisions. The gravity of Neptune's existing moons keeps the rings in place.

◆ AMAZING FACT ◆

Since Neptune was first seen from Earth in 1846, it still has not made a full orbit around the Sun. The trip takes 165 Earth years, so it completes the trip in 2011.

TRITON'S SURFACE
Triton is volcanically active, with geysers shooting plumes of dark material 5 miles (8 km) high. With few craters, Triton's surface is covered in frosts of nitrogen, methane, and other ices.

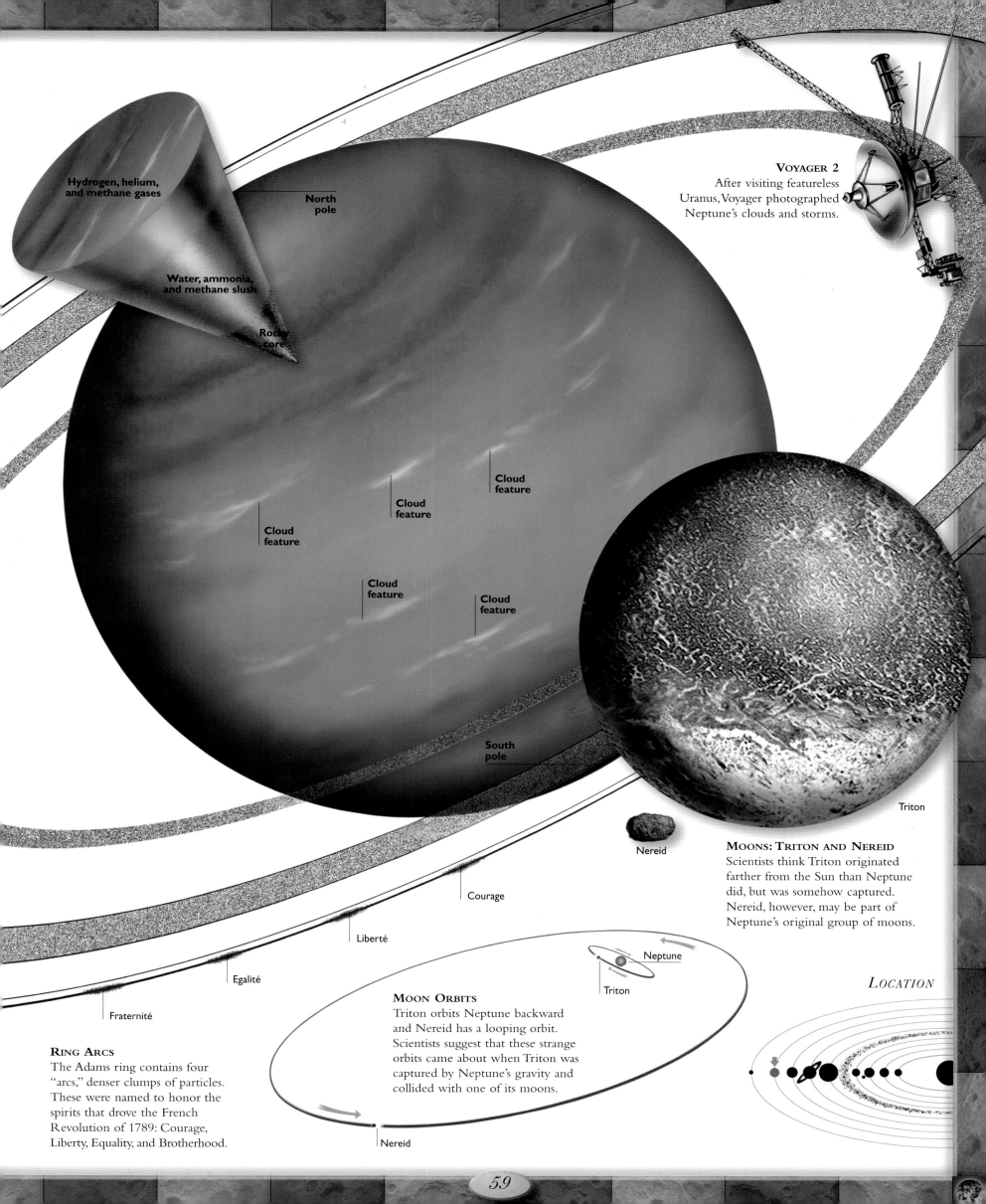

Hydrogen, helium, and methane gases

Water, ammonia, and methane slush

Rocky core

North pole

Cloud feature

Cloud feature

Cloud feature

Cloud feature

Cloud feature

South pole

VOYAGER 2
After visiting featureless Uranus, Voyager photographed Neptune's clouds and storms.

Triton

Nereid

MOONS: TRITON AND NEREID
Scientists think Triton originated farther from the Sun than Neptune did, but was somehow captured. Nereid, however, may be part of Neptune's original group of moons.

Courage

Liberté

Egalité

Fraternité

RING ARCS
The Adams ring contains four "arcs," denser clumps of particles. These were named to honor the spirits that drove the French Revolution of 1789: Courage, Liberty, Equality, and Brotherhood.

MOON ORBITS
Triton orbits Neptune backward and Nereid has a looping orbit. Scientists suggest that these strange orbits came about when Triton was captured by Neptune's gravity and collided with one of its moons.

Neptune

Triton

Nereid

LOCATION

Pluto

ONCE CONSIDERED THE NINTH PLANET, Pluto was downgraded to a dwarf planet in 2006. It was discovered in 1930 by Clyde Tombaugh, after a long search. In 1978, James Christy found that Pluto has a large moon, now called Charon. Pluto is very small and icy, unlike either the rocky planets or the gas giants. Scientists think Pluto is a different kind of Solar System object—an icy planetesimal.

Icy planetesimals probably formed in the Kuiper Belt, a region beyond the orbit of Neptune. From there, the gravity of the gas giants sent most of them careening among the planets. Some planetesimals were destroyed in collisions. Others were captured and became moons (Neptune's big moon Triton may be an icy planetesimal captured in this way). Some planetesimals were thrown out and formed the distant Oort Cloud (see page 62), and some became comets. And one, perhaps, became Pluto.

During its long year, Pluto's distance from the Sun varies from about 30-50 times Earth's distance from the Sun. As it nears the Sun and grows warmer, its atmosphere springs into existence. The rest of the time, Pluto's temperature hovers around −396°F (−238°C). This is so cold that its atmosphere stays frozen as a layer of frost and snow on the surface.

The first spacecraft to visit Pluto is on its way. After passing Pluto, New Horizons will continue deeper into the Kuiper Belt.

NAME
PLUTO, THE ROMAN GOD OF THE UNDERWORLD

DISTANCE FROM THE SUN
3,675 MILLION MILES (5,914 MILLION KM)

DIAMETER
1,432 MILES (2,304 KM)

MASS
0.2% x EARTH'S MASS

MOONS
3—LARGEST IS CHARON

LENGTH OF DAY (in Earth days/hours/minutes)
ROTATION TIME AND SOLAR DAY: BOTH 6 D 9 H 17 M

LENGTH OF YEAR
248 EARTH YEARS

◆ PROJECT: *Weighing It Up* ◆

❶ Weigh yourself on a household scale and write down your weight on Earth at the top of a piece of paper.

❷ Write down the name of every planet you want to visit. (Draw its picture too if you like!)

❸ Go to the Universe Fact File on pages 110–11 and find the surface gravity of each planet. Write it next to the planet's name.

❹ Multiply your weight on Earth by the surface gravity for each planet. That's what you'd weigh on each body. (Of course, you wouldn't actually be able to stand on the gas-giant planets because their surfaces aren't solid!)

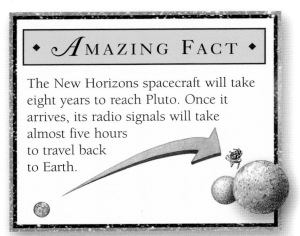

◆ AMAZING FACT ◆

The New Horizons spacecraft will take eight years to reach Pluto. Once it arrives, its radio signals will take almost five hours to travel back to Earth.

PLUTO AND CHARON
Charon's diameter is about half Pluto's, making almost a double planet. Scientists speculate that Pluto and Charon may have formed together after a catastrophic collision.

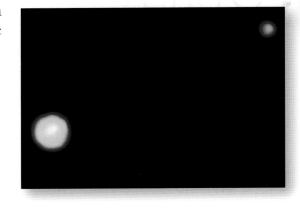

MAP OF PLUTO
Scientists don't know what Pluto's surface features look like, but observations show that it has a thin crust of nitrogen and methane ice. What lies below the surface is also guesswork until a probe visits, but there may be a mantle of water ice and a large rocky core.

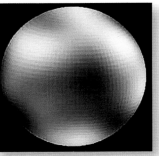

PLUTO SNAPSHOT
Images taken by the Hubble Space Telescope suggest that Pluto is much like Neptune's moon Triton. They are nearly the same size and temperature and have similar surface ices.

Pluto's orbit   Pluto   Kuiper Belt

THE OUTER REACHES
This cutaway view shows planet orbits and the Kuiper Belt. Pluto's eccentric orbit tilts 17 degrees to the orbits of the other planets. Scientists think Pluto came from the Kuiper Belt, a region beyond Neptune populated by small, icy bodies.

Pluto   Moon   Ganymede

SIZE COMPARISON
Pluto is smaller than all the planets of the Solar System—it is even smaller than some of the moons, including Earth's Moon and Jupiter's moon Ganymede (shown here to scale).

Water-methane-nitrogen ice

Water ice

Rocky core

THE EXPRESS
On its way to Pluto, New Horizons is about a quarter the size of the Voyager 2 spacecraft.

PLUTO'S DAY AND MONTH
Pluto and Charon keep the same faces turned toward each other. Charon revolves around Pluto in exactly the time that Pluto rotates on its axis. So Pluto's day and its month have the same length—about 6.4 Earth days.

MOON: CHARON
Charon, shown here in scale to Pluto, is a mystery. Its surface seems entirely covered in water ice with none of Pluto's methane or nitrogen. Inside it probably has a rocky core.

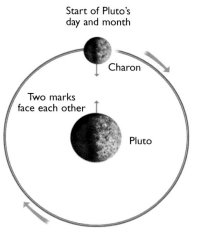

Start of Pluto's
day and month

Charon

Two marks
face each other

Pluto

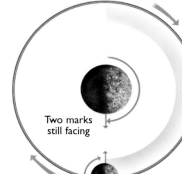

3.2 Earth days later:
Pluto is halfway through its
rotation and Charon is halfway
through its orbit

Two marks
still facing

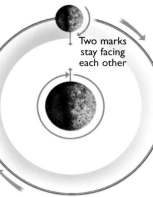

6.4 Earth days later:
Pluto has completed its
rotation and Charon
has completed its orbit

Two marks
stay facing
each other

LOCATION

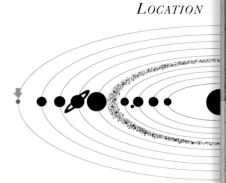

Comets

MOST COMETS EXIST in the icy-cold regions beyond Neptune. Here they are loosely packed lumps of frozen water and other ices mixed with dust. Many are only the size of houses, but others measure a dozen miles (about 20 km) or more across. Sometimes one of these lumps is pulled by gravity or pushed by a collision toward the center of the Solar System. As the comet approaches the Sun, its ices grow warm and begin to boil away, forming a cloud of dusty gas called a coma. The coma can be thousands of miles wide, much bigger than the nucleus (core) of the comet. Sunlight and solar radiation pressing on the coma drive its dust and gas into two separate tails, which may be millions of miles long. The tail of gas is bluish and always points away from the Sun. The dust tail is yellowish or white. It looks smooth and is often curved.

Comets sometimes meet dramatic ends. Satellites have seen more than 60 small comets evaporate as they approached the Sun. In 1994, 20 or so pieces of comet Shoemaker-Levy 9 struck Jupiter, causing bright explosions. Jupiter wore dusty marks in its clouds for months afterward.

Scientists think that comets are leftovers from the formation of the Solar System and that they contain a frozen record of this time. Space probes such as Giotto, which flew past comet Halley in 1986, have provided close-up views of comets. The Stardust probe flew to comet Wild 2 in 2004, snatched a sample of dust, and brought it back to Earth two years later.

COMET ORBITS
Short-period comets such as Halley and Encke orbit the Sun in 200 years or less and travel among the planets. Comets that take longer than 200 years are long-period comets. Comet Hale-Bopp will return in 2,400 years.

Uranus

ORIGIN OF NAME
COMET IS FROM THE GREEK WORDS FOR "HAIRY STAR."

SIZE OF NUCLEUS
COMET NUCLEI RANGE FROM ABOUT 100 YARDS TO 25 MILES (100 M TO 40 KM) IN DIAMETER.

LENGTH OF TAIL
CAN BE OVER 300 MILLION MILES (482.8 MILLION KM) LONG

COMPOSITION
FROZEN WATER AND OTHER ICES, WITH DUST RICH IN CARBON AND SILICATES

NUMBER OF COMETS IN THE SOLAR SYSTEM
UNKNOWN—PROBABLY IN THE TRILLIONS

COMET HALE-BOPP
Comet Hale-Bopp was a striking sight in early 1997. This photograph clearly shows the comet's broad, white dust tail and bluish gas tail.

◆ LOOK AGAIN ◆

- Which comet tail always points away from the Sun?
- If you melted a comet, what would you have?
- Where do most comets come from?

WHERE COMETS COME FROM
The Oort Cloud is an enormous region surrounding the Solar System. It contains trillions of icy objects and is the source of long-period comets (ones that take more than 200 years to orbit the Sun). Short-period comets come from the Kuiper Belt, an inner region that begins near the orbit of Neptune.

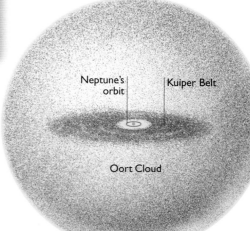

Neptune's orbit

Kuiper Belt

Oort Cloud

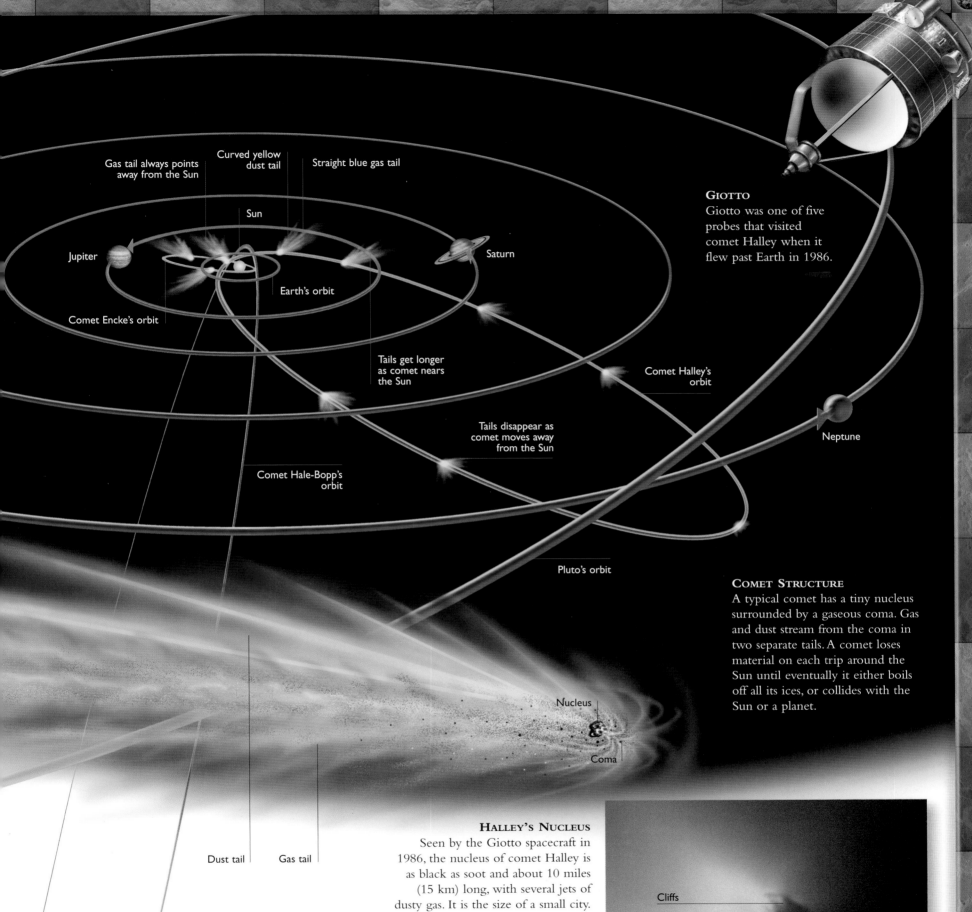

Gas tail always points away from the Sun

Curved yellow dust tail

Straight blue gas tail

Sun

Jupiter

Comet Encke's orbit

Earth's orbit

Saturn

Tails get longer as comet nears the Sun

Tails disappear as comet moves away from the Sun

Comet Hale-Bopp's orbit

Pluto's orbit

Comet Halley's orbit

Neptune

Nucleus

Coma

Dust tail

Gas tail

GIOTTO

Giotto was one of five probes that visited comet Halley when it flew past Earth in 1986.

COMET STRUCTURE

A typical comet has a tiny nucleus surrounded by a gaseous coma. Gas and dust stream from the coma in two separate tails. A comet loses material on each trip around the Sun until eventually it either boils off all its ices, or collides with the Sun or a planet.

HALLEY'S NUCLEUS

Seen by the Giotto spacecraft in 1986, the nucleus of comet Halley is as black as soot and about 10 miles (15 km) long, with several jets of dusty gas. It is the size of a small city.

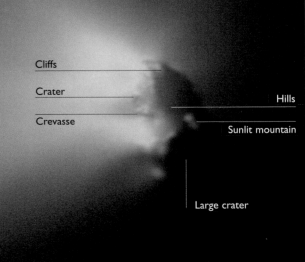

Cliffs

Crater

Crevasse

Hills

Sunlit mountain

Large crater

COMET HALLEY

In 1705, Edmond Halley discovered that one comet kept returning about every 76 years. When it came back on schedule after Halley's death, it was named for him. Comet Halley's last visit was in 1986. Its next is in 2061.

Deep Space

BIG AS IT SEEMS TO US, the Solar System is just Earth's backyard. Beyond lies the rest of the universe—deep space. There are stars and other solar systems in deep space, but that's not all. Even though space looks dark and empty, astronomers have discovered that gas and dust drift through it. This interstellar matter is normally invisible, but it can be detected if a bright star lies behind it.

Some interstellar matter collects in thick clouds of dust and gas called nebulas. These are places where stars (and planets) are born. Typically, a large nebula creates an open cluster of several hundred stars. Another kind of cluster is the globular cluster, containing up to a million stars. Larger in scale are the galaxies, usually vast assemblies of billions of stars. Galaxies take different forms such as spiral, elliptical, and irregular. On the largest scales, galaxies themselves cluster into groups.

Distances in deep space are much greater than within the Solar System, so astronomers use the light-year, the distance that light travels in one year—roughly 6 trillion miles (10 trillion km). This is an enormous distance. If the distance between Earth and the Sun were 1 inch (2.5 cm), a light-year would be 1 mile (1.6 km). The star nearest the Sun, Alpha Centauri, is about 4.3 light-years away, while the most distant galaxy detected is 12 to 15 billion light-years away.

LEAST MASSIVE STAR KNOWN
GLIESE 623B, ONLY 10% AS MASSIVE AS THE SUN

MOST MASSIVE STAR KNOWN
ETA CARINAE, ABOUT 150 TIMES AS MASSIVE AS THE SUN

LEAST MASSIVE GALAXY KNOWN
PEGASUS II, A DWARF ELLIPTICAL GALAXY WITH PERHAPS 10 MILLION STARS

MOST MASSIVE GALAXY KNOWN
M87, A GIANT ELLIPTICAL GALAXY WITH ABOUT 800 BILLION STARS

A TOUR OF DEEP SPACE
Beyond our Solar System, there are nebulas where stars are born (below left), stars of all sizes, clusters of stars, galaxies of various shapes, and clusters of galaxies. Astronomers use giant telescopes on Earth and orbiting telescopes in space to study these spectacular objects.

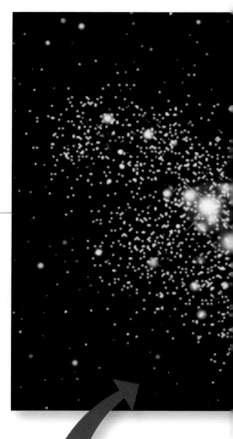

Star Cluster
Star clusters such as the Jewel Box are common in deep space. When clouds of gas and dust collapse, they make clusters of stars. The stars have different masses and age at various speeds, the most massive aging fastest.

Nebula
Stars are born in giant clouds of dust and hydrogen gas such as the Lagoon nebula (shown here). This giant cloud may produce thousands of stars.

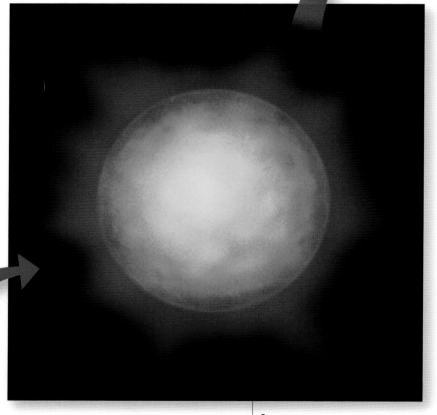

Star
After shining for billions of years, stars like the Sun start to run out of their hydrogen fuel supply. They grow larger and redder, becoming red giants or supergiants such as Betelgeuse (pictured).

ROSAT
The ROSAT space telescope detected the X-ray energy coming from stars, nebulas, and galaxies.

◆ **LOOK AGAIN** ◆

● Where are stars born?
● What kinds of stars age fastest?
● How far away is the most distant known galaxy?

Spiral Galaxy
Spiral galaxies have a nucleus of older yellow and reddish stars, and a spiral-armed disk with dusty gas clouds where new stars emerge.

◆ **AMAZING FACT** ◆

If you could travel to the nearest star—Alpha Centauri—in a space shuttle at 5 miles per second (8 km/s), the journey would take you roughly 162,000 years.

HORSEHEAD NEBULA
This dark nebula gets its name from its shape. It can be seen outlined against a cloud of red hydrogen.

Galaxy Cluster
Like stars, galaxies gather in groups known as clusters. Astronomers are studying whether galaxies form in a cluster first or whether the clusters grow from galaxies that are born separately.

STARRY SKY
The stars you can see with the naked eye all lie relatively close to Earth. Binoculars or a telescope will show you more, such as the dense star field pictured here.

Nebulas

Clouds of dust and gas in space are known as nebulas, from the Latin word for "cloud." In some nebulas, gravity packs the dust and gas so tightly that parts of the nebula condense into stars. By studying these star-making "factories," astronomers have caught stars in the act of being born.

Nebulas are usually cold and do not shine, so they can be hard to see. But a nebula that lies near a hot star absorbs energy from the star and its gases glow like a vivid red fluorescent light. This is called an emission nebula. Because they are bright, emission nebulas can be seen for great distances. For example, astronomers have detected emission nebulas in the Andromeda galaxy, some 2.5 million light-years away.

Another kind of nebula is made of tiny dust grains. These are just the right size to reflect starlight, so this nebula shines by reflecting the light of nearby stars. Reflection nebulas often appear blue because the dust grains reflect blue starlight especially well. Some dark dust nebulas are visible only because we see them against a bright background. The Horsehead nebula, for example, is a big cloud of dusty gas thick enough to block the light from the emission nebula behind it (see page 65).

While many nebulas are the birthplace of stars, others represent a star's final stages. When stars like the Sun grow old, they throw off their outer layers. The layers become a glowing shell of gas that expands into space, lit by the hot core of the star. These gas clouds are called planetary nebulas, but they have no relation to planets. They just looked like planets to the 19th century astronomers who came up with the name.

EMISSION NEBULA
The Orion nebula is a beautiful example of an emission nebula. It can be faintly seen with the naked eye, but looks best in a telescope. Astronomers have detected dozens of newborn stars within it.

REFLECTION NEBULA
Starlight reflecting from tiny dust grains produces this reflection nebula, seen in the constellation of Corona Australis. The bluish color comes from the light of the hot stars inside the nebula, and also from the dust grains, which reflect blue light especially well.

EAGLE NEBULA (main image)
Type: emission; Distance: 7,000 light-years; Diameter: 315 light-years

ORION NEBULA (page 66, top)
Type: emission; Distance: 1,500 light-years; Diameter: 40 light-years

REFLECTION NEBULA IN CORONA AUSTRALIS (page 66, middle)
Type: reflection; Distance: 445 light-years; Diameter: 0.13 light-years

CONE NEBULA (page 67, bottom center)
Type: dark; Distance: 3,000 light-years; Length: 50 light-years

HELIX NEBULA (page 67, lower right)
Type: planetary; Distance: 600 light-years; Diameter: 2 light-years

◆ Amazing Fact ◆

Only about 0.1 percent of a nebula ends up making stars (and their planets, if they have any). The rest gets blown back into space, where it will eventually end up in another nebula.

Nebula

Star forming

A STARRY EAGLE

The Eagle nebula is an emission nebula surrounding a cluster of stars. It is 7,000 light-years away and appears in the constellation of Serpens. This photo taken through a telescope on Earth (right) shows dust clouds and gas being lit up by the light from hot, young stars. Our Sun and planets formed out of a similar nebula about 4.6 billion years ago.

PILLARS OF DUST AND GAS

The Hubble Space Telescope peered into the Eagle nebula and revealed pillars of dust and gas. The left-hand pillar (above) is about one light-year high. The light from newborn stars is eroding the gas in the pillars, much as wind moves dust on Earth. Little spikes emerging from the pillars (left) are denser globules of dusty gas. Each is about the size of the Solar System.

PLANETARY NEBULA

The Helix nebula in the constellation of Aquarius is the closest planetary nebula to the Sun. It is only about 10,000 years old. Eventually the gas cloud will drift away and disappear, leaving just the white-hot central star.

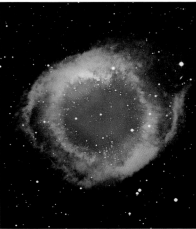

DARK NEBULA

The Cone nebula in the constellation of Monoceros is a cloud of dense dust visible against a bright emission nebula.

Stars

EVERY STAR IS A BIG BALL of extremely hot gas. Stars are mostly hydrogen (about 90 percent) and helium (roughly 10 percent), with tiny amounts of other gases. In its core, a true star must be hot enough—at least 11 million degrees Fahrenheit (6 million degrees Celsius)—to have nuclear reactions. These reactions fuse hydrogen into helium and release energy. The outward push of energy keeps the star from collapsing under its own weight. As each bit of energy reaches the surface, it flies into space—and the star shines.

The smallest true stars have about 10 percent of the Sun's mass. Smaller than these are the brown dwarfs, star-like bodies that never became hot enough to fuse hydrogen into helium. They give off a little heat but they cannot shine like a true star. The most massive stars known seem to have about 150 times the Sun's mass. Astronomers think that if a star bigger than this tried to form, the cloud that gave birth to it would probably break apart and produce two or more stars.

Many common stars, in fact, are really two stars that orbit each other. The nearest star to the Sun is a triple-star system known as Alpha Centauri, with two stars, each about the Sun's size—Alpha Centauri A and B—and a much smaller third star—Proxima Centauri. The brightest star system in the sky, Sirius, is made up of two stars—Sirius A, also known as the Dog Star, and Sirius B, the Pup. Astronomers can estimate the mass of multiple stars by closely observing how they orbit one another.

SUN
TYPE: YELLOW MAIN SEQUENCE; DISTANCE: 8 LIGHT-MINUTES; DIAMETER: 865,000 MILES (1,392,000 KM)

ALPHA CENTAURI
TYPE: YELLOW MAIN SEQUENCE; DISTANCE: 4.3 LIGHT-YEARS; DIAMETER: 1 X THE SUN'S DIAMETER

SIRIUS
TYPE: WHITE MAIN SEQUENCE; DISTANCE: 8.6 LIGHT-YEARS; DIAMETER: 2.4 X THE SUN'S DIAMETER

BETELGEUSE
TYPE: RED SUPERGIANT; DISTANCE: 427 LIGHT-YEARS; DIAMETER: 800 X THE SUN'S DIAMETER

AN ORDINARY LIFE
From dust to dust—a star is born from a lump of dusty gas in a nebula. And at the end of its life, millions or billions of years later, it will throw some of its material back into space. The more massive a star is, the hotter it becomes and the faster its life runs. This sequence shows the life cycle of an average-size star like the Sun.

Red Giant Star
After another 10 billion years, the star runs low on hydrogen fuel. It swells into a red giant that starts to pulsate. If the star has planets, the innermost ones are destroyed.

Main Sequence Star
About 40 million years later, the star is fully formed and living a normal existence, perhaps with a system of planets.

Starbirth Nebula
An ordinary star like the Sun is born in a nebula when a cloud of gas and dust starts to collapse and grow hotter.

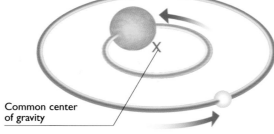

Common center of gravity

DOUBLE-STAR SYSTEM
The two stars in the Sirius system orbit each other every 50 years. When astronomers computed the mass of each star, they found that the smaller star, Sirius B, was very massive for its size. It was the first white dwarf star ever found.

White Dwarf Star
In less than 50,000 years, the planetary nebula disperses into space. It leaves behind a white dwarf, the star's white-hot core.

Planetary Nebula
Three billion years later, the pulsations grow stronger, and the bloated star sheds its outer layers to form a planetary nebula.

Red supergiant

Red giant

HERTZSPRUNG–RUSSELL DIAGRAM

The diagram arranges stars according to their brightness (scale at left) and temperature (scale along bottom). Most stars fall in the main sequence, which runs from top left to bottom right. Not surprisingly, most stars that are hotter are also brighter. In the upper right are red supergiants—cool but very bright because of their great size. White dwarfs, near the bottom, can be hot but still very dim.

STAR SIZE COMPARISON

Compared to a white dwarf star, the Sun is a giant. But a red giant star has a diameter 20 to 40 times greater than the Sun's, and a red supergiant is roughly 800 times larger.

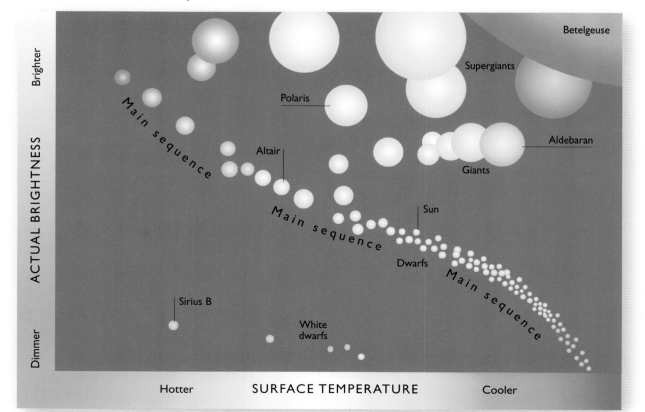

ACTUAL BRIGHTNESS

Brighter

Dimmer

Main sequence

Main sequence

Main sequence

Betelgeuse

Supergiants

Polaris

Altair

Aldebaran

Giants

Sun

Dwarfs

Sirius B

White dwarfs

Hotter   SURFACE TEMPERATURE   Cooler

Sun

White dwarf

Variable Stars

WHILE MANY STARS SHINE STEADILY year after year, others seem to change in brightness. One kind of variable star is called an eclipsing binary. It is really a double-star system in which one star passes in front of the other. When the two are side by side, they are at their brightest. When one is in front of the other, the system appears dimmer. These stars' actual brightness remains the same, but they appear dimmer because they eclipse each other.

The actual brightness of some stars changes as well. Giants and supergiants regularly grow larger and smaller, changing color and brightness. They are called pulsating variables and are classified by how much their brightness changes and by their period—how long they take to go from bright to dim to bright again.

The Cepheids are a group of pulsating stars that change in brightness over periods ranging from 1 day to 70 days. Any two Cepheids with the same period have the same actual brightness. The longer a Cepheid's period is, the brighter the star actually is. In the 1920s, American astronomer Edwin Hubble found Cepheids in the Andromeda galaxy. By measuring their period, he could tell their actual brightness. Then, by comparing their apparent brightness to their actual brightness, he could estimate how far away they are. He proved that the Cepheids and Andromeda are too far away to be part of the Milky Way—and that the universe is larger than anyone had expected.

Some variables change dramatically. In a double-star system, the star with stronger gravity may pull so much gas from its companion that it sets off an explosion known as a nova. The system suddenly brightens enormously and then fades slowly. The explosions can happen again and again.

NOVA EXPLOSION

In a double-star system, things can get complicated! As one star ages, it swells into a red giant and some of its gas may be captured by its companion star, a white dwarf. When the captured material crashes onto the white dwarf, the gas can become hot enough to touch off a nuclear explosion. The resulting blast of energy is called a nova. If the bloated red giant keeps feeding gas to the white dwarf, the nova will erupt repeatedly.

Red giant

Gas streamimg to white dwarf

ALGOL
TYPE: ECLIPSING BINARY; MAGNITUDE: VARIES FROM 2.1 TO 3.4; PERIOD: 2 DAYS 20 HOURS 49 MINUTES

MIRA
TYPE: PULSATING VARIABLE; MAGNITUDE: VARIES FROM 3.4 TO 9.3; PERIOD: 332 DAYS

ETA CARINAE
TYPE: IRREGULAR VARIABLE; MAGNITUDE: WAS 2ND MAGNITUDE IN THE 1840S, THEN DIMMED GREATLY, BUT IS NOW BRIGHTENING AGAIN

White dwarf

ECLIPSING BINARY

In eclipsing binaries such as Algol, two stars orbit each other. If the orbit is tipped just right, when one star passes behind the other, its light is blocked and the total light from the pair dims.

Bright white star blocks some light from orange star— medium brightness

White star beside orange star—maximum brightness

CATACLYSMIC VARIABLE

In 1841, the star known as Eta Carinae suffered a violent outburst and blew off two giant clouds of gas. Since then, the clouds have been expanding. This strange cataclysmic variable recently doubled in brightness. It will explode as a supernova (see page 72) sometime in the next few thousand years.

Orange star blocks all light from white star— minimum brightness

PULSATING VARIABLE

A pulsating variable star expands and contracts regularly. As it swells, the star's surface becomes cooler, redder, and dimmer. The reverse happens when it shrinks. The time it takes for one complete cycle of swelling and shrinking is called the period, and it may last hours or months.

• AMAZING FACT •

One of the most spectacular novas ever observed was nova Cygni 1975. Before it erupted, it was too faint to be seen. At its peak, on August 31, 1975, it had an apparent magnitude of 1.8. Astronomers calculated that its actual brightness must have increased by at least 20 million times, making it 1 million times more luminous than the Sun.

MAGNITUDE SCALE

Astronomers measure star brightness in magnitudes. Lower numbers mean a brighter star. The brightest stars use negative numbers—Sirius is −1.4 magnitude. The faintest stars your eyes can see are 6th magnitude.

APPARENT BRIGHTNESS

In the constellation of Orion, red Betelgeuse (upper left) and blue Rigel (lower right) appear nearly the same brightness. But Rigel lies almost twice as far away, so in reality it is much brighter. Astronomers compare stars' actual brightnesses by measuring how each would appear at a standard distance of 32.6 light-years.

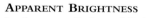

−1　0　1　2　3　4　5　6　7　8

• PROJECT: *Follow a Variable* •

Follow a star's brightness as it changes. A good star to observe in the Northern Hemisphere is Algol in the constellation of Perseus—observe it every night for a week if you can. In the Southern Hemisphere, try looking at Mira in Cetus once every two weeks for a couple of months.

❶ Locate the star on one of the star maps in this book (see pages 94–109), then find it in the night sky. Note how bright it looks compared to the stars around it. Draw a picture of the stars, indicating whether the variable is brighter or dimmer than each of the nearby stars.

❷ When you next observe, compare the variable to the nearby stars and note whether its brightness has changed.

Supernovas

A SUPERNOVA IS THE EXPLOSION of a massive star. In a supernova, a single star can briefly outshine all the rest of its galaxy. There are two types of star that can become a supernova. The first is a white dwarf in a double-star system (see diagram, below). If the white dwarf's companion swells to become a red giant, some of its gas can be captured by the white dwarf. As this material falls on the white dwarf, it steadily adds mass. If the white dwarf grows to be 1.4 times more massive than the Sun, it becomes unstable. Runaway nuclear reactions cause the white dwarf to explode, producing a supernova that destroys the stars.

The second star that can become a supernova is a massive star at least eight times larger than the Sun (see diagram, right). Such stars are very hot and have short, intense lives. The end comes when the star runs out of fuel and its nuclear reactions stop. In a second, the core collapses and sends a shock wave through the outer layers. When the shock wave reaches the surface, the supernova explodes. In this kind of supernova, the star's core survives as a neutron star—a very dense, city-size sphere—or collapses further to become a black hole—an infinitely dense object with such powerful gravity that even light cannot escape.

Each supernova throws off a supernova remnant—a cloud of gas and dust that will help to make new stars. Earth contains elements created in hot stars that died before the Sun was born. When the stars exploded as supernovas, these elements were tossed back into the Milky Way, where some of them formed the solar system. We are literally made of recycled star-stuff.

MASSIVE-STAR SUPERNOVA

One type of supernova signals the explosive death of a massive star. Such stars have at least eight times the Sun's mass. Their high temperatures cause them to race through their fuel supplies and then explode. They leave behind either a neutron star or, if the original star was very massive, a black hole.

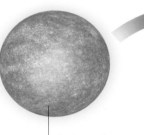

Ordinary Star
A star with at least eight times the Sun's mass evolves quickly. It shines as an ordinary star for only about 30 million years.

Supergiant Star
The massive star swells to become a supergiant star and begins to pulsate. This pulsating stage may last for 70 million years.

SUPERNOVA REMNANT

About 120,000 years ago, a massive star exploded in the constellation of Vela. By now, the expanding wisps of gas look almost like spiderwebs. Supernova explosions return gas and dust to space, where they will help to build new stars.

SUPERNOVA 1987A
SEEN EXPLODING: FEBRUARY 23, 1987; NOW: A YOUNG SUPERNOVA REMNANT; DISTANCE: 179,000 LIGHT-YEARS; DIAMETER: 0.2 LIGHT-YEAR

CRAB NEBULA
SEEN EXPLODING: 1054; NOW: A SUPERNOVA REMNANT; DISTANCE: 6,300 LIGHT-YEARS; SIZE: 8.8 BY 13.7 LIGHT-YEARS

SAX J1808.4-3658
SEEN EXPLODING: IN PREHISTORIC TIMES; NOW: A PULSAR; DISTANCE: 13,000 LIGHT-YEARS

A RECENT SUPERNOVA

In 1987, a massive star known as supernova 1987A was seen exploding in the Large Magellanic Cloud. The expanding bubble of gas is still small, but eventually it will look like the Vela remnant.

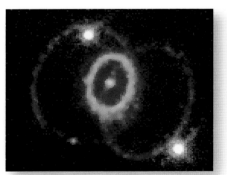

Mass Transfer
A white dwarf star attracts gas from its red giant companion.

Unstable Dwarf
The white dwarf grows in mass and becomes unstable.

DOUBLE-STAR SUPERNOVA

A supernova can occur in some kinds of double-star system. Here the gas flows from one star to its companion. Made unstable by the extra mass, the companion star explodes. Both stars are destroyed in the explosion and all that is left of them is a supernova remnant—a shell of hot gas.

Supernova Explosion
Eventually, the white dwarf explodes as a supernova.

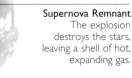

Supernova Remnant
The explosion destroys the stars, leaving a shell of hot, expanding gas.

Supernova Explosion

The star runs out of fuel and no longer has nuclear reactions to support its upper layers. The star explodes as a supernova.

Black Hole

If the original star had much more than 10 times the Sun's mass, its surviving core collapses into a black hole. This is so compact that even light can't escape. The hole is surrounded by a supernova remnant of gas and dust.

Neutron Star

A star that began with a mass up to 10 times greater than the Sun's leaves behind a neutron star. Surrounding the neutron star is a supernova remnant—an expanding shell of hot gas.

PULSARS

A neutron star, the collapsed core of a supernova, is only a few miles across but it spins very rapidly and turns some of its momentum into beams of energy. If Earth lies in the beam, we see a repeating signal like a light from a lighthouse. The pulses of energy give neutron stars their other name—pulsars.

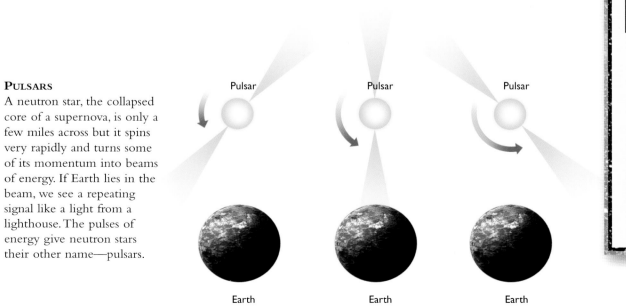

Pulsar   Pulsar   Pulsar

Earth   Earth   Earth

◆ AMAZING FACT ◆

A huge supernova in AD 1054 was seen in many parts of the world. The starburst (bottom left) was scratched into stone by Native Americans in present-day New Mexico soon after. It is believed to be a record of the exploding star in the night sky.

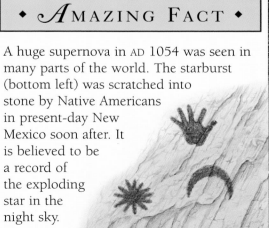

Other Solar Systems

THE SUN ISN'T THE ONLY STAR with planets. In October 1995, astronomers discovered that a star called 51 Pegasi has a planet with about half the mass of Jupiter orbiting close to it. Since then, more than 200 planets orbiting normal stars have been found. Astronomers think they will eventually find that lots of stars have their own families of planets.

The search is difficult because it is impossible to see these planets directly. Viewed from Earth, the planets appear close to their star, so they are lost in its glare. To find the planets, astronomers look for tiny movements of the star, indicated by subtle changes in the color of the star's light produced by the Doppler shift (see page 19). These changes occur because when a planet orbits a star, its gravity causes the star to move back and forth a little. Current telescopes limit how small a shift can be detected. Astronomers have found massive, Jupiter-size planets with strong gravity orbiting fairly close to their star. In 2007, an Earth-size planet was discovered orbiting around a red dwarf star.

A look at the other planetary systems shows that they are built differently from the Sun's. Our Solar System has small-mass planets such as Earth orbiting near the Sun, while the big planets such as Jupiter orbit much farther out. But the other solar systems have big planets close to their star. Perhaps as these solar systems were forming, something happened that moved the large planets inward. In any case, astronomers expect that other solar systems will have small planets as well. Earth-size planets would be the most likely places to look for alien life.

NUMBER OF OTHER SOLAR SYSTEMS DISCOVERED
MORE THAN 70 CONFIRMED (OTHERS HAVE BROWN DWARFS INSTEAD OF PLANETS)

ESTIMATED NUMBER OF OTHER SOLAR SYSTEMS
MOST STARS THAT ARE SINGLE (RATHER THAN MULTIPLE) PROBABLY HAVE PLANETS.

SMALLEST PLANET FOUND OUTSIDE THE SOLAR SYSTEM
A PLANET WITH 5.5 x EARTH'S MASS THAT ORBITS THE STAR GLIESE 876

LARGEST PLANET FOUND OUTSIDE THE SOLAR SYSTEM
A PLANET WITH 11 x JUPITER'S MASS THAT ORBITS THE STAR HD 114762

◆ PROJECT: *Making a Solar System* ◆

For this project, you need several sheets of paper, crayons or colored pencils, and the information contained in the Planet Comparison chart on the facing page.

❶ Pick one of the other planetary systems in the chart.

❷ Draw what you think its planets would look like if you approached them in a spaceship. Keep in mind that big planets will probably have thick atmospheres like Jupiter's. Each planetary system probably also has undiscovered planets the size of Earth.

❸ For comparison, draw in some members of our Solar System, such as Mercury, Earth, and Jupiter.

◆ AMAZING FACT ◆

If you lived on a planet that orbited a double star, you would see two suns in the sky at least part of the time. Everyday objects would have two shadows when both suns were visible. And if the suns were very different from each other, the shadows might have different colors.

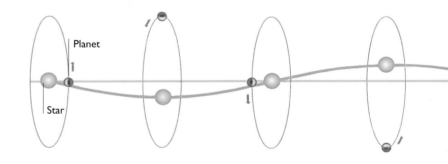

Planet

Star

COROT
The French space telescope COROT was launched in 2006. Its main purpose was to study small pulsations in stars, but it found an extrasolar planet.

KEPLER
The proposed Kepler space telescope will search for Earth-size planets by looking for a slight dimming of the star as a planet moves in front of it.

LOOK AGAIN

- Why have astronomers found only massive planets so far?
- How do astronomers discover planets they can't see?
- How do other solar systems differ from ours?

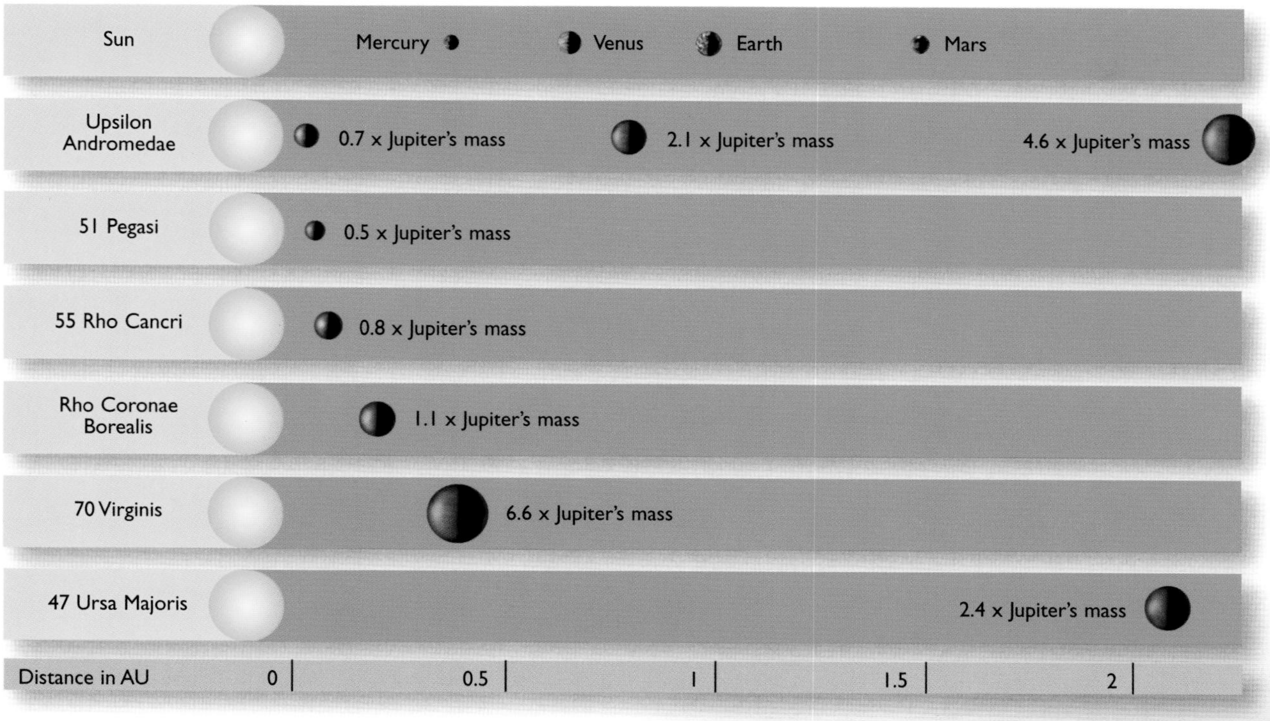

Sun	Mercury	Venus	Earth	Mars
Upsilon Andromedae	0.7 x Jupiter's mass	2.1 x Jupiter's mass	4.6 x Jupiter's mass	
51 Pegasi	0.5 x Jupiter's mass			
55 Rho Cancri	0.8 x Jupiter's mass			
Rho Coronae Borealis	1.1 x Jupiter's mass			
70 Virginis	6.6 x Jupiter's mass			
47 Ursa Majoris			2.4 x Jupiter's mass	
Distance in AU	0 0.5	1	1.5	2

PLANET COMPARISON
This chart shows some of the other known planetary systems, along with our inner Solar System. The differences are striking—the star 70 Virginis, for example, has a planet with more than six times Jupiter's mass orbiting about as close as Mercury orbits the Sun. Perhaps these other systems formed in a different way than the Sun's planets did.

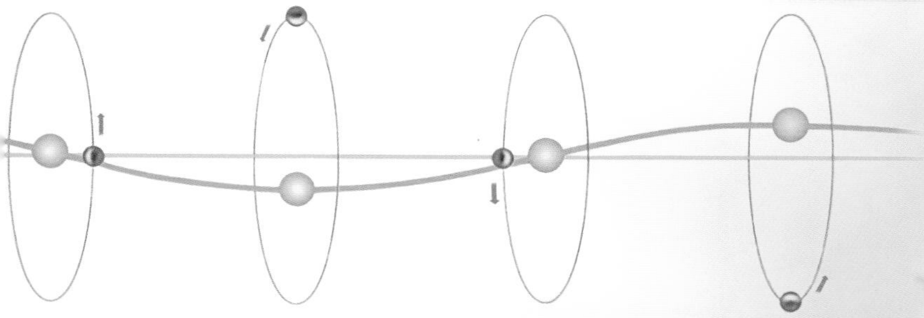

WOBBLING STAR
When careful observation reveals a slight wobble in a star's path, this suggests that a planet is orbiting the star—even if the planet is too small to see. If the planet is massive or close to its star, the effect is greater.

ANOTHER SOLAR SYSTEM
What would an alien planet system look like? So far, all the planets found around other stars are large bodies with masses roughly similar to Jupiter's. Astronomers believe that such planets would probably resemble Jupiter and have cloud belts and swirling storms.

Star Clusters

MOST STARS OCCUR IN GROUPS, which astronomers call associations or clusters. The group with the smallest number of stars is the stellar association. An association has up to a hundred young stars scattered across hundreds of light-years. The brightest members are hot, blue-white stars, each more massive than the Sun. Some associations, however, contain mostly smaller stars that are still forming. The bright stars of the constellation Perseus belong to three associations. No association is more than a few million years old.

Open clusters have many more stars than an association—several hundred to a thousand. They cluster in a much smaller space than an association—only tens of light-years instead of hundreds. Two open clusters near our Solar System are the Pleiades and Hyades. The Sun is also part of an open cluster, but the cluster is hard to identify because it is all around us. Some of our fellow cluster members are stars in the Big Dipper. Open clusters can be as much as 500 million years old.

The giants of the star-cluster kingdom are the globular clusters. They can have up to a million stars concentrated in a region smaller than that taken up by a hundred stars in an association. Stars in a globular cluster are old and well evolved, and include many red giants and white dwarfs. Because the red giants are so much brighter than white dwarfs, they are the most visible stars in a globular cluster.

STELLAR ASSOCIATIONS IN MILKY WAY
ABOUT 150 ARE KNOWN

SIZE OF THE LARGEST ASSOCIATION IN PERSEUS
LESS THAN 100 STARS; ABOUT 800 LIGHT-YEARS IN DIAMETER

OPEN CLUSTERS IN MILKY WAY
OVER 1,000 ARE KNOWN

SIZE OF PLEIADES OPEN CLUSTER
ABOUT 500 STARS; ABOUT 12 LIGHT-YEARS IN DIAMETER

GLOBULAR CLUSTERS IN MILKY WAY
ABOUT 150 ARE KNOWN

SIZE OF OMEGA CENTAURI GLOBULAR CLUSTER
OVER 1 MILLION STARS; ABOUT 150 LIGHT-YEARS IN DIAMETER

• PROJECT: *Collecting Clusters* •

You can collect star clusters. All you need is the star maps on pages 94–109 and a pair of binoculars.

❶ Find the right star maps for the season and your part of the world.

❷ Look for the globular and open cluster symbols on the maps. Make a list of all the clusters that should be visible tonight.

❸ Go outside with the star map and try to locate the clusters on your list. (Start with the easy, bright ones!) Tick them off when you find them.

❹ Sketch what you see and label the sketch with the date and time.

OMEGA CENTAURI
Omega Centauri is the most massive globular star cluster known in the Milky Way. Astronomers estimate that it contains about a million stars. Imagine what the night sky would look like from a planet near its center.

Pleione

Atlas

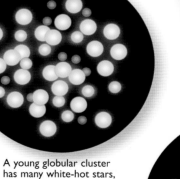

A young globular cluster has many white-hot stars, plus yellow stars like the Sun and dim red dwarfs.

GLOBULAR CLUSTERS
Because they have so much mass and gravity, globular clusters hold onto most of their stars for a long time. A few stars are ejected, however, when cluster stars move randomly and almost collide.

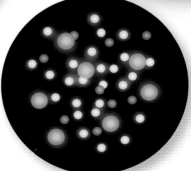

In an old globular, the stars in the original population have evolved, becoming red giants and white dwarfs.

Asterope

Maia

Taygeta

Celaeno

Electra

Merope

THE PLEIADES
The Pleiades is a beautiful open cluster in the constellation of Taurus. It lies 375 light-years away and contains several hundred stars. The cluster is dominated by young, hot blue stars, and surrounded by a blue reflection nebula. Although you can see the Pleiades easily with the naked eye, it looks especially beautiful in binoculars.

Alcyone

OPEN CLUSTERS
When an open cluster forms, it is less than about 30 light-years in diameter and has a broad range of stars, with many being hotter and more massive than the Sun.

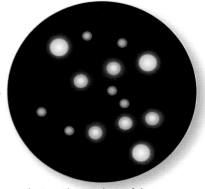

In time, the members of the open cluster drift apart as the gravity of the rest of the galaxy pulls on them.

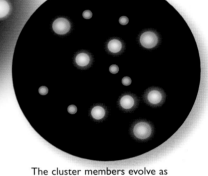

The cluster members evolve as all stars do, with the more massive stars becoming red giants.

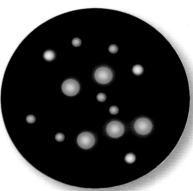

As the open cluster becomes fainter and more scattered, its red giants become white dwarfs and its yellow stars become the new red giants.

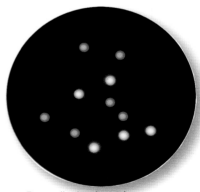

Eventually, the cluster becomes hard to tell apart from the rest of the galaxy's stars. Its smallest stars will hardly have changed.

◆ LOOK AGAIN ◆

● Which cluster type is the oldest?

● How large is the Pleiades cluster?

● What is the most massive globular cluster?

CLUSTERS IN THE MILKY WAY
In this side-on view of the Milky Way, open clusters lie in or near the disk of the galaxy. Globular clusters, on the other hand, orbit the Milky Way's central bulge like a cloud of moons.

Cloud of globular clusters

Open clusters in spiral arms

Open clusters in spiral arms

Cloud of globular clusters

Central bulge of Milky Way

The Milky Way

If the solar system is like a neighborhood, the Milky Way galaxy is like a gigantic city. In fact, it is larger than most galaxies astronomers have found. Our galaxy's name comes from how it looks in the night sky. Ancient people saw a smooth band dividing the sky like a milky stream and pondered what it was made of. About 400 years ago, Galileo studied the band with his telescope and saw that it contained countless tiny stars, just like the ones your naked eye can see, but fainter.

It took astronomers hundreds of years to figure out the actual shape and size of the Milky Way galaxy—and many details are still unclear. Because the Solar System lies within the Milky Way, surveying the galaxy is like studying a big grassy field while lying down in it. In the 1930s, astronomers found the Sun was not at the galaxy's center, but about two-thirds of the way toward one edge. Later, radio telescopes peered through the galaxy's dust clouds to reveal that the Milky Way has several spiral arms. The Sun lies in the Orion arm, part of which is what we see in the sky. The Perseus arm is ahead of the Orion arm, while the Sagittarius arm is behind. Stars, clusters, and gas clouds all orbit the center of the galaxy as planets orbit the Sun. Our star takes 226 million years to complete one trip around the Milky Way.

At the center of the Milky Way lies a supermassive black hole, probably containing a million times more material than the Sun. Around this swirls the galactic bulge, a huge collection of older red and yellow stars. Surrounding the bulge like a wide collar is the many-armed disk, which is turning slowly. Recent studies show the disk may be warped like a hat-brim, although astronomers don't yet know why. Floating above both bulge and disk is the galactic halo, sparsely populated by old red stars and globular clusters. These probably formed at the same time as the galaxy itself.

SIZE OF MILKY WAY
100,000 light-years in diameter

STARS IN MILKY WAY
About 200 billion

STAR CLUSTERS IN MILKY WAY
About 150 globular clusters and over 1,000 open clusters are known.

DUST AND GAS IN MILKY WAY
About 5% of the Milky Way's visible matter is gas and dust.

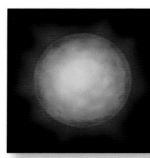

BETELGEUSE
Aged red stars like Betelgeuse are more common in the Milky Way's central bulge than in the spiral arms.

ORION NEBULA
The Orion nebula is part of a giant cloud of gas and dust—a "star factory" that has been at work for the last 12 million years.

THE PLEIADES
Open clusters such as the Pleiades are slowly being pulled apart by the tug of gravity from other stars and clouds of dust and gas.

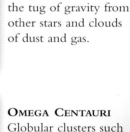

OMEGA CENTAURI
Globular clusters such as Omega Centauri formed along with the Milky Way's first stars. Both are now billions of years old.

EAGLE NEBULA
Clouds of gas and new stars such as the Eagle nebula are found only in the galaxy's central bulge and spiral arms.

• Amazing Fact •

If you were to leave Earth on a space shuttle, traveling at 5 miles per second (8 km/s), it would you take 1.2 billion years to reach the center of the galaxy. That's about one-tenth the age of the universe.

SIDE-ON GALAXY
If we could see the Milky Way in profile, its disk would look much thinner than its central bulge. Above and below the disk is a halo made of globular clusters and old red stars.

THE MILKY WAY

The Milky Way looks like a vast pinwheel and has a broad disk. Marked by hot, young stars, its spiral arms wrap around a central bulge full of old red stars. All the prominent objects in our night sky come from a small part of the galaxy near the Sun, indicated by the white box.

IRAS SPACE TELESCOPE
The InfraRed Astronomy Satellite (IRAS) surveyed the dust of the Milky Way.

Perseus arm

Orion arm

Orion nebula

Betelgeuse

The Pleiades

SUN

Eagle nebula

Omega Centauri

Cygnus arm

Crux-Centaurus arm

Sagittarius arm

Central bulge

Nucleus

Black hole

Halo of globular clusters

INFRARED MILKY WAY
This infrared image highlights the warmest areas of the Milky Way. The infrared radiation comes mostly from the dust that lies all through the disk. The dust glows with the heat of starlight, and clumps of dust contain new stars.

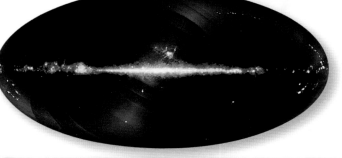

A BAND OF STARS
The Milky Way in the sky is not completely smooth to the eye. The darker patches are places where vast clouds of dust block the light of faraway stars.

Galaxies

GALAXIES VARY IN APPEARANCE, size, and shape. Astronomers, however, fit them into three basic patterns—spirals, ellipticals, and irregulars. Spiral galaxies are easy to identify with their sweeping arms, which contain gas and dust that make new stars. An important subclass of the spirals are barred spirals. These have a roughly oblong-shaped center and may be ordinary spiral galaxies that have collided with or devoured smaller galaxies. Astronomers believe that the Milky Way has absorbed several small galaxies already, and that its central bulge may be bar-like in shape. It could be that we live in a barred spiral galaxy.

Elliptical galaxies contain mostly older stars and little or no gas to make new ones. These ball- or oval-shaped galaxies may have formed early in the universe's history and stopped making new stars when they ran out of gas. A subclass, the dwarf elliptical, may be the most numerous of all galaxies. But because these small galaxies of dim stars are more difficult to see than larger, brighter galaxies, we have discovered only a few of them.

Irregular galaxies are small and shapeless, but many are still actively making stars. The Small Magellanic Cloud is an irregular galaxy that is being distorted by the Large Magellanic Cloud and the Milky Way.

Galaxies gather in clusters, just as stars do. Here, they often collide or interact, pulling one another out of shape. When a galaxy's dust and gas clouds are disturbed by a collision, bright new stars may be born, leading to a spectacular fireworks display.

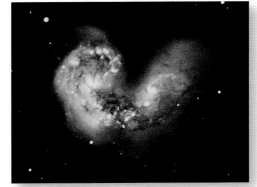

COLLIDING GALAXIES
When galaxies collide, they pass right through each other because their stars lie far apart. But the gravitational tugs of such a collision usually trigger each galaxy's gas clouds to begin making new stars. The Antennae galaxies, which began colliding 500 million years ago, feature bright areas of young stars.

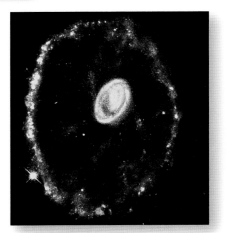

RING OF STARS
When a small galaxy collided with the larger Cartwheel galaxy, a wave of star formation—the blue ring—spread outward through the Cartwheel's disk. The ring of young stars is now big enough to encircle the whole Milky Way.

POPULATIONS OF KNOWN GALAXIES
SPIRAL GALAXIES: 63%; BARRED SPIRAL GALAXIES: 15%; ELLIPTICAL GALAXIES: 18%; IRREGULAR GALAXIES: 4%

WHIRLPOOL/M51 (page 80)
TYPE: SPIRAL; DISTANCE: 15 MILLION LIGHT-YEARS; DIAMETER: 50,000 LIGHT-YEARS

GREAT BARRED SPIRAL/NGC 1365 (page 81)
TYPE: BARRED SPIRAL; DISTANCE: 55 MILLION LIGHT-YEARS; DIAMETER: 157,800 LIGHT-YEARS

M87 (page 81, top)
TYPE: GIANT ELLIPTICAL; DISTANCE: 55 MILLION LIGHT-YEARS; DIAMETER: 147,000 LIGHT-YEARS

SMALL MAGELLANIC CLOUD (page 81, right)
TYPE: IRREGULAR; DISTANCE: 210,000 LIGHT YEARS; DIAMETER: 17,000 LIGHT-YEARS

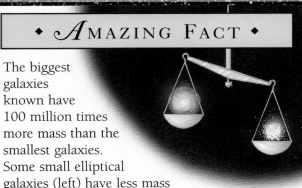

❖ AMAZING FACT ❖

The biggest galaxies known have 100 million times more mass than the smallest galaxies. Some small elliptical galaxies (left) have less mass than the largest globular clusters (right).

ELLIPTICAL GALAXY

As you can see in this illustration of M87, an elliptical galaxy looks like the central bulge of a spiral galaxy. Ellipticals can be more massive than the Milky Way, but range down to tiny dwarf ellipticals, which can be smaller than the largest globular star cluster.

IRREGULAR GALAXY

Like many other irregular galaxies, the Small Magellanic Cloud is small but contains many bright nebulas and hot, young stars. Astronomers think most irregular galaxies will eventually be absorbed by larger galaxies.

BARRED SPIRAL GALAXY

A regular spiral galaxy has a circular bulge at its center, but the center of a barred spiral is longer than it is wide. Obvious barred spirals, such as the Great Barred Spiral (NGC 1365) shown here, make up only a fraction of all spirals, but many ordinary spirals seem to have weak bars.

SPIRAL GALAXY

The Whirlpool (M51) is a spectacular spiral galaxy. All spiral galaxies feature the trademark arms, but some have tightly wound arms, while others are more open. Spiral galaxies also differ in how much dust and gas they contain.

GALAXY CLASSIFICATION

Edwin Hubble developed this scheme for classifying galaxies by shape, which is still used. Hubble thought ellipticals evolved to become spirals, but today's astronomers think most spirals are born that way.

Spirals

Ellipticals

Barred spirals

◆ PROJECT: *Pie-pan Spiral* ◆

You need a round glass or aluminum pie-pan, a coin, and a sprinkle of dots from a paper punch.

1. Place the coin under the center of the pie-pan on a kitchen counter, so the pan turns easily.
2. Pour about half an inch (about 1 cm) of tap water into the pan.
3. Carefully sprinkle the paper-punch dots in the center of the pan.
4. Spin the pan slowly. Notice how the dots stream into spiral arms.

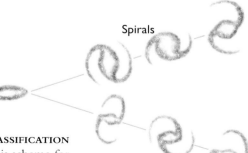

The Local Group

THE LOCAL GROUP IS THE NAME Edwin Hubble gave to the galaxies nearest the Milky Way. Today, astronomers know of about 35 Local Group galaxies spread across roughly 10 million light-years of space. This is not a random collection of galaxies that just happen to lie nearby. Linked by the pull of gravity, the Local Group members form a cluster of galaxies, just as the Pleiades forms a cluster of stars.

Two big galaxies dominate the Local Group—the Milky Way and the Andromeda galaxy, which is slightly larger. Each has attracted a collection of smaller Local Group galaxies. Belonging to the Andromeda galaxy are M32, NGC 147, NGC 185, NGC 205, and 14 dwarf galaxies. The Pinwheel (M33), the third-largest galaxy in the group, also lies near Andromeda. The Milky Way's satellite galaxies are the Large and Small Magellanic Clouds and several dwarf galaxies. The rest of the Local Group galaxies appear to stand alone.

Because the Local Group is our local cluster, astronomers can study it in detail. They have found 3 spiral galaxies, 2 ellipticals, 12 irregulars, and about 14 dwarf ellipticals. Several of the smaller member-galaxies were discovered only recently. An unsolved question is whether the Local Group has a bigger share of small galaxies than the universe as a whole. If the Local Group is typical, then the universe has a great many more small galaxies waiting to be discovered.

Several other "local groups" surround ours, each cluster held together by its own gravity. The largest galaxy cluster near us lies in the constellation of Virgo. Together with many other clusters, the Local Group and Virgo cluster form a bigger group called the Local Supercluster, some 60 million light-years across.

SIZE OF LOCAL GROUP
ABOUT 10 MILLION LIGHT-YEARS IN DIAMETER, WITH ABOUT 35 MEMBERS

MAGELLANIC CLOUDS
LARGE CLOUD—DISTANCE: 179,000 LIGHT-YEARS; DIAMETER: 34,000 LIGHT-YEARS
SMALL CLOUD—DISTANCE: 210,000 LIGHT-YEARS; DIAMETER: 17,000 LIGHT-YEARS

ANDROMEDA GALAXY (M31)
DISTANCE: 2.9 MILLION LIGHT-YEARS; DIAMETER: 128,000 LIGHT-YEARS

PINWHEEL GALAXY (M33)
DISTANCE: 2.6 MILLION LIGHT-YEARS; DIAMETER: 50,000 LIGHT-YEARS

SCULPTOR DWARF
DISTANCE: 284,000 LIGHT-YEARS; DIAMETER: 1,400 LIGHT-YEARS

FORNAX CLUSTER
In the same constellation as the Fornax dwarf galaxy, the Fornax cluster of galaxies is hundreds of times farther away. Like the Local Group, it is an immense area of empty space dotted with galaxies clustered in strings and sheets.

NGC 6822
irregular

IC 1613
irregular

GALACTIC NEIGHBORS
The Local Group has a few big, bright member-galaxies and a lot of small ones. The 17 largest members of the cluster are illustrated here. To be a Local Group member, a galaxy must lie nearby and must not be moving so fast that it can escape the cluster's gravity.

M32
elliptical

Pinwheel (M33)
spiral

NGC 147
dwarf elliptical

NGC 185
dwarf elliptical

Andromeda (M31)
spiral

◆ LOOK AGAIN ◆

● How many galaxies does the Local Group contain?

● What is the most common type of galaxy in the Group?

● What does the Local Group belong to?

VIRGO CLUSTER
The Local Group sits on the edge of a large supercluster of galaxies that surrounds the Virgo cluster (shown here). The Virgo cluster contains the giant elliptical galaxy M87, which is a powerful radio and X-ray source.

SMALL MAGELLANIC CLOUD
The Small Magellanic Cloud is the second-largest satellite galaxy of the Milky Way. Studying its irregular shape, astronomers found that it has been distorted by the gravity of the Milky Way and the Large Magellanic Cloud.

ANDROMEDA GALAXY
The Andromeda galaxy is the most distant object we can see with the naked eye, some 2.9 million light-years away. Like the Milky Way, it is a spiral, but it is more massive than the Milky Way.

Fornax dwarf
dwarf elliptical

Sculptor dwarf
irregular

NGC 205
elliptical

Leo I
dwarf elliptical

Leo II
dwarf elliptical

Draco dwarf
dwarf elliptical

Ursa Minor dwarf
dwarf elliptical

Small Magellanic Cloud
dwarf irregular

Large Magellanic Cloud
irregular

Milky Way
spiral

◆ AMAZING FACT ◆

The life of a small galaxy in a cluster of galaxies isn't easy. The biggest galaxies attract and devour the smaller ones, usually by pulling them apart and absorbing their stars.

Black Holes

SOME GALAXIES HAVE SMALL, BRIGHT CENTERS that emit lots of energy. These are known as active galaxies, and astronomers believe their energy is generated by a small but extremely massive object, most likely a black hole. Black holes are so dense that they swallow everything that comes near them—even light cannot escape their incredible gravity. A stellar black hole, one that forms after a supernova, has about the mass of a star (see page 73), but a galactic black hole in the heart of a galaxy can be as massive as a billion Suns.

Since black holes pull in light, astronomers can't see them directly. Instead, they pinpoint black holes by looking for the effects of extremely strong gravity. An active galaxy's energy comes not from inside the black hole, but from the region just outside. Swirling around a black hole like water going down a drain is a disk of material made from torn-apart stars and clouds of gas. The black hole's powerful gravity squeezes this disk with extreme force, heating it to hundreds of thousands of degrees. Before the matter is sucked into the black hole, it radiates X-rays, radio waves, and lots of visible energy.

Astronomers have found several kinds of active galaxies that harbor a black hole in their center. The activity differs depending on how compressed the gas is near the black hole and whether we are looking at the disk from one side or from above. In some active galaxies, the disk around the black hole is very thick. This lets some energy and hot gas shoot out from the disk, producing enormous jets that can stretch thousands of light-years.

DIAMETER OF A STELLAR BLACK HOLE
A BLACK HOLE WITH AS MUCH MASS AS THE SUN WOULD BE 3.6 MILES (6 KM) ACROSS.

DIAMETER OF A GALACTIC BLACK HOLE
A BLACK HOLE WITH AS MUCH MASS AS 1 MILLION SUNS WOULD BE 3.6 MILLION MILES (6 MILLION KM) ACROSS.

QUASAR PKS 0637-752 (page 84, top)
DISTANCE: 6 BILLION LIGHT-YEARS; DIAMETER: UNKNOWN

EINSTEIN CROSS (page 84, center right)
DISTANCE: 10 BILLION LIGHT-YEARS; DIAMETER: UNKNOWN

CENTAURUS A/NGC 5128 (page 84, center left)
DISTANCE: 26 MILLION LIGHT-YEARS; DIAMETER: 138,000 LIGHT-YEARS

SEYFERT NGC 1275 (page 84, bottom)
DISTANCE: 230 MILLION LIGHT-YEARS; DIAMETER: 175,000 LIGHT-YEARS

◆ PROJECT: *Gravitational Lens* ◆

A gravitational lens works because strong gravity can bend and focus light. For this project, you need a simple lens (such as one from a magnifying glass) that you can hold in your hand. It works better if the lens isn't perfect.

❶ Hold the lens about an inch (2 or 3 cm) above a sheet of newspaper. Move it back and forth slowly.

❷ The distortions you see are what astronomers see (in very slow motion!) as a black hole or a massive galaxy moves in front of a more distant object.

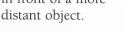

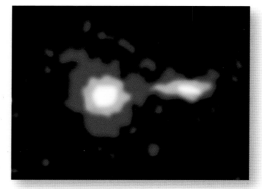

QUASAR
The bright cores of active galaxies that vary in brightness over weeks or days are known as quasars, short for quasi-stellar object. Quasar PKS 0637-752 gives off the energy of 10 trillion Suns. This X-ray image shows a powerful jet thousands of light-years long.

GRAVITATIONAL LENS
In the Einstein Cross, the four outside objects are all images of the same quasar! In the middle is a massive galaxy whose gravity works like a lens to bend the quasar's light, creating four images instead of one (see diagram, facing page). The galaxy lies 20 times closer to us than the quasar does.

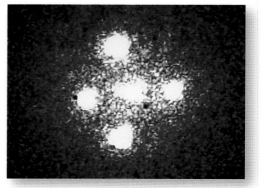

RADIO GALAXY
Centaurus A (NGC 5128) is the nearest active galaxy to Earth. Here the optical image at the center shows it as a large elliptical galaxy. The colorful radio image shows two enormous lobes of radio energy, flowing north and south from the central galaxy.

SEYFERT GALAXY
NGC 1275, shown here in an X-ray image, is a type of active galaxy called a Seyfert galaxy, after the astronomer who first discovered them. Seyfert galaxies have star-like centers and show evidence of hot gas moving at high speeds.

SHOOTING JETS
Radio astronomers long ago detected enormous jets of hot gas and energy shooting from some galaxies. But the jets remained a mystery until theorists worked out how a black hole at the center of a galaxy could produce them.

Image of distant galaxy

Earth

Path of light

Path of light

Active galaxy with black hole at center

Path of light

Actual position of distant galaxy

Path of light

Path of light

Image of distant galaxy

MULTIPLE IMAGES

A black hole is so powerful that it can bend light traveling near it. Here a galaxy with a black hole bends light from a distant galaxy, creating the optical illusion of a double galaxy for observers on Earth. In some cases, such as the Einstein Cross (see facing page), this effect produces four images of the distant object.

GALACTIC BLACK HOLE

Active galaxies produce a huge amount of energy in a very small space. Astronomers believe such galaxies contain a black hole devouring a disk of gas. As the gas falls into the black hole, it becomes extremely hot and emits lots of energy.

◆ LOOK AGAIN ◆

● How does a black hole "shine"?

● Can galaxies make optical illusions?

● Why do some active galaxies produce jets?

The Universe

THE UNIVERSE WAS BORN SOME 12 to 15 billion years ago in a gigantic explosion that astronomers call the Big Bang. It began as a super-hot, super-compressed speck containing all the matter in the universe today. This churning, seething soup of exotic particles had a temperature of more than a trillion degrees.

As the universe expanded, it cooled and more familiar kinds of matter, such as protons, electrons, and neutrons, began to appear. As time continued, these particles merged to make simple chemical elements—first hydrogen, then helium. The earliest stars and galaxies took shape from these elements. Once stars formed, their nuclear reactions began creating more complex elements, such as oxygen, carbon, lead, and gold. These included the elements that would later form the Sun and the Solar System—and us! In the meantime, stars clumped together to form galaxies, and galaxies merged into clusters and superclusters.

The Big Bang created a universe that is expanding along with space itself. Wherever they look, astronomers find that the farther away a galaxy is, the faster it is moving away from us. Will this expansion continue forever? That depends on how much matter the universe has within it, which is very hard to determine. Astronomers make estimates from the light given off by stars and nebulas. This shows only one-tenth of the mass needed to stop the expansion, so many believe the universe will expand forever. But astronomers are also looking for "dark matter"—stars too dim to see, black holes, and exotic particles. If there's enough dark matter, gravity will halt the expansion and someday the universe will fall back on itself, producing a Big Crunch. Most astronomers now think this is unlikely, but some believe there might be enough extra matter to slow down the expansion so that the universe eventually stabilizes.

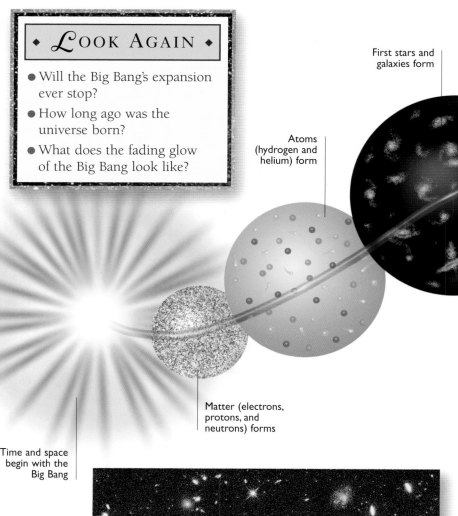

First stars and galaxies form

Atoms (hydrogen and helium) form

Matter (electrons, protons, and neutrons) forms

Time and space begin with the Big Bang

ANCIENT GALAXIES
In 1995, the Hubble Space Telescope took a long stare into deep space and photographed the oldest galaxies ever seen. Astronomers are studying these ancient galaxies to see how today's galaxies formed and evolved.

◆ AMAZING FACT ◆

As the universe expands, the galaxies are all moving away from one another—just as galaxies drawn on a balloon get farther apart as you blow up the balloon. Unlike the balloon, however, the universe is not expanding into anything. There is no "outside" because the universe contains everything there is, including space itself.

WALLS OF GALAXIES
The universe shows structure even on very large scales. Astronomers are studying whether galaxies formed first and then merged into clusters—or whether vast chains and sheets of matter appeared before turning into galaxies.

Void

Void

Great Wall of Galaxies

450

450

Millions of light-years

300

300

150

150

Local Supercluster

Today's universe
has perhaps
50 billion galaxies

THE BIG CRUNCH

A cramped fate awaits the universe if it
contains enough matter to stop the expansion
altogether. As the universe implodes, galaxies
squeeze together and time may flow backward.
In the end, everything crunches into a black
hole. Recent evidence, however, indicates that
the expansion of the universe is accelerating,
not slowing down. The universe could expand
forever.

THE BIG BANG

The Big Bang explains how matter
and energy combined to make the
stars and galaxies of today. The universe
is still expanding and its future depends
on how much matter it contains.
There might be enough matter to
slow down the expansion, so that the
universe eventually stabilizes. But if
the universe keeps expanding at the
same rate, galaxies will drift farther
apart, stars will eventually burn out,
and ordinary matter will disintegrate,
leaving a boundless "sea" of particles.

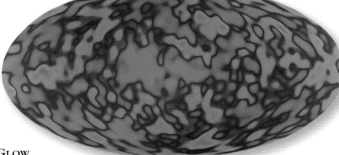

FADING GLOW

This map by the COBE satellite
shows ripples in the cosmic
background radiation—the fading
glow of the Big Bang. The blue
regions, which are slightly denser,
became the first stars and galaxies.

COSMIC EXPLORER

The Cosmic Background
Explorer (COBE) satellite was
launched to study the radiation
left over from the Big Bang.
The map it produced (above)
revealed ripples in this radiation.

Stargazing

STARGAZING IS EASY—you can start in your own backyard this evening if the sky is clear. Many skywatchers, however, choose a spot that has an uninterrupted view of the sky, such as a park or a schoolyard. Find a safe, dark place away from distractions such as streetlights and lights from houses. Then pick the best star map from pages 94 to 109 for your location and season.

Before you begin stargazing, give your eyes at least 15 minutes to adjust to the dark. You will need a small flashlight to see the star map. White light will take away your night vision for many minutes, so cover the flashlight lens with red cellophane. Once your eyes have adjusted, try to match the bright stars in the sky with those on the star map. After you locate the brighter stars, find dimmer ones by drawing imaginary lines to them on the map and then looking for the same pattern in the sky.

The naked eye is ideal for some skywatching, such as finding constellations and observing meteor showers. If you want to see more, try using binoculars. These give a better view than most cheap telescopes do. The Milky Way becomes thousands of individual stars. Big star clusters such as the Pleiades look best in binoculars, and brighter galaxies show as patches of fuzzy light.

The next step is a good telescope. This will show craters on the Moon, the rings of Saturn, glowing nebulas, and more. Buying a telescope is a big decision—it calls for careful research to avoid wasting money. If you don't already own a telescope, check whether a local astronomy club, observatory, or science center will let you look through theirs.

With the star maps in this book, you can learn your way around the sky. Once you've mastered this, you may want to consult a star atlas that shows even more stars and objects. Star atlases are like road maps for a journey through space that you can follow for the rest of your life.

NAKED-EYE PLANETS
Just as in ancient times, five of the planets can be easily seen with the unaided eye—Mercury, Venus, Mars, Jupiter, and Saturn. This evening sky shows the crescent Moon with Venus above it, near the top of the photo, and Jupiter below.

LIGHT POLLUTION
The glow from streetlights and other outdoor lighting washes out stars and makes it impossible to see faint objects in the night sky. Your best view of the night sky will be in the country on clear, moonless nights.

NIGHT-SKY EVENTS
Some special events in the night sky can be predicted. Lunar eclipses usually occur at least once a year (see page 113 for dates). This time-exposure photo shows the Moon before, during, and after an eclipse.

◆ PROJECT: *Daytime Stars* ◆

Stars shine day and night but we can see them only at night. During the day, the atmosphere catches the bright light of the Sun and makes a brilliant blue sky that hides the stars. To see how this works, try a simple experiment.

❶ Use a paper punch to make holes in an index card representing stars. You can copy a favorite constellation.

❷ Put the card inside an ordinary white envelope.

❸ In a dark room, shine a light on the front of the envelope. The envelope reflects the light so you can't see the "stars."

❹ Now shine the light from behind the envelope. When the envelope is dark, the "stars" can shine through.

A GOOD TELESCOPE
The most important quality in a telescope—much more important than how much it magnifies—is a sturdy, shake-free mount.

SETTING UP FOR STARGAZING

You'll see more in the sky if you are comfortable. Depending on the season, comfort may mean wearing long underwear and a ski cap—or using bug repellent! (But even summer nights can become chilly, so be prepared.) A lawn chair lets you relax and makes holding binoculars easier. And a flask of hot cocoa or soup tastes great when you've been outside for a while.

♦ AMAZING FACT ♦

Under a dark sky in the countryside, you can't really see "millions" of stars, although it might look like it! Instead, under good conditions, the naked eye is able to spot about 2,000 stars.

Constellations

CONSTELLATIONS DIVIDE THE SKY into easy-to-remember pieces. In ancient times, when few people could read, constellations were like heavenly storybooks. They helped people remember important tales about the gods. Astronomers now recognize a total of 88 constellations.

The major constellations come from Greek and Roman civilization, more than 2,000 years ago. But even then, some constellations were already old, having been created in ancient Mesopotamia (today's Iraq). Astronomers think that Taurus the Bull, Leo the Lion, and Scorpius the Scorpion may have been among the very first constellations. They marked where the Sun appeared during important seasons for crops.

Stars have been named in various ways. Ptolemy named stars for their place in the constellation. Rigel, a star in the constellation of Orion the Hunter, means "foot" in Arabic. (The name is Arabic because Ptolemy's names came to us in the Middle Ages through an Arabic translation.) Somewhat later, astronomers began to identify stars using Greek letters, with Alpha being the brightest star in a constellation, Beta the second-brightest, and so on. Other astronomers gave stars numbers.

Star clusters, galaxies, and nebulas usually have names like M35 or NGC 1365. M-numbers were assigned by Charles Messier, who lived in the late 1700s and discovered many of these objects. NGC-numbers come from the *New General Catalogue,* a giant list of discoveries collected in the late 1800s. Astronomical names sometimes seem complicated, but this is because they combine the efforts of countless skywatchers, working together over thousands of years.

◆ AMAZING FACT ◆

Other cultures have grouped the same stars in different ways. For example, where we see the Big Dipper, the ancient Egyptians saw these same stars as the hind leg of an ox—and the Sioux Indians of North America saw a skunk!

MOVING STARS
Stars are always moving, but because distances in space are so enormous, the stars in a constellation appear fixed in place. Gradually, however, their movements will make today's constellations unrecognizable.

Big Dipper
100,000
years ago

Big Dipper
today

Big Dipper
100,000 years
from now

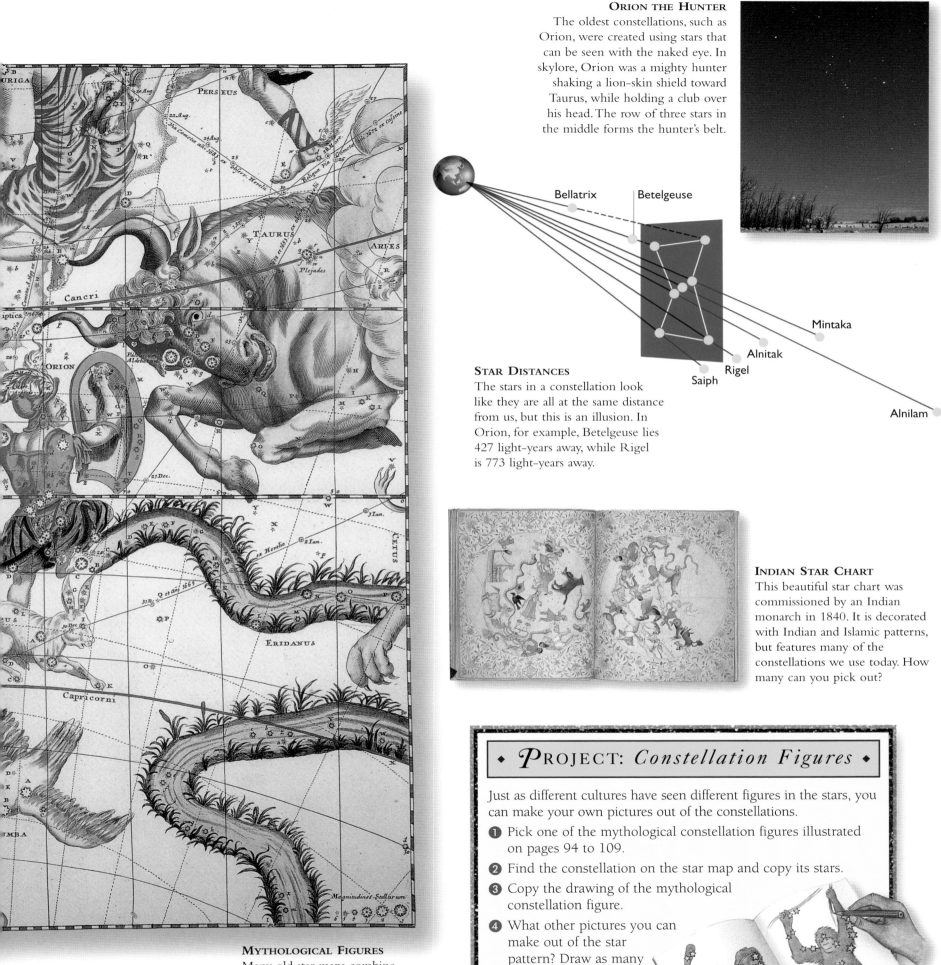

ORION THE HUNTER

The oldest constellations, such as Orion, were created using stars that can be seen with the naked eye. In skylore, Orion was a mighty hunter shaking a lion-skin shield toward Taurus, while holding a club over his head. The row of three stars in the middle forms the hunter's belt.

Bellatrix Betelgeuse

Mintaka

Alnitak

Rigel

Saiph

Alnilam

STAR DISTANCES

The stars in a constellation look like they are all at the same distance from us, but this is an illusion. In Orion, for example, Betelgeuse lies 427 light-years away, while Rigel is 773 light-years away.

INDIAN STAR CHART

This beautiful star chart was commissioned by an Indian monarch in 1840. It is decorated with Indian and Islamic patterns, but features many of the constellations we use today. How many can you pick out?

MYTHOLOGICAL FIGURES

Many old star maps combine carefully plotted stars with colorful figures from mythology. The constellations illustrated on this map include Gemini the Twins, Orion the Hunter, Taurus the Bull, and Eridanus the River.

◆ PROJECT: *Constellation Figures* ◆

Just as different cultures have seen different figures in the stars, you can make your own pictures out of the constellations.

❶ Pick one of the mythological constellation figures illustrated on pages 94 to 109.

❷ Find the constellation on the star map and copy its stars.

❸ Copy the drawing of the mythological constellation figure.

❹ What other pictures you can make out of the star pattern? Draw as many as you can imagine.

Our example shows two different figures based on the constellation of Orion.

Using a Star Map

THE FOLLOWING PAGES SHOW STAR MAPS for the Northern and Southern hemispheres and for each of the four seasons in the year. Just turn to the page that shows the current season for the hemisphere where you live. The two maps on each spread show the stars and constellations of the evening sky that you'll see when looking north or south. The maps also wrap around to the east and west points on the horizon, so together they show the entire sky.

Star maps change with the seasons because constellations move in and out of view as Earth travels around the Sun. For example, the stars visible on a March evening are different from those you see on a September evening. As Earth travels its orbit through the year, we look out at different stellar backgrounds. The change from one night to the next isn't much, but it adds up. After a month has passed, any constellation or star is rising and setting two hours earlier. This means that when you use a star map for a given season, you may find that the constellations do not lie exactly as shown on the map. Early in the season they may lie more to the east, while late in the season they will be over toward the west. (Similarly, if you observe late at night, try the next season's chart.)

The maps show stars, the Milky Way, clusters, nebulas, and even galaxies. Planets and objects such as comets are not shown because these are constantly moving. Constellations always return to view every year at the same season, but planets don't. To find where to look for a given planet, you need to check with an astronomy magazine, newspaper, or Web sites such as *www.skypub.com* and *www.astronomy.com*.

OVER ONE HOUR
Earth's rotation makes the sky appear to move from east to west—over an hour, you can see Orion shift westward. If you are looking south, as shown here, the movement is from left to right. Looking north, it is from right to left.

OVER TWO WEEKS
Earth's movement around the Sun has the same effect as its rotation—if you look south at Orion at the same time of night two weeks apart, you'll see a similar shift to the one shown here, with Orion appearing farther west.

STAR MAPS
Each half-circular star map shows half of the sky that is visible at a given season. The horizon runs along the bottom with either north or south in the center. East and west are marked, and overhead is at the top. Turn the map to match the compass direction you are facing.

Open star clusters use this symbol, and are identified by name.

This is the name of a star.

Thin lines connect the brighter stars in major constellations to help you trace the patterns.

The Milky Way is shown in light blue.

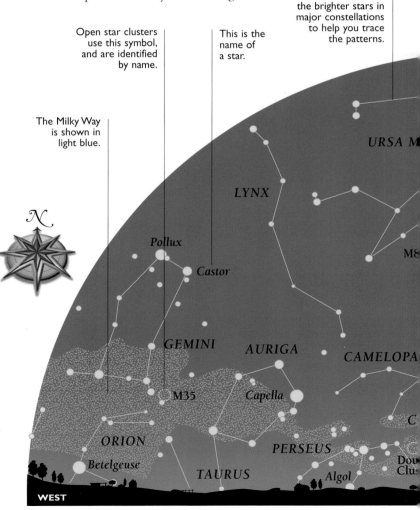

STAR TRAILS
As Earth rotates, stars around the celestial pole appear to travel in a circle. This time-exposure photo captures the movement.

FINDING YOUR WAY
To use the star maps, you need to locate the four main compass directions: north, south, east, and west. In some communities, streets follow the compass. In other places, you have to find directions from the sky—or by asking an adult.

KEY TO MAP SYMBOLS
Sky maps show star brightnesses using dots sized according to their magnitude. Fainter stars have higher magnitude numbers, while the brightest stars have negative magnitudes. Objects such as clusters, nebulas, and galaxies are plotted using special symbols.

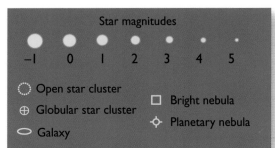

Star magnitudes

−1	0	1	2	3	4	5

○ Open star cluster
⊕ Globular star cluster
◯ Galaxy
☐ Bright nebula
✧ Planetary nebula

FINDING NORTH

In the Northern Hemisphere, use the Big Dipper to find the north celestial pole, which is near the star Polaris in Ursa Minor. First locate the Dipper using the correct map from pages 94 to 101 for your location and season. Then draw an imaginary line from the end of the Dipper's bowl to Polaris.

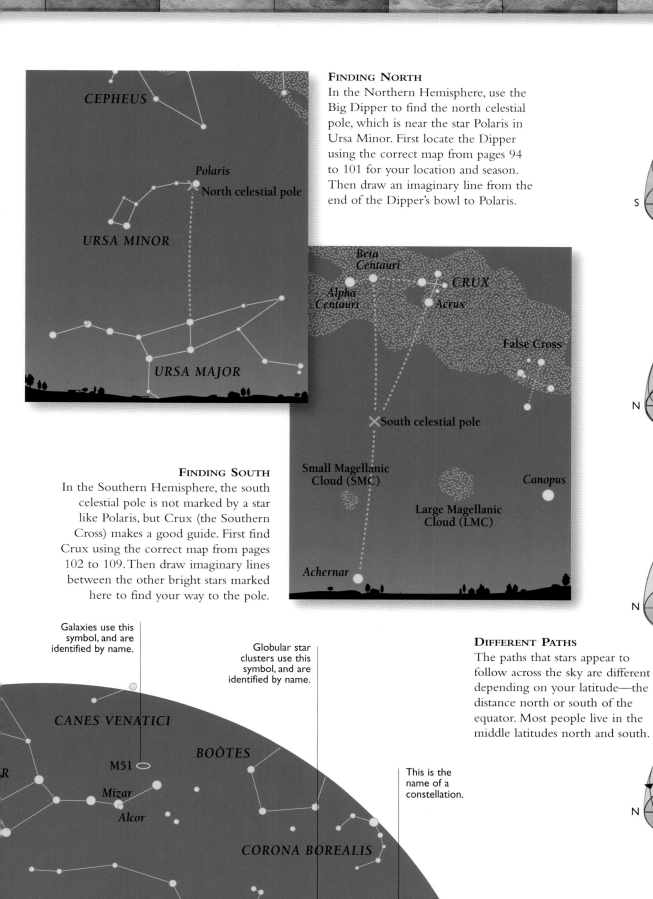

CEPHEUS

Polaris
North celestial pole

URSA MINOR

URSA MAJOR

Beta Centauri
Alpha Centauri
CRUX
Acrux

False Cross

X South celestial pole

Small Magellanic Cloud (SMC)

Large Magellanic Cloud (LMC)

Canopus

Achernar

FINDING SOUTH

In the Southern Hemisphere, the south celestial pole is not marked by a star like Polaris, but Crux (the Southern Cross) makes a good guide. First find Crux using the correct map from pages 102 to 109. Then draw imaginary lines between the other bright stars marked here to find your way to the pole.

Galaxies use this symbol, and are identified by name.

Globular star clusters use this symbol, and are identified by name.

CANES VENATICI

M51

BOÖTES

Mizar

Alcor

This is the name of a constellation.

CORONA BOREALIS

RSA MINOR

M13

Polaris

DRACO

NGC 6543

LIS

HERCULES

Vega

The horizon is indicated by a black silhouette of buildings and landscape.

OPEIA

CEPHEUS

LYRA

M57

OPHIUCHUS

Dcneb

CYGNUS

LACERTA

This map shows the stars for spring skies in the Northern Hemisphere, looking north (see page 96).

EAST

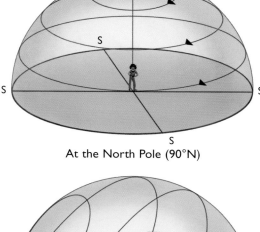
At the North Pole (90°N)

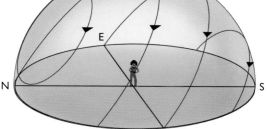
At the northern middle latitudes (40°N)

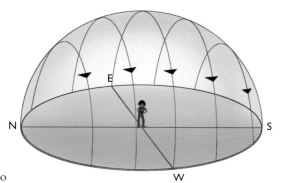
At the equator (0°)

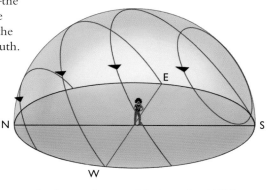
At the southern middle latitudes (40°S)

DIFFERENT PATHS

The paths that stars appear to follow across the sky are different depending on your latitude—the distance north or south of the equator. Most people live in the middle latitudes north and south.

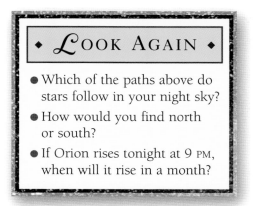

◆ *L*OOK AGAIN ◆

- Which of the paths above do stars follow in your night sky?
- How would you find north or south?
- If Orion rises tonight at 9 PM, when will it rise in a month?

Winter Stars of the Northern Skies

LOOKING NORTH Many people can recognize the Big Dipper (known as the Plough in Europe). The Dipper is made from the seven bright stars that mark out the back and tail of Ursa Major, the Big Bear. This evening, the Dipper seems to be standing on its handle in the northeast. An imaginary line pointing left from the two top stars of its bowl leads to Polaris in Ursa Minor, the Little Bear. As the Dipper rises, Cassiopeia the Queen sinks in the northwest. Cassiopeia is shaped like the letter M. Nearby are Cassiopeia's mythological companions: Cepheus the King (her husband), Andromeda (her daughter), Perseus (Andromeda's hero and rescuer), and Pegasus (Perseus's horse). Cetus the Sea Monster, who was about to eat Andromeda when Perseus saved her, is setting in the southwest (see Looking South map, facing page). Use the naked eye or binoculars to look for the Andromeda galaxy (M31) in Andromeda. Under dark skies it looks like an oval smudge of light.

WHERE YOU CAN SEE THIS SKY FROM
NORTHERN HEMISPHERE AREAS SUCH AS EUROPE, UNITED STATES, CANADA, AND JAPAN

WHEN YOU CAN SEE THIS SKY BEST
JANUARY THROUGH MARCH

BEST NAKED-EYE SIGHTS
ALGOL IN PERSEUS, BIG DIPPER IN URSA MAJOR, POLARIS IN URSA MINOR

BEST BINOCULAR SIGHTS
DOUBLE CLUSTER IN PERSEUS, DOUBLE STAR MIZAR AND ALCOR AND GALAXY M81 IN URSA MAJOR

BEST TELESCOPE SIGHTS
ANDROMEDA GALAXY (M31) IN ANDROMEDA, WHIRLPOOL GALAXY (M51) IN CANES VENATICI

DOUBLE CLUSTER
Lying close together in space, these two open star clusters can just be seen by eye between the constellations of Perseus and Cassiopeia.

URSA MAJOR
The Big Bear includes more than just the Big Dipper, but you need dark skies to see the entire figure.

PERSEUS THE HERO
According to legend, the hero Perseus married Andromeda after rescuing her from the sea monster Cetus.

BIG DIPPER
Europeans describe the Big Dipper as a Plough or a Cart, with the stars in the Dipper's handle representing the oxen pulling it along.

◆ LOOK AGAIN ◆

- Which star is the night sky's brightest?
- The Big Dipper is part of what constellation?
- Who did Perseus rescue? From whom?

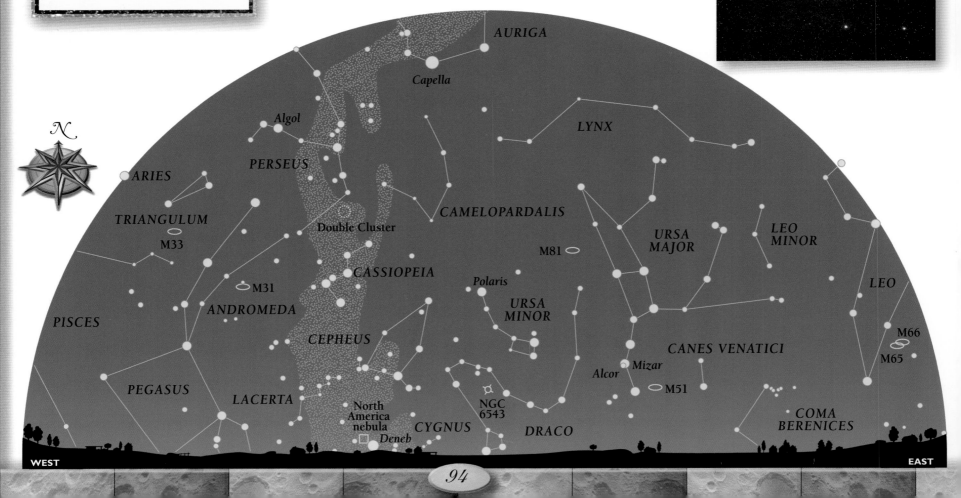

LOOKING SOUTH   Orion the Hunter stands high above the horizon, showing a belt of three stars. From the middle of Orion's belt hangs his sword, which contains the Orion nebula (M42), just visible to the eye. Two bright stars, Betelgeuse and Rigel, mark Orion's shoulder and foot. Orion is driving back Taurus the Bull, which has the beautiful Pleiades star cluster on its shoulder. Another star cluster, the Hyades, makes up Taurus's face. Below Orion crouches Lepus the Hare. To the lower left of Orion, you can see Canis Major, the Big Dog, with the blazing star Sirius as its eye. Above Sirius, the star Procyon marks Canis Minor, the Little Dog, while the stars Castor and Pollux stand at the head of Gemini the Twins. Overhead in the Milky Way, look for Auriga the Charioteer, with its brightest star Capella (shown on the Looking North map, facing page).

WHERE YOU CAN SEE THIS SKY FROM
NORTHERN HEMISPHERE AREAS SUCH AS EUROPE, UNITED STATES, CANADA, AND JAPAN

WHEN YOU CAN SEE THIS SKY BEST
JANUARY THROUGH MARCH

BEST NAKED-EYE SIGHTS
SIRIUS IN CANIS MAJOR, RIGEL AND BETELGEUSE IN ORION, MIRA IN CETUS

BEST BINOCULAR SIGHTS
PLEIADES AND HYADES STAR CLUSTERS IN TAURUS, BEEHIVE STAR CLUSTER IN CANCER

BEST TELESCOPE SIGHTS
ORION NEBULA (M42) IN ORION, M35 STAR CLUSTER IN GEMINI

CANIS MAJOR
In mythology, the Big Dog was one of two hunting dogs who always accompanied Orion on his hunts.

SIRIUS
Sirius, which forms the eye of the dog Canis Major, is the night sky's brightest star. Ancient Egyptians knew the annual Nile flood was coming when Sirius rose just before the Sun.

ORION THE HUNTER
The Hunter makes a handy signpost for skywatchers. Find other constellations by extending imaginary lines out from Orion.

ORION NEBULA (M42)
You can just spot this famous nebula by eye, but it is much easier to see in binoculars. In a small telescope, this gas cloud becomes a grand sight.

TAURUS THE BULL
The Bull is one of the oldest constellations. Pictures of it appear on Mesopotamian tablets that are more than 3,000 years old.

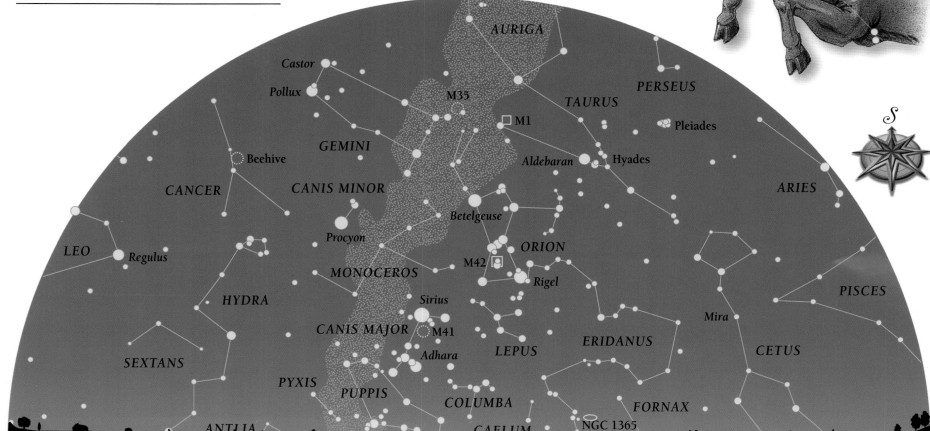

EAST

WEST

Spring Stars of the Northern Skies

LOOKING NORTH   Tonight the Big Dipper (part of Ursa Major, the Big Bear) is upside down high in the northern sky. The left-hand stars in the Dipper's bowl point down to Polaris, the Pole Star, in the constellation of Ursa Minor, the Little Bear. Between the Dipper and Polaris winds the snaky form of Draco the Dragon. Below the Pole Star, the W shape of Cassiopeia the Queen sits just above the trees. Setting in the northwest are Gemini the Twins, with the stars Castor and Pollux. Rising in the northeast, the bright star Vega marks Lyra, which represents a lyre (a stringed musical instrument). Above Lyra, look for Hercules. In mythology, Hercules was the half-mortal son of Jupiter, the ruler of the gods. Finally, follow the curved handle of the Dipper as it "arcs to Arcturus," the brightest star in Boötes the Herdsman, high in the southeast (see Looking South map, facing page).

WHERE YOU CAN SEE THIS SKY FROM
NORTHERN HEMISPHERE AREAS SUCH AS EUROPE, UNITED STATES, CANADA, AND JAPAN

WHEN YOU CAN SEE THIS SKY BEST
APRIL THROUGH JUNE

BEST NAKED-EYE SIGHTS
VEGA IN LYRA, CASTOR AND POLLUX IN GEMINI

BEST BINOCULAR SIGHTS
HERCULES CLUSTER (M13) IN HERCULES, DOUBLE STAR MIZAR AND ALCOR IN URSA MAJOR

BEST TELESCOPE SIGHTS
GALAXY M81 IN URSA MAJOR, WHIRLPOOL GALAXY (M51) IN CANES VENATICI

URSA MINOR
The Little Bear is also called the Little Dipper. Find Polaris, then the two stars of the small bowl—the rest lie in between.

HERCULES CLUSTER (M13)
This globular star cluster is just visible by eye on a dark night, and is easy to see in binoculars.

WHIRLPOOL GALAXY (M51)
The Whirlpool galaxy (near the Big Dipper's handle) has its spiral arms distorted by the passage of a smaller galaxy nearby.

HERCULES
In mythology, Hercules was famed for his feats of strength. Among them was cleaning out the stables where the Sun god's horses lived!

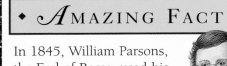

◆ AMAZING FACT ◆

In 1845, William Parsons, the Earl of Rosse, used his giant telescope to discover that the Whirlpool galaxy (M51) had a spiral shape. It was the first time a galaxy had been seen as a spiral.

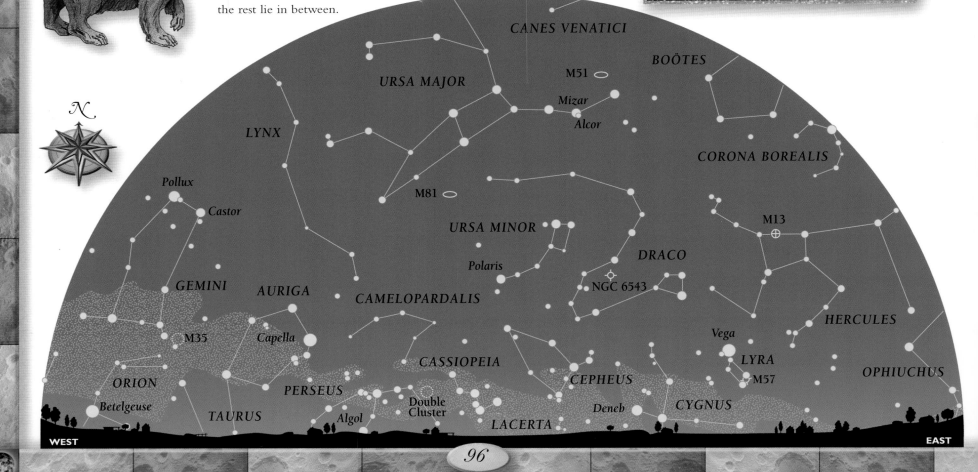

CANES VENATICI

BOÖTES

URSA MAJOR

M51

Mizar

Alcor

LYNX

CORONA BOREALIS

M81

Pollux

Castor

URSA MINOR

M13

Polaris

DRACO

NGC 6543

GEMINI

AURIGA

CAMELOPARDALIS

HERCULES

M35

Capella

Vega

LYRA

M57

CASSIOPEIA

ORION

PERSEUS

CEPHEUS

OPHIUCHUS

Betelgeuse

TAURUS

Algol

Double Cluster

Deneb

CYGNUS

LACERTA

WEST

EAST

N

96

LOOKING SOUTH With the Milky Way wrapped around the horizon, where it is hard to see, spring skies are relatively dark. Yet four bright stars light the southern half of the sky. Arcturus in Boötes the Herdsman stands high in the southeast, while Spica in Virgo the Maiden lies in the south. In the southwest, look for Regulus in Leo the Lion, and setting in the west you'll find Procyon in Canis Minor, the Little Dog. Leo also contains two spiral galaxies, M65 and M66, which you can spot in binoculars or a telescope. Below Leo and Virgo stretches the figure of Hydra the Sea Serpent, the sky's longest constellation. Hydra's stars are dim, so it is a difficult constellation to find except on dark, moonless nights. Between Virgo and the tail of Leo lies the Virgo cluster of galaxies, a nearby group of spiral and elliptical galaxies about 60 million light-years away.

LEO THE LION
The Lion is one of the oldest constellations known. The Sumerians of nearly 6,000 years ago showed it in pictures of the zodiac.

WHERE YOU CAN SEE THIS SKY FROM
NORTHERN HEMISPHERE AREAS SUCH AS EUROPE, UNITED STATES, CANADA, AND JAPAN

WHEN YOU CAN SEE THIS SKY BEST
APRIL THROUGH JUNE

BEST NAKED-EYE SIGHTS
ARCTURUS IN BOÖTES, SPICA IN VIRGO, REGULUS IN LEO, PROCYON IN CANIS MINOR

BEST BINOCULAR SIGHTS
BEEHIVE STAR CLUSTER IN CANCER

BEST TELESCOPE SIGHTS
GALAXIES M65 AND M66 IN LEO, VIRGO CLUSTER OF GALAXIES

BEEHIVE CLUSTER
Ancient skylore said that when Cancer's Beehive star cluster disappeared from the sky, rain would follow in a day or two.

◆ LOOK AGAIN ◆

- Where would you look to find a cluster of galaxies?
- How do you find the Pole Star using the Big Dipper?
- What constellation does the star Capella belong to?

CANCER THE CRAB
The Crab is hard to see in city skies. Try looking halfway between Regulus in Leo (on this map), and Castor and Pollux in Gemini (in the west on the Looking North map, facing page).

HYDRA
Hydra the Sea Serpent winds its way across the sky. In mythology, Hercules had to kill a nine-headed Hydra.

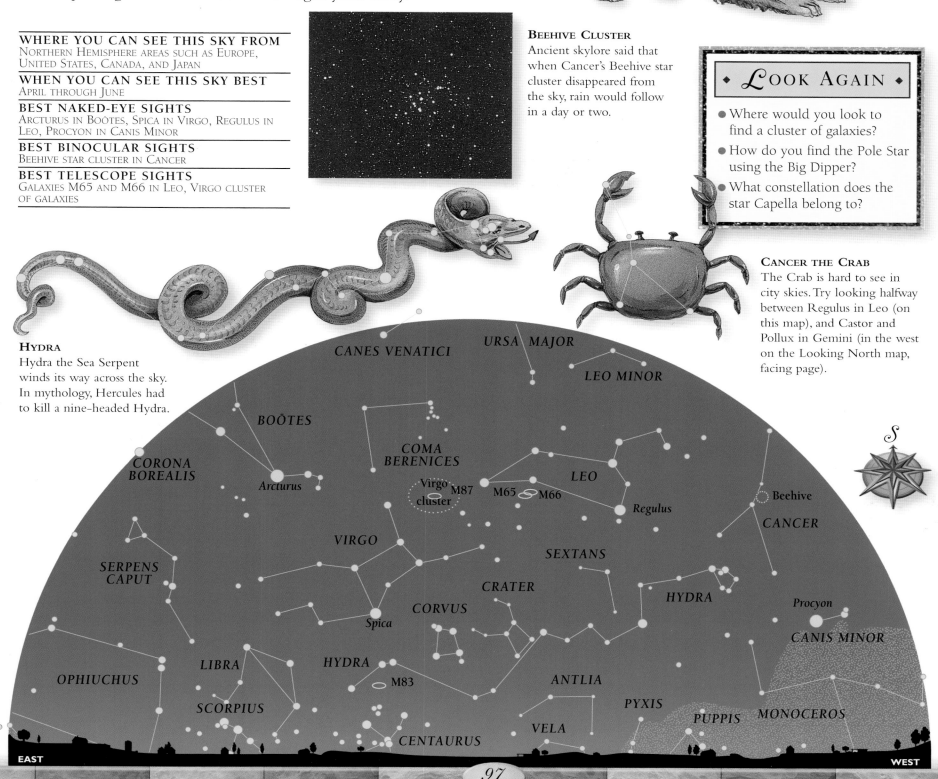

CANES VENATICI · URSA MAJOR · LEO MINOR · BOÖTES · COMA BERENICES · CORONA BOREALIS · Arcturus · Virgo cluster · M87 · M65 · M66 · LEO · Regulus · Beehive · CANCER · SERPENS CAPUT · VIRGO · SEXTANS · HYDRA · Procyon · CRATER · CANIS MINOR · CORVUS · Spica · OPHIUCHUS · LIBRA · HYDRA · M83 · ANTLIA · SCORPIUS · PYXIS · PUPPIS · MONOCEROS · VELA · CENTAURUS

S

EAST · **WEST**

Summer Stars of the Northern Skies

LOOKING NORTH This evening, the Big Dipper (in Ursa Major, the Big Bear) lies to the left of Polaris, the Pole Star, opposite Cassiopeia the Queen, which is rising on the right. Ursa Minor, the Little Bear, curves upward from Polaris. It is often called the Little Dipper. Above Ursa Minor, the dim form of Draco the Dragon wraps around the Pole Star. This is the best time of year to see the Milky Way in the Northern Hemisphere. If the night is moonless and dark, look for the Milky Way crossing the sky from northeast to south. It passes from Cassiopeia, through her husband, Cepheus the King, to Cygnus the Swan overhead. The stars of Cygnus continue onto the Looking South map (see facing page) and form a cross that resembles a bird flying south along the Milky Way. This constellation is sometimes called the Northern Cross.

WHERE YOU CAN SEE THIS SKY FROM
NORTHERN HEMISPHERE AREAS SUCH AS EUROPE, UNITED STATES, CANADA, AND JAPAN

WHEN YOU CAN SEE THIS SKY BEST
JULY THROUGH SEPTEMBER

BEST NAKED-EYE SIGHTS
SUMMER TRIANGLE (MADE UP OF THREE STARS: DENEB IN CYGNUS, VEGA IN LYRA, AND ALTAIR IN AQUILA)

BEST BINOCULAR SIGHTS
MILKY WAY FROM CASSIOPEIA THROUGH CYGNUS, GALAXY M81 IN URSA MAJOR

BEST TELESCOPE SIGHTS
ANDROMEDA GALAXY (M31) IN ANDROMEDA, PLANETARY NEBULA NGC 6543 IN DRACO

CEPHEUS THE KING
A mythical king of Ethiopia, Cepheus saw his daughter Andromeda rescued by the hero Perseus from the sea monster Cetus.

DRACO THE DRAGON
In Greek mythology, the Dragon was defeated by Hercules. Some old star charts show Draco under one of Hercules' feet.

CYGNUS THE SWAN
The Swan's shape has suggested a bird in flight to many cultures. Our figure comes from Greek mythology.

ANDROMEDA GALAXY (M31)
The Andromeda galaxy is a spiral much like the Milky Way. The nearest major galaxy to us, it can just be seen with the naked eye, but looks better in binoculars or a telescope.

M81
Seen as a smudge of light in binoculars, this spiral galaxy in Ursa Major has about as many stars as the Milky Way.

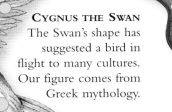

Vega
LYRA
HERCULES
CYGNUS
Deneb
North America nebula
DRACO
NGC 6543
BOÖTES
CEPHEUS
M51
Alcor
Mizar
LACERTA
URSA MINOR
COMA BERENICES
CANES VENATICI
Polaris
CASSIOPEIA
M81
CAMELOPARDALIS
Double Cluster
M31
PEGASUS
URSA MAJOR
LEO
PERSEUS
ANDROMEDA
PISCES
LEO MINOR
LYNX
PISCES

WEST

EAST

LOOKING SOUTH The brightest part of the Milky Way parades across the southern sky on summer nights. The most star-rich constellations are Scorpius the Scorpion and Sagittarius the Archer. Behind their stars lies the center of the Milky Way galaxy. More than 30,000 light-years of dusty gas hide it from view. To the right of the Milky Way, look for the large but faint constellation of Ophiuchus the Serpent Carrier. In Greek legend, Ophiuchus learned about the healing powers of plants from a serpent. He appears in the sky with the constellation Serpens the Serpent. If you look farther north, you'll see that the Milky Way divides in two near Aquila the Eagle and Cygnus the Swan. The dark rift is caused by a cloud of dust near the Sun that obscures the distant Milky Way stars. Three bright stars make up the Summer Triangle—Deneb in Cygnus (see Looking North map, facing page), Vega in Lyra, and Altair in Aquila.

WHERE YOU CAN SEE THIS SKY FROM
NORTHERN HEMISPHERE AREAS SUCH AS EUROPE, UNITED STATES, CANADA, AND JAPAN

WHEN YOU CAN SEE THIS SKY BEST
JULY THROUGH SEPTEMBER

BEST NAKED-EYE SIGHTS
DARK RIFT IN THE MILKY WAY, ANTARES IN SCORPIUS

BEST BINOCULAR SIGHTS
STAR CLOUDS IN SCORPIUS AND SAGITTARIUS

BEST TELESCOPE SIGHTS
LAGOON (M8) AND TRIFID (M20) NEBULAS IN SAGITTARIUS, EAGLE NEBULA (M16) IN SERPENS, DUMBBELL NEBULA (M27) IN VULPECULA

OPHIUCHUS
Ophiuchus the Serpent Carrier appears between the two halves of the constellation Serpens the Serpent—Serpens Cauda and Serpens Caput.

AQUILA THE EAGLE
In ancient myth, the Eagle was sent by the chief of the gods to rescue people—or to punish them.

LAGOON NEBULA (M8)
The Lagoon nebula (in the Milky Way near the horizon) can be seen with binoculars and makes a beautiful sight in a small telescope. Stars are being born inside its dusty gas clouds.

DUMBBELL NEBULA (M27)
The constellation of Vulpecula the Little Fox is home to the Dumbbell nebula, a cloud of gas thrown off by an old star.

◆ **LOOK AGAIN** ◆

- What three stars make up the Summer Triangle?
- How far away is the center of the Milky Way?
- What did a serpent teach Ophiuchus?

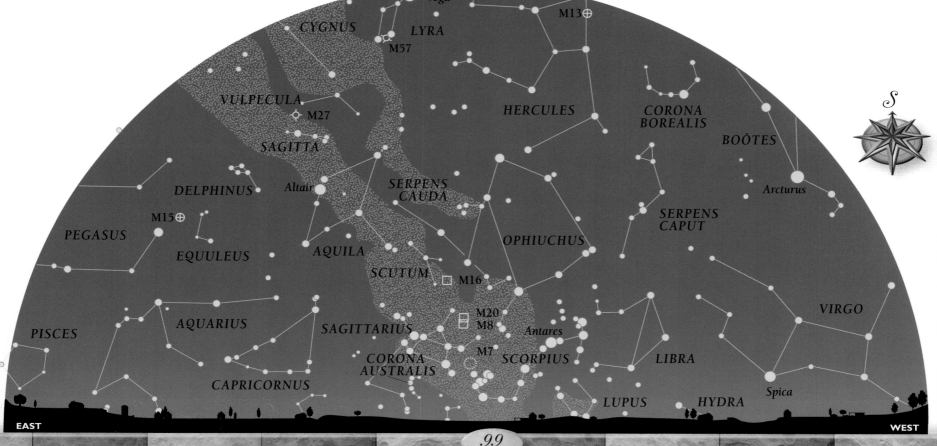

Vega
CYGNUS
LYRA
M57
M13⊕
VULPECULA
M27
HERCULES
CORONA BOREALIS
BOÔTES
SAGITTA
Altair
SERPENS CAUDA
DELPHINUS
Arcturus
SERPENS CAPUT
M15⊕
PEGASUS
AQUILA
OPHIUCHUS
EQUULEUS
SCUTUM
M16
VIRGO
M20
M8
SAGITTARIUS
Antares
PISCES
AQUARIUS
M7
LIBRA
CORONA AUSTRALIS
SCORPIUS
Spica
CAPRICORNUS
LUPUS
HYDRA

EAST

WEST

Autumn Stars of the Northern Skies

LOOKING NORTH On autumn evenings, the Big Dipper (in Ursa Major, the Big Bear) lies on the northern horizon below Polaris, the Pole Star. Polaris is part of Ursa Minor, the Little Bear. Above Polaris, you can see Cassiopeia the Queen, which resembles a slightly bent M. Cepheus the King lies to the lower left of Cassiopeia. Auriga the Charioteer is rising in the northeast, dominated by a bright yellowish star, Capella. Above Auriga, Perseus the Hero lies in the band of the Milky Way. Perseus's bright star Algol is a famous variable. Over in the west, the Summer Triangle of the stars Deneb in Cygnus, Vega in Lyra, and Altair in Aquila (which is shown on the Looking South map, facing page) is setting. Cassiopeia's daughter, Andromeda, stands overhead, with the Andromeda galaxy (M31) visible to the naked eye as a small oval patch of light. This spiral galaxy is the most distant object we can see with the naked eye. It is similar in size to our own Milky Way galaxy.

WHERE YOU CAN SEE THIS SKY FROM
NORTHERN HEMISPHERE AREAS SUCH AS EUROPE, UNITED STATES, CANADA, AND JAPAN

WHEN YOU CAN SEE THIS SKY BEST
OCTOBER THROUGH DECEMBER

BEST NAKED-EYE SIGHTS
VARIABLE STAR ALGOL IN PERSEUS, SUMMER TRIANGLE (MADE UP OF THREE STARS: DENEB IN CYGNUS, VEGA IN LYRA, AND ALTAIR IN AQUILA)

BEST BINOCULAR SIGHTS
DOUBLE CLUSTER IN PERSEUS, NORTH AMERICA NEBULA IN CYGNUS

BEST TELESCOPE SIGHTS
ANDROMEDA GALAXY (M31) IN ANDROMEDA, RING NEBULA (M57) IN LYRA

◆ LOOK AGAIN ◆

- Two Local Group galaxies are visible tonight. What are they?
- Which nebula can be seen near the star Deneb?
- Who was Cassiopeia's daughter?

LYRA THE LYRE
This small constellation is easy to spot because it has a bright star, Vega, and a distinct shape.

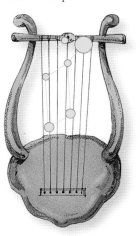

RING NEBULA (M57)
The Ring nebula in Lyra is a planetary nebula—a shell of gas surrounding a white dwarf star. A similar fate awaits the Sun.

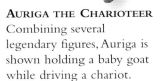

AURIGA THE CHARIOTEER
Combining several legendary figures, Auriga is shown holding a baby goat while driving a chariot.

NORTH AMERICA NEBULA
This cloud of hydrogen gas in Cygnus the Swan got its name because it resembles a map of North America.

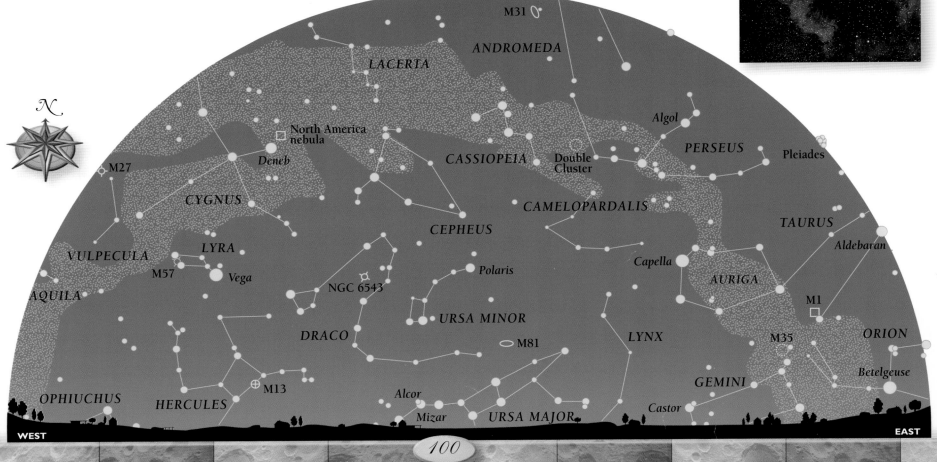

LOOKING SOUTH   High in the southern sky, the Great Square of Pegasus, with a bright star at each corner, makes a guidepost to other constellations. In mythology, Pegasus is the Flying Horse ridden by Perseus the Hero. The horse sprang from the blood of Medusa, a snake-haired monster whom Perseus decapitated. In tonight's sky, the constellation appears upside down, with the stars to the lower right of the Square marking the horse's neck. Pegasus reaches west toward the star Altair in Aquila the Eagle, which lies in the Milky Way. Nearby is tiny Delphinus the Dolphin, a small group of faint stars that looks a little like a kite. Below the Square lie several other "watery" constellations: Aquarius (the Water Carrier), Piscis Austrinus (the Southern Fish), Pisces (the Fishes), and Cetus (the Sea Monster). You can spot Piscis Austrinus by looking for the bright star Fomalhaut, but the other figures lack bright stars and can be difficult to trace. Cetus has the famed variable star Mira in its neck. In the east, Taurus the Bull is rising, followed by winter's Orion the Hunter, which is still half below the horizon.

WHERE YOU CAN SEE THIS SKY FROM
NORTHERN HEMISPHERE AREAS SUCH AS EUROPE, UNITED STATES, CANADA, AND JAPAN

WHEN YOU CAN SEE THIS SKY BEST
OCTOBER THROUGH DECEMBER

BEST NAKED-EYE SIGHTS
FOMALHAUT IN PISCIS AUSTRINUS, VARIABLE STAR MIRA IN CETUS

BEST BINOCULAR SIGHTS
HYADES STAR CLUSTER IN TAURUS, HELIX NEBULA IN AQUARIUS, PINWHEEL GALAXY (M33) IN TRIANGULUM

BEST TELESCOPE SIGHTS
GLOBULAR CLUSTER M15 IN PEGASUS

PINWHEEL GALAXY (M33)
Like the Andromeda galaxy (M31) and our own Milky Way, the Pinwheel in Triangulum (high in the southeast sky) is a spiral galaxy in the Local Group.

AQUARIUS
In old star atlases, Aquarius the Water Carrier is usually shown pouring a jug of water into the mouth of the Southern Fish.

PISCES THE FISHES
Pisces is one of the 12 zodiac constellations. Since it is relatively dim, it is easiest to spot on a dark, moonless night.

HYADES
This loose open star cluster in Taurus (in the eastern sky) lies only about 150 light-years away.

EAST

WEST

Winter Stars of the Southern Skies

LOOKING NORTH   Three bright stars are visible, two of them low in the sky. In the northwest, yellowish Arcturus is setting along with Boötes the Herdsman. Lying due north near the horizon is white Vega, the brightest star in Lyra the Lyre, a small but distinct constellation. In the northeast and higher up is the white star Altair in Aquila the Eagle. It lies close to a great rift in the Milky Way that runs from Cygnus the Swan up to Serpens Cauda. The rift is caused by a huge cloud of dust. To Vega's lower right, you may be able to find Deneb in Cygnus, almost on the horizon. If you look to the left of Vega, you'll see Hercules and the curve of stars that marks Corona Borealis, the Northern Crown. High in the western sky, you might spot the faint stars of Libra the Scales, one of the zodiac constellations. Overhead near Sagittarius the Archer, the Milky Way widens because that is where the center of our galaxy lies. This region contains beautiful dense star clouds.

WHERE YOU CAN SEE THIS SKY FROM
SOUTHERN HEMISPHERE AREAS SUCH AS AUSTRALIA, NEW ZEALAND, SOUTH AMERICA, AND SOUTH AFRICA

WHEN YOU CAN SEE THIS SKY BEST
JULY THROUGH SEPTEMBER

BEST NAKED-EYE SIGHTS
DARK RIFT IN MILKY WAY FROM CYGNUS TO SERPENS CAUDA AND SCUTUM

BEST BINOCULAR SIGHTS
STAR CLOUDS IN SCORPIUS AND SAGITTARIUS

BEST TELESCOPE SIGHTS
LAGOON (M8) AND TRIFID (M20) NEBULAS IN SAGITTARIUS, EAGLE NEBULA (M16) IN SERPENS, DUMBBELL NEBULA (M27) IN VULPECULA, HERCULES CLUSTER (M13) IN HERCULES

LIBRA THE SCALES
Libra's stars once formed the claws of Scorpius the Scorpion. But around 50 BC, astronomers made them into a separate constellation.

SAGITTARIUS THE ARCHER
The half-man, half-horse Sagittarius is one of two centaurs in the sky (the other is Centaurus). Its brightest stars actually look a bit like a teapot.

TRIFID NEBULA (M20)
The Trifid nebula in Sagittarius features dark dust lanes that split it into three parts.

EAGLE NEBULA (M16)
The Eagle nebula lies in Serpens at the edge of the Milky Way. Seen through a telescope, this cloud of gas resembles a crouching bird.

SERPENS THE SERPENT
Serpens the Serpent is the only constellation in two halves (Caput, which means "head" in Latin, and Cauda, which means "tail"). It is divided by Ophiuchus the Serpent Carrier (see page 99).

LOOKING SOUTH The Milky Way is setting in the southwest. Along with it go a number of bright stars. Crux, the Southern Cross, is easy to identify by its shape. Next to it lies the dark Coalsack nebula, a large patch of interstellar dust that you can see with the naked eye. In the south, to the left of Crux, the Small Magellanic Cloud (SMC) looks like a piece of detached Milky Way. Curving above Crux is Centaurus the Centaur, a mythical half-man, half-horse creature. The stars Alpha and Beta Centauri mark the Centaur's forelegs. Above the Centaur lies Lupus the Wolf, and above the Wolf is a stretch of Milky Way that runs up to Scorpius the Scorpion, at the very top of the map. Here, and in nearby Sagittarius the Archer (who is also a centaur), lie many of the Milky Way's greatest sights. They are perfect for exploring with binoculars or a telescope on a moonless night.

CORONA AUSTRALIS
The Southern Crown (below Sagittarius on the map) originally represented a crown of leaves.

◆ LOOK AGAIN ◆
- Which constellation is in two pieces?
- Why does the Milky Way look wider in Sagittarius and Scorpius?
- Can you see the Northern and Southern Crowns at the same time?

WHERE YOU CAN SEE THIS SKY FROM
SOUTHERN HEMISPHERE AREAS SUCH AS AUSTRALIA, NEW ZEALAND, SOUTH AMERICA, AND SOUTH AFRICA

WHEN YOU CAN SEE THIS SKY BEST
JULY THROUGH SEPTEMBER

BEST NAKED-EYE SIGHTS
ALPHA AND BETA CENTAURI IN CENTAURUS

BEST BINOCULAR SIGHTS
OPEN CLUSTER M7 IN SCORPIUS, GLOBULAR CLUSTERS 47 TUCANAE (47 TUC) IN THE SMALL MAGELLANIC CLOUD AND OMEGA CENTAURI IN CENTAURUS, SMALL MAGELLANIC CLOUD (SMC)

BEST TELESCOPE SIGHTS
JEWEL BOX CLUSTER IN CRUX

47 TUCANAE (47 TUC)
This splendid globular cluster near the Small Magellanic Cloud (SMC) looks beautiful in binoculars or a telescope. It lies 16,000 light-years away.

MILKY WAY
Seeing the Milky Way in binoculars on a moonless night away from city lights is a sight no one forgets.

LUPUS THE WOLF
In Greek mythology, the Wolf was speared by the Centaur (Centaurus) and placed on the Altar (Ara) as a sacrifice.

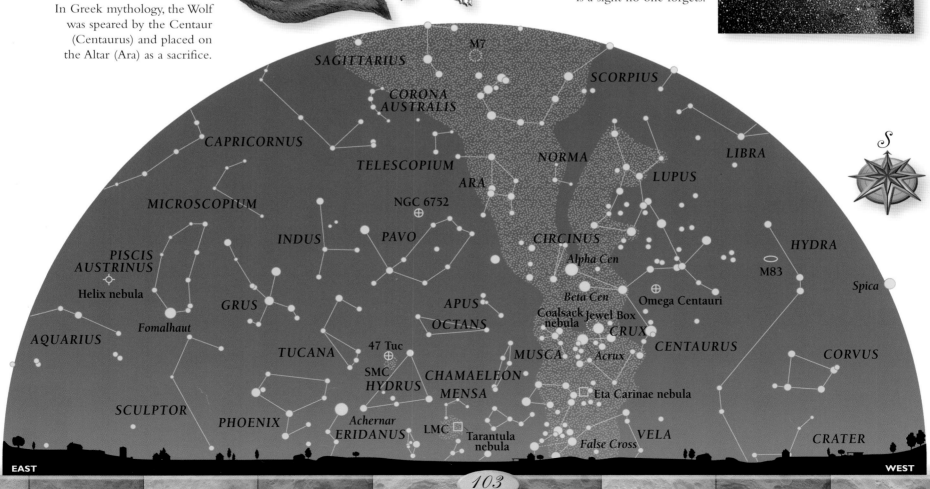

Spring Stars of the Southern Skies

LOOKING NORTH The Great Square of Pegasus, the Flying Horse, makes a guidepost tonight as it "gallops" west across the northern horizon. The two lower stars in the Square point left toward the bright white star Altair in Aquila the Eagle. The two stars on the left side of the Square point upward to Fomalhaut in Piscis Austrinus, the Southern Fish, which is high overhead. Between Pegasus and Fomalhaut lie three dim constellations with watery themes: Pisces the Fishes, Cetus the Sea Monster, and Aquarius the Water Carrier. These are seen most easily on moonless nights, preferably well away from city lights. Rising in the east is the bright star Aldebaran, which forms the eye of Taurus the Bull. To the left of Aldebaran is the pretty Pleiades star cluster, also known as the Seven Sisters. Orion the Hunter is on the eastern horizon, half-risen into view.

WHERE YOU CAN SEE THIS SKY FROM
SOUTHERN HEMISPHERE AREAS SUCH AS AUSTRALIA, NEW ZEALAND, SOUTH AMERICA, AND SOUTH AFRICA

WHEN YOU CAN SEE THIS SKY BEST
OCTOBER THROUGH DECEMBER

BEST NAKED-EYE SIGHTS
GREAT SQUARE OF PEGASUS, FOMALHAUT IN PISCIS AUSTRINUS, VARIABLE STAR MIRA IN CETUS

BEST BINOCULAR SIGHTS
PLEIADES AND HYADES STAR CLUSTERS IN TAURUS

BEST TELESCOPE SIGHTS
GLOBULAR CLUSTER M15 IN PEGASUS, ANDROMEDA GALAXY (M31) IN ANDROMEDA

FOMALHAUT
In ancient mythology, the star Fomalhaut was seen as a bright bubble in the mouth of the Southern Fish.

CETUS
In the neck of Cetus the Sea Monster lies the variable star Mira, which brightens and fades from view every 11 months.

SQUARE OF PEGASUS
If you find the Great Square and extend imaginary lines drawn between its four stars, you can locate many of tonight's constellations.

PEGASUS
In Greek mythology, Pegasus the Flying Horse grew from the blood of a monster slain by the hero Perseus.

✦ AMAZING FACT ✦

The Magellanic Clouds (shown on the Looking South map, facing page) are named for explorer Ferdinand Magellan, whose sailors likely saw the galaxies on their round-the-world voyage in the early 1500s.

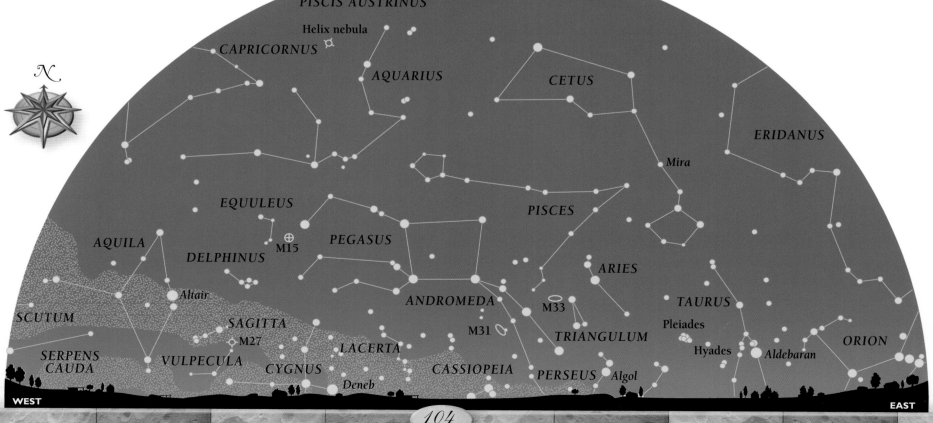

PISCIS AUSTRINUS — Fomalhaut — SCULPTOR — Helix nebula — CAPRICORNUS — AQUARIUS — CETUS — ERIDANUS — Mira — EQUULEUS — PISCES — AQUILA — PEGASUS — M15 — DELPHINUS — ARIES — Altair — ANDROMEDA — M33 — TAURUS — SCUTUM — SAGITTA — M31 — Pleiades — M27 — TRIANGULUM — Hyades — ORION — SERPENS CAUDA — VULPECULA — LACERTA — CASSIOPEIA — PERSEUS — Algol — Aldebaran — CYGNUS — Deneb

N

LOOKING SOUTH   In this sky, two bright stars catch your eye, one high in the south, the other low in the southeast. The higher star is Achernar in Eridanus the River. This is a long, winding figure that runs from Achernar at one end over to the eastern horizon, where Orion is rising. The star low in the southeast is Canopus in Carina the Keel. Canopus is the sky's second-brightest star, after Sirius. Between Canopus and Achernar lies the Large Magellanic Cloud (LMC), with the Small Magellanic Cloud (SMC) to its upper right. Both are satellite galaxies of the Milky Way and, in the night sky, look like stray Milky Way pieces. Several celestial birds flock here. Phoenix the Firebird is above Achernar, and Grus the Crane stands to the right of Phoenix. Tucana the Toucan and Pavo the Peacock crouch below both. The setting Milky Way lies on the western horizon.

TUCANA THE TOUCAN
This bird from the tropics of America was added to the list of constellations in the early 1600s.

GREAT BARRED SPIRAL (NGC 1365)
The Great Barred Spiral is one of the brightest of a cluster of galaxies in the constellation of Fornax the Furnace.

WHERE YOU CAN SEE THIS SKY FROM
SOUTHERN HEMISPHERE AREAS SUCH AS AUSTRALIA, NEW ZEALAND, SOUTH AMERICA, AND SOUTH AFRICA

WHEN YOU CAN SEE THIS SKY BEST
OCTOBER THROUGH DECEMBER

BEST NAKED-EYE SIGHTS
CANOPUS IN CARINA, ACHERNAR IN ERIDANUS

BEST BINOCULAR SIGHTS
SMALL MAGELLANIC CLOUD (SMC), LARGE MAGELLANIC CLOUD (LMC)

BEST TELESCOPE SIGHTS
GLOBULAR CLUSTER 47 TUCANAE (47 TUC) IN THE SMALL MAGELLANIC CLOUD, GREAT BARRED SPIRAL (NGC 1365) IN FORNAX

MAGELLANIC CLOUDS
These two satellite galaxies of the Milky Way will one day collide with our galaxy, which will then swallow up their stars.

GRUS THE CRANE
Like Tucana, the Crane is a "new" constellation that does not date from ancient times. It was invented in 1603.

◆ LOOK AGAIN ◆

- Name at least three night-sky birds visible this evening.
- What is the second-brightest star in the whole night sky?
- Where will you find the variable star Mira?

SCULPTOR · Fomalhaut · PISCIS AUSTRINUS · PHOENIX · FORNAX · GRUS · ERIDANUS · MICROSCOPIUM · CAPRICORNUS · S · NGC 1365 · Achernar · HOROLOGIUM · TUCANA · INDUS · 47 Tuc · SMC · RETICULUM · HYDRUS · PAVO · CORONA AUSTRALIS · CAELUM · DORADO · NGC 6752 · TELESCOPIUM · SAGITTARIUS · LEPUS · Tarantula nebula · MENSA · OCTANS · APUS · SCUTUM · PICTOR · LMC · CHAMAELEON · M8 · Rigel · Canopus · VOLANS · ARA · M7 · M16 · M42 · COLUMBA · MUSCA · M20 · SERPENS CAUDA · ORION · CANIS MAJOR · PUPPIS · CARINA · CIRCINUS · SCORPIUS · OPHIUCHUS · Adhara · VELA · CRUX · NORMA

EAST · WEST

Summer Stars of the Southern Skies

LOOKING NORTH To explore the sky this evening, use the tall figure of Orion the Hunter, standing high in the north. Notice how the colors of the stars Betelgeuse (a cool, red star) and Rigel (a hot, blue one) differ. A row of three dimmer stars in the middle of Orion makes up the Hunter's belt. Extending the belt down to the left points to Taurus the Bull, with the ruddy star Aldebaran and the Hyades and Pleiades star clusters. Aldebaran forms the Bull's angry eye and the Hyades form his face. Extend Orion's belt up to the right and it points to Sirius, the sky's brightest star, in Canis Major, the Big Dog. From Sirius, a line down to the northeast horizon passes Procyon in Canis Minor, the Little Dog, then reaches Regulus in Leo the Lion. Below Orion, the yellow star Capella arcs low in the north with Auriga the Charioteer. To its right stands Gemini the Twins, with the two bright stars Castor and Pollux. The highlight of Cancer the Crab is the Beehive star cluster, which can be seen just to the right of Pollux. This beautiful open cluster contains more than 200 stars and looks best through binoculars.

WHERE YOU CAN SEE THIS SKY FROM
SOUTHERN HEMISPHERE AREAS SUCH AS AUSTRALIA, NEW ZEALAND, SOUTH AMERICA, AND SOUTH AFRICA

WHEN YOU CAN SEE THIS SKY BEST
JANUARY THROUGH MARCH

BEST NAKED-EYE SIGHTS
SIRIUS IN CANIS MAJOR, ORION THE HUNTER

BEST BINOCULAR SIGHTS
BEEHIVE STAR CLUSTER IN CANCER, PLEIADES AND HYADES STAR CLUSTERS IN TAURUS

BEST TELESCOPE SIGHTS
OPEN STAR CLUSTERS M35 IN GEMINI AND M41 IN CANIS MAJOR, CRAB NEBULA (M1) IN TAURUS, ORION NEBULA (M42) IN ORION

GEMINI THE TWINS
Castor and Pollux, the two brightest stars in Gemini the Twins, were named after the twins in Greek mythology who hatched from an egg.

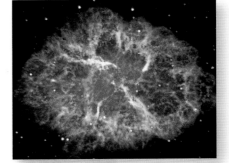

PLEIADES
The Pleiades are sometimes called "the Seven Sisters," but most people can see only six stars by eye. Those with sharp eyesight may see nine stars.

MONOCEROS THE UNICORN
The Unicorn was created in the early 1600s, using dim stars. It appears upside down on the star map below.

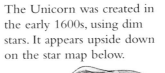

CRAB NEBULA (M1)
The Crab nebula in Taurus is the expanding cloud of hot gas left by a star that was seen exploding in AD 1054.

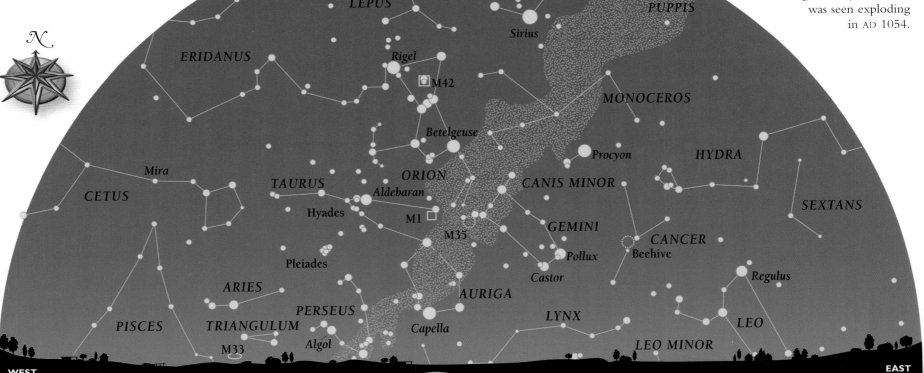

LOOKING SOUTH High in the south, the bright star Canopus marks the rudder of Carina the Keel. Carina is part of the mythical ship *Argo*. This ship was sailed by Jason and the Argonauts in their quest for the Golden Fleece, a ram's coat of gold kept in a dragon-guarded grove. Other parts of the *Argo* include Vela the Sails, Puppis the Stern, and Pyxis the Compass, all of which lie in the Milky Way. Rising in the southeast below Vela is tiny Crux, the Southern Cross. Centaurus the Centaur partly wraps around it. In the southwestern sky, you'll see a single bright star, Achernar. It marks the end of Eridanus the River, which begins at a point next to Rigel in Orion (see Looking North map, facing page). Look between Achernar and Canopus for a misty patch. This is the Large Magellanic Cloud (LMC), one of two satellite galaxies that orbit our own Milky Way galaxy. The other, the Small Magellanic Cloud (SMC), makes a triangle with Achernar and the Large Cloud.

WHERE YOU CAN SEE THIS SKY FROM
SOUTHERN HEMISPHERE AREAS SUCH AS AUSTRALIA, NEW ZEALAND, SOUTH AMERICA, AND SOUTH AFRICA

WHEN YOU CAN SEE THIS SKY BEST
JANUARY THROUGH MARCH

BEST NAKED-EYE SIGHTS
CANOPUS IN CARINA, CRUX (THE SOUTHERN CROSS)

BEST BINOCULAR SIGHTS
LARGE MAGELLANIC CLOUD (LMC), SMALL MAGELLANIC CLOUD (SMC)

BEST TELESCOPE SIGHTS
JEWEL BOX STAR CLUSTER IN CRUX, GLOBULAR CLUSTER 47 TUCANAE (47 TUC) IN THE SMALL MAGELLANIC CLOUD (SMC), TARANTULA NEBULA IN THE LARGE MAGELLANIC CLOUD (LMC)

ERIDANUS THE RIVER
The meandering celestial River commemorates Oceanus, a mythical stream once believed to circle the ancient world.

ETA CARINAE NEBULA
In the center of this gas cloud in Carina lies the unstable star Eta Carinae. Astronomers expect to see the star explode any time in the next few thousand years.

COLUMBA THE DOVE
The Dove, near the top of the map, was invented around 1600. It honors the biblical bird that Noah sent from the ark to look for land.

◆ LOOK AGAIN ◆

- What happened in 1987 in the Large Magellanic Cloud?
- Where is "Oceanus" in tonight's sky?
- What is the Crab nebula?

LARGE MAGELLANIC CLOUD (LMC)
In 1987, astronomers saw a star explode in this small irregular galaxy. It was the first bright supernova seen since the telescope was invented about 400 years ago.

EAST

WEST

Autumn Stars of the Southern Skies

LOOKING NORTH Four bright stars make easy jumping-off points for finding constellations this evening. Look for Procyon in Canis Minor, the Little Dog, setting in the northwest. In the north, Regulus marks the heart of Leo the Lion. Then over in the northeast at about the same height as Regulus, you'll see reddish Arcturus. It stands in the constellation of Boötes the Herdsman. Directly above Arcturus, and with a marked contrast in color, is white Spica in Virgo the Maiden. The patch of sky between Leo and Virgo contains the Virgo cluster of galaxies. At about 55 million light-years away, this is the nearest large galaxy cluster to our own Local Group. The long figure of Hydra the Sea Serpent has his head near Procyon. His body weaves high overhead past Crater the Cup and Corvus the Crow, ending not far from Spica.

WHERE YOU CAN SEE THIS SKY FROM
SOUTHERN HEMISPHERE AREAS SUCH AS AUSTRALIA, NEW ZEALAND, SOUTH AMERICA, AND SOUTH AFRICA

WHEN YOU CAN SEE THIS SKY BEST
APRIL THROUGH JUNE

BEST NAKED-EYE SIGHTS
REGULUS IN LEO, ARCTURUS IN BOÖTES, SPICA IN VIRGO

BEST BINOCULAR SIGHTS
BEEHIVE STAR CLUSTER IN CANCER

BEST TELESCOPE SIGHTS
GALAXIES M65 AND M66 IN LEO, M83 IN HYDRA, M87 IN VIRGO, VIRGO CLUSTER OF GALAXIES

VIRGO THE MAIDEN
Virgo is the only female figure to be found among the 12 constellations of the zodiac.

BOÖTES THE HERDSMAN
According to ancient legend, when Boötes invented the plow, the gods honored him with a place in the heavens.

M87
An elliptical galaxy, M87 in Virgo is one of the most massive galaxies known. In a small telescope, it looks like a hazy patch of light.

M83
M83 is a barred spiral galaxy that is turned so we see its disk face-on. You can observe it high in the northeastern sky through binoculars.

◆ LOOK AGAIN ◆

- What ship has Vela for its sails?
- When did Crux become a separate constellation?
- How did Boötes earn his place in the night sky?

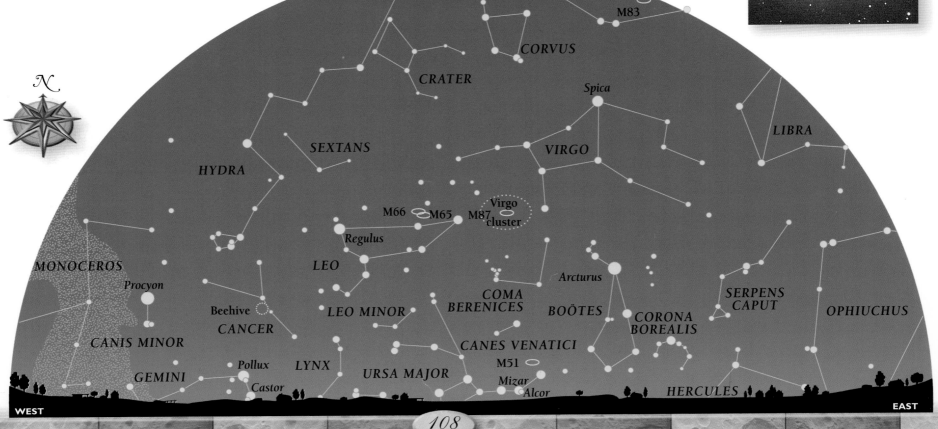

HYDRA
M83
CORVUS
CRATER
Spica
LIBRA
SEXTANS
VIRGO
HYDRA
Virgo cluster
M66 M65 M87
Regulus
MONOCEROS
LEO
Arcturus
Procyon
Beehive
LEO MINOR
COMA BERENICES
BOÖTES
SERPENS CAPUT
OPHIUCHUS
CANIS MINOR
CANCER
CANES VENATICI
CORONA BOREALIS
GEMINI
Pollux
Castor
LYNX
URSA MAJOR
M51
Mizar
Alcor
HERCULES

LOOKING SOUTH To fully appreciate the glories of the Milky Way arching across the southern sky, try to get away from city lights on a moonless evening at this time of year. If you have a pair of binoculars or a small telescope, take the opportunity to sweep through the band of Milky Way stars. The band runs from the dazzling star Sirius in Canis Major, the Big Dog, which is setting in the west, to ruddy Antares in Scorpius the Scorpion, rising in the southeast. In the southwest, look above the bright star Canopus for Carina the Keel, Vela the Sails, and Puppis the Stern—all constellations that were once part of Jason and the Argonauts' mythical ship *Argo*. To the left of these stand the bright stars of tiny Crux, the Southern Cross, which Centaurus the Centaur so nimbly hops over, his forefeet marked by Alpha and Beta Centauri.

SCORPIUS THE SCORPION
Greek mythology said that Scorpius killed Orion, which is why one is always setting as the other rises.

THE JEWEL BOX
Seen in a telescope, this small but rich open cluster near Crux shows stars of different colors. It lies about 6,800 light-years away.

WHERE YOU CAN SEE THIS SKY FROM
SOUTHERN HEMISPHERE AREAS SUCH AS AUSTRALIA, NEW ZEALAND, SOUTH AMERICA, AND SOUTH AFRICA

WHEN YOU CAN SEE THIS SKY BEST
APRIL THROUGH JUNE

BEST NAKED-EYE SIGHTS
MILKY WAY, CRUX, COALSACK NEBULA IN CRUX

BEST BINOCULAR SIGHTS
MILKY WAY, LARGE MAGELLANIC CLOUD (LMC)

BEST TELESCOPE SIGHTS
JEWEL BOX STAR CLUSTER IN CRUX, OMEGA CENTAURI GLOBULAR CLUSTER IN CENTAURUS, ETA CARINAE NEBULA IN CARINA, TARANTULA NEBULA IN LARGE MAGELLANIC CLOUD (LMC)

TARANTULA NEBULA
The Tarantula nebula got its name because its gas clouds look a bit like the hairy legs of a spider. You can find it to the left of the star Canopus.

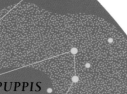

CENTAURUS THE CENTAUR
Centaurs were half-man and half-horse. Centaurus honors Chiron, the wisest of these mythical beasts. Sagittarius the Archer is also a centaur.

CRUX
Crux, the Southern Cross, dates only from 1592. Before then, its stars were part of Centaurus.

EAST

HYDRA

ANTLIA

CENTAURUS

Omega
Centauri

PYXIS

S

LIBRA

LUPUS

CRUX

Eta Carinae
nebula

VELA

Jewel
Box

Coalsack
nebula

Acrux

PUPPIS

Alpha Cen

Beta
Cen

False Cross

Antares

MUSCA

CIRCINUS

CARINA

CANIS MAJOR

NORMA

VOLANS

Adhara

OPHIUCHUS

SCORPIUS

CHAMAELEON

Tarantula
nebula

Canopus

M41

Sirius

ARA

APUS

OCTANS

MENSA

PICTOR

COLUMBA

M7

NGC
6752

PAVO

LMC

RETICULUM

SERPENS
CAUDA

M8

TELESCOPIUM

DORADO

LEPUS

SAGITTARIUS

CORONA AUSTRALIS

47 Tuc

SMC

HYDRUS

M20

M16

TUCANA

HOROLOGIUM

CAELUM

ORION

INDUS

WEST

Universe Fact File

SUN FACTS

APPARENT MAGNITUDE: −26.8
ABSOLUTE (ACTUAL) MAGNITUDE: 4.8
ROTATION TIME: 25 Earth days at equator, 34 Earth days near poles
DIAMETER: 865,000 miles (1,392,000 km)
MASS: 332,946 x Earth's
DENSITY: 1.4 x water's density
SURFACE GRAVITY: 27.9 x Earth's
COMPOSITION: 92.1% hydrogen, 7.8% helium, 1% other elements
SURFACE TEMPERATURE: 9,900°F (5,500°C)
CORE TEMPERATURE: 27,900,000°F (15,500,000°C)
MAGNETIC FIELD STRENGTH: up to 10,000 x Earth's

MERCURY FACTS

WHEN DISCOVERED: prehistoric
WHO DISCOVERED IT: unknown
HOW WE CAN SEE IT: naked eye
APPARENT MAGNITUDE: −2 to +3
DISTANCE FROM SUN: 0.4 AU, or 36 million miles (58 million km)
LENGTH OF YEAR: 88 Earth days
AVERAGE SPEED: 30 miles per second (48 km/s)
INCLINATION OF ORBIT: 7.0°
ECCENTRICITY OF ORBIT: 0.21
TILT OF AXIS: 0.5°
ROTATION TIME: 59 Earth days
SOLAR DAY: 176 Earth days
DIAMETER: 3,029 miles (4,875 km)
MASS: 55% x Earth's
DENSITY: 5.4 x water's density
SURFACE GRAVITY: 0.38 x Earth's
COMPOSITION: iron and rock
ATMOSPHERE: essentially none
AVERAGE TEMPERATURE: −274°F to 873°F (−170°C to 467°C)
MAGNETIC FIELD STRENGTH: 0.5% x Earth's
NUMBER OF MOONS: none
NUMBER OF RINGS: none
NUMBER OF PROBE VISITS: 2

VENUS FACTS

WHEN DISCOVERED: prehistoric
WHO DISCOVERED IT: unknown
HOW WE CAN SEE IT: naked eye
APPARENT MAGNITUDE: −4.0 to −4.6
DISTANCE FROM SUN: 0.7 AU, or 67 million miles (108 million km)
LENGTH OF YEAR: 225 Earth days
AVERAGE SPEED: 22 miles per second (35 km/s)
INCLINATION OF ORBIT: 3.4°
ECCENTRICITY OF ORBIT: 0.01
TILT OF AXIS: 177.4°
ROTATION TIME: 243 Earth days
SOLAR DAY: 117 Earth days
DIAMETER: 7,521 miles (12,104 km)
MASS: 82% x Earth's
DENSITY: 5.2 x water's density
SURFACE GRAVITY: 0.90 x Earth's
COMPOSITION: mostly rock
ATMOSPHERE: 97% carbon dioxide, 3% nitrogen
PRESSURE OF ATMOSPHERE: 96 x Earth's
AVERAGE TEMPERATURE: 880°F (470°C)
MAGNETIC FIELD STRENGTH: less than 0.05% x Earth's
NUMBER OF MOONS: none
NUMBER OF RINGS: none
NUMBER OF PROBE VISITS: 32

EARTH FACTS

WHEN DISCOVERED: prehistoric
WHO DISCOVERED IT: unknown
DISTANCE FROM SUN: 1.0 AU, or 93 million miles (150 million km)
LENGTH OF YEAR: 365.25 days
AVERAGE SPEED: 18.5 miles per second (30 km/s)
INCLINATION OF ORBIT: 0°
ECCENTRICITY OF ORBIT: 0.02
TILT OF AXIS: 23.5°
ROTATION TIME: 23 hours 56 minutes
SOLAR DAY: 24 hours
DIAMETER: 7,926 miles (12,756 km)
MASS: 1.3×10^{25} pounds (6×10^{24} kg)
DENSITY: 5.5 x water's density
COMPOSITION: mostly rock
ATMOSPHERE: 78% nitrogen, 21% oxygen, plus water, argon, carbon dioxide
AVERAGE TEMPERATURE: 63°F (17°C)
NUMBER OF MOONS: 1
NUMBER OF RINGS: none

MARS FACTS

WHEN DISCOVERED: prehistoric
WHO DISCOVERED IT: unknown
HOW WE CAN SEE IT: naked eye
APPARENT MAGNITUDE: −2.6 to +1.8
DISTANCE FROM SUN: 1.5 AU, or 142 million miles (228 million km)
LENGTH OF YEAR: 687 Earth days
AVERAGE SPEED: 15 miles per second (24 km/s)
INCLINATION OF ORBIT: 1.9°
ECCENTRICITY OF ORBIT: 0.09
TILT OF AXIS: 25.2°
ROTATION TIME: 24 hours 37 minutes
SOLAR DAY: 24 hours 40 minutes
DIAMETER: 4,213 miles (6,780 km)
MASS: 10.7% x Earth's
DENSITY: 3.9 x water's density
SURFACE GRAVITY: 0.38 x Earth's
COMPOSITION: mostly rock
ATMOSPHERE: 95% carbon dioxide, 2.7% nitrogen, 1.6% argon, plus others
PRESSURE OF ATMOSPHERE: 0.6% x Earth's
AVERAGE TEMPERATURE: −74°F (−59°C)
MAGNETIC FIELD STRENGTH: less than 0.1% x Earth's
NUMBER OF MOONS: 2
NUMBER OF RINGS: none
NUMBER OF PROBE VISITS: 28

JUPITER FACTS

WHEN DISCOVERED: prehistoric
WHO DISCOVERED IT: unknown
HOW WE CAN SEE IT: naked eye
APPARENT MAGNITUDE: −2.5 to −1.2
DISTANCE FROM SUN: 5.2 AU, or 483 million miles (778 million km)
LENGTH OF YEAR: 11.9 Earth years
AVERAGE SPEED: 8 miles per second (13 km/s)
INCLINATION OF ORBIT: 1.3°
ECCENTRICITY OF ORBIT: 0.05
TILT OF AXIS: 3.1°
ROTATION TIME: 9 hours 55 minutes
SOLAR DAY: same as rotation time
DIAMETER: 88,846 miles (142,984 km)
MASS: 317.8 x Earth's mass
DENSITY: 1.3 x water's density
GRAVITY AT CLOUDTOPS: 2.6 x Earth's surface gravity
COMPOSITION: mostly gaseous
ATMOSPHERE: 86% hydrogen, 13.6% helium, plus methane, ammonia, water
AVERAGE TEMPERATURE AT CLOUDTOPS: −162°F (−108°C)
MAGNETIC FIELD STRENGTH: 7.1 x Earth's
NUMBER OF MOONS: 49
NUMBER OF RINGS: 3
NUMBER OF PROBE VISITS: 5

NOTES ON PLANET FACTS

APPARENT MAGNITUDE: How bright an object looks in the sky. Brighter objects have smaller numbers than dimmer ones.
DISTANCE FROM SUN: The planet's average distance from the Sun.
INCLINATION OF ORBIT: The angle of the planet's orbit relative to the plane of Earth's orbit.
ECCENTRICITY OF ORBIT: How elliptical the planet's orbit is. The larger the number, the more elliptical the orbit is.

NOTES ON ASTEROID FACTS

DISTANCE FROM SUN: The asteroid's average distance from the Sun.
ORBIT TIME: All years listed are Earth years.

NOTES ON COMET FACTS

NAME: Comets are named for their discoverers.
ORBIT TIME: All years listed are Earth years.
ORBIT INCLIN.: The inclination of the comet's orbit relative to the plane of Earth's orbit.
ORBIT ECCENT.: The eccentricity of the comet's orbit. The larger the number, the more elliptical the orbit is.

GENERAL NOTES

- 1 AU (astronomical unit) is the average distance between Earth and the Sun, about 93 million miles (150 million km).
- A tonne is a metric ton, equal to 1,000 kg or about 2,200 pounds.

SATURN FACTS

WHEN DISCOVERED: prehistoric
WHO DISCOVERED IT: unknown
HOW WE CAN SEE IT: naked eye
APPARENT MAGNITUDE: 0.6 to 1.5
DISTANCE FROM SUN: 9.6 AU, or 890 million miles (1,432 million km)
LENGTH OF YEAR: 29.4 Earth years
AVERAGE SPEED: 6 miles per second (10 km/s)
INCLINATION OF ORBIT: 2.5°
ECCENTRICITY OF ORBIT: 0.05
TILT OF AXIS: 26.7°
ROTATION TIME: 10 hours 39 minutes
SOLAR DAY: same as rotation time
DIAMETER: 74,896 miles (120,533 km)
MASS: 95.2 x Earth's
DENSITY: 0.7 x water's density
GRAVITY AT CLOUDTOPS: 1.1 x Earth's surface gravity
COMPOSITION: mostly gaseous
ATMOSPHERE: 96% hydrogen, 3.3% helium, plus methane, ammonia, and others
AVERAGE TEMPERATURE AT CLOUDTOPS: −218°F (−139°C)
MAGNETIC FIELD STRENGTH: 0.34 x Earth's
NUMBER OF MOONS: 48
NUMBER OF RINGS: 7
NUMBER OF PROBE VISITS: 4

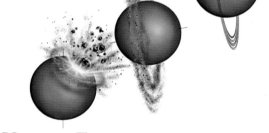

URANUS FACTS

WHEN DISCOVERED: March 1781
WHO DISCOVERED IT: William Herschel
HOW WE CAN SEE IT: barely visible to the naked eye, but easy to see with a telescope
APPARENT MAGNITUDE: 5.5 to 5.9
DISTANCE FROM SUN: 19.2 AU, or 1,784 million miles (2,871 million km)
LENGTH OF YEAR: 84.1 Earth years
AVERAGE SPEED: 4 miles per second (7 km/s)
INCLINATION OF ORBIT: 0.8°
ECCENTRICITY OF ORBIT: 0.04
TILT OF AXIS: 97.9°
ROTATION TIME: 17 hours 14 minutes
SOLAR DAY: same as rotation time
DIAMETER: 31,763 miles (51,118 km)
MASS: 14.5 x Earth's
DENSITY: 1.3 x water's density
GRAVITY AT CLOUDTOPS: 0.90 x Earth's surface gravity
COMPOSITION: mostly gaseous
ATMOSPHERE: 83% hydrogen, 15% helium, 2% methane
AVERAGE TEMPERATURE AT CLOUDTOPS: −323°F (−197°C)
MAGNETIC FIELD STRENGTH: 0.38 x Earth's
NUMBER OF MOONS: 27
NUMBER OF RINGS: 11
NUMBER OF PROBE VISITS: 1

PLANET FEATURES

The names of geological features on rocky planets and moons come from Latin and Greek.
Chasma: a deep, long depression with steep sides
Corona: an oval-shaped feature
Fossae: depressions that are long, narrow, and shallow
Mons, montes: a mountain or range of mountains
Patera: an irregular crater
Planitia: a low plain
Planum: a plateau or high plain
Regio: a large area distinct from surrounding ones
Rupes: a long cliff caused by geological faulting
Terra: an extensive landmass
Tessera: terrain that is heavily broken up by faulting
Tholus: a small domed mountain or hill
Vallis, valles: a valley or set of connected valleys
Vastitas: an extensive plain

NEPTUNE FACTS

WHEN DISCOVERED: September 1846
WHO DISCOVERED IT: Urbain Leverrier, John Couch Adams, Johann Galle, and Heinrich d'Arrest
HOW WE CAN SEE IT: telescope
APPARENT MAGNITUDE: 7.9
DISTANCE FROM SUN: 30.1 AU, or 2,795 million miles (4,498 million km)
LENGTH OF YEAR: 164.9 Earth years
AVERAGE SPEED: 3.5 miles per second (5.5 km/s)
INCLINATION OF ORBIT: 1.8°
ECCENTRICITY OF ORBIT: 0.01
TILT OF AXIS: 29.6°
ROTATION TIME: 16 hours 7 minutes
SOLAR DAY: same as rotation time
DIAMETER: 30,775 miles (49,528 km)
MASS: 17.2 x Earth's
DENSITY: 1.6 x water's density
GRAVITY AT CLOUDTOPS: 1.1 x Earth's surface gravity
COMPOSITION: mostly gaseous
ATMOSPHERE: 80% hydrogen, 19% helium, 1% methane
AVERAGE TEMPERATURE AT CLOUDTOPS: −330°F (−201°C)
MAGNETIC FIELD STRENGTH: 22% x Earth's
NUMBER OF MOONS: 13
NUMBER OF RINGS: 6
NUMBER OF PROBE VISITS: 1

PLUTO FACTS

WHEN DISCOVERED: February 1930
WHO DISCOVERED IT: Clyde Tombaugh
HOW WE CAN SEE IT: telescope
APPARENT MAGNITUDE: 13.7
DISTANCE FROM SUN: 39.5 AU, or 3,675 million miles (5,914 million km)
LENGTH OF YEAR: 248 Earth years
AVERAGE SPEED: 3 miles per second (5 km/s)
INCLINATION OF ORBIT: 17.1°
ECCENTRICITY OF ORBIT: 0.25
TILT OF AXIS: 122.5°
ROTATION TIME: 6.4 Earth days
SOLAR DAY: same as rotation time
DIAMETER: 1,432 miles (2,304 km)
MASS: 0.2% x Earth's
DENSITY: 2.1 x water's density
SURFACE GRAVITY: 0.065 x Earth's
COMPOSITION: rock and ice
ATMOSPHERE: methane, nitrogen
PRESSURE OF ATMOSPHERE: about 3 millionths x Earth's
AVERAGE TEMPERATURE: −387°F (−233°C)
MAGNETIC FIELD STRENGTH: unknown
NUMBER OF MOONS: 3
NUMBER OF RINGS: none
NUMBER OF PROBE VISITS: 1

ASTEROID FACTS

NAME	DISCOVERY	DISTANCE FROM SUN	ORBIT TIME	ROTATION TIME	DIAMETER
1 Ceres	Piazzi, 1801	2.76 AU	4.6 yrs	9h 5m	567 miles (913 km)
2 Pallas	Olbers, 1802	2.77 AU	4.6 yrs	7h 49m	325 miles (523 km)
4 Vesta	Olbers, 1807	2.36 AU	3.6 yrs	5h 21m	323 miles (520 km)
10 Hygeia	De Gasparis, 1849	3.14 AU	5.6 yrs	27h 40m	267 miles (429 km)
511 Davida	Dugan, 1903	3.18 AU	5.7 yrs	5h 8m	209 miles (337 km)
704 Interamnia	Cerulli, 1910	3.06 AU	5.4 yrs	8h 44m	207 miles (333 km)
253 Mathilde	Palisa, 1885	2.65 AU	4.3 yrs	17h 24m	41 miles (66 km)
243 Ida	Palisa, 1884	2.86 AU	4.9 yrs	4h 38m	37 miles (60 km)
433 Eros	Witt & Charlois, 1898	1.46 AU	1.8 yrs	5h 18m	21 miles (33 km)
951 Gaspra	Neujmin, 1916	2.21 AU	3.3 yrs	7h 3m	11 miles (18 km)

COMET FACTS

NAME	FIRST RECORDED	FARTHEST FROM SUN	CLOSEST TO SUN	TYPE	ORBIT TIME	ORBIT INCLIN.	ORBIT ECCENT.
Encke	1786	4.1 AU	0.3 AU	short period	3.3 yrs	11.9°	0.85
Wirtanen	1954	5.1 AU	1.1 AU	short period	5.5 yrs	11.7°	0.65
Wild 2	1978	5.3 AU	1.6 AU	short period	6.4 yrs	3.2°	0.54
d'Arrest	1851	5.6 AU	1.4 AU	short period	6.5 yrs	19.5°	0.61
Tempel-Tuttle	1866	19.5 AU	1.0 AU	short period	32.9 yrs	163°	0.90
Halley	239 BC	35.0 AU	0.6 AU	short period	76.0 yrs	162°	0.97
Swift-Tuttle	1862	52.3 AU	1.0 AU	short period	137.3 yrs	113°	0.96
Bennett	1970	281.8 AU	0.5 AU	long period	1,678 yrs	90.0°	0.99
Donati	1858	311.6 AU	0.6 AU	long period	1,950 yrs	117°	0.99
Hale-Bopp	1995	370.6 AU	0.9 AU	long period	2,529 yrs	89.4°	0.99
Hyakutake	1996	2,006 AU	0.2 AU	long period	31,781 yrs	125°	0.99
Ikeya-Seki	1965	4,000 AU	0.01 AU	long period	89,443 yrs	129°	0.99

NAME	DISCOVERY	DISTANCE FROM PLANET IN MILES (KM)	ORBIT TIME	DIAMETER IN MILES (KM)	MASS IN TONS (TONNES)	SURFACE COMPOSITION
Earth						
the Moon	prehistoric	238,856 (384,401)	27.3 days	2,160 (3,476)	8.0×10^{19} (7.3×10^{19})	anorthosite & basalt rock, dust
Mars						
Phobos	Hall, 1877	5,827 (9,378)	0.3 day	17 (27)	1.1×10^{13} (9.6×10^{12})	carbon-rich rock, dust
Deimos	Hall, 1877	14,577 (23,459)	1.3 days	9 (15)	2.0×10^{12} (1.8×10^{12})	carbon-rich rock, dust
45 Eugenia						
S/1998(45)1	Merline, 1998	771 (1,240)?	4.7 days	6 (10)?	unknown	rock?
243 Ida						
Dactyl	Galileo spacecraft, 1993	56 (90)	unknown	1 (1.6)	4.1×10^{9} (3.7×10^{9})	carbon-rich rock, dust
Jupiter						
Metis	Synnott, 1979	79,511 (127,960)	0.3 day	25 (40)	1.0×10^{14} (9.5×10^{13})	rock
Adrastea	Jewitt & Danielson, 1979	80,145 (128,980)	0.3 day	16 (25)	2.1×10^{13} (1.9×10^{13})	rock
Amalthea	Barnard, 1892	112,655 (181,300)	0.5 day	168 (270)	7.9×10^{15} (7.2×10^{15})	rock, sulfur coating?
Thebe	Synnott, 1979	137,882 (221,900)	0.7 day	68 (110)	8.4×10^{14} (7.6×10^{14})	rock
Io	Galileo, 1610	261,970 (421,600)	1.8 days	2,264 (3,643)	9.8×10^{19} (8.9×10^{19})	rock
Europa	Galileo, 1610	416,880 (670,900)	3.5 days	1,939 (3,120)	5.3×10^{19} (4.8×10^{19})	rock
Ganymede	Galileo, 1610	664,870 (1,070,000)	7.2 days	3,273 (5,268)	1.7×10^{20} (1.5×10^{20})	rock
Callisto	Galileo, 1610	1,170,000 (1,883,000)	16.7 days	2,983 (4,800)	1.2×10^{20} (1.1×10^{20})	rock
Leda	Kowal, 1974	6,893,500 (11,094,000)	238.7 days	10 (16)	6.3×10^{12} (5.7×10^{12})	carbon-rich dirt, ice
Himalia	Perrine, 1904	7,133,300 (11,480,000)	250.6 days	116 (186)	1.0×10^{16} (9.5×10^{15})	carbon-rich dirt, ice
Lysithea	Nicholson, 1938	7,282,500 (11,720,000)	259.2 days	22 (36)	8.4×10^{13} (7.6×10^{13})	carbon-rich dirt, ice
Elara	Perrine, 1905	7,293,000 (11,737,000)	259.6 days	47 (76)	8.4×10^{14} (7.6×10^{14})	carbon-rich dirt, ice
Ananke	Nicholson, 1951	13,173,100 (21,200,000)	631 days	19 (30)	4.2×10^{13} (3.8×10^{13})	carbon-rich dirt, ice
Carme	Nicholson, 1938	14,043,000 (22,600,000)	692 days	25 (40)	1.0×10^{14} (9.5×10^{13})	carbon-rich dirt, ice
Pasiphae	Melotte, 1908	14,602,200 (23,500,000)	735 days	31 (50)	2.1×10^{14} (1.9×10^{14})	carbon-rich dirt, ice
Sinope	Nicholson, 1914	14,726,500 (23,700,000)	758 days	22 (36)	8.4×10^{13} (7.6×10^{13})	carbon-rich dirt, ice
Saturn						
Pan	Showalter, 1990	83,005 (133,583)	0.6 day	12 (20)	unknown	ice?
Atlas	Terrile, 1980	85,544 (137,670)	0.6 day	24 (38)	unknown	dirty ice?
Prometheus	Collins & others, 1980	86,590 (139,353)	0.6 day	87 (140)	1.5×10^{14} (1.4×10^{14})	ice?
Pandora	Collins & others, 1980	88,048 (141,700)	0.6 day	68 (110)	1.4×10^{14} (1.3×10^{14})	ice?
Epimetheus	Walker & others, 1966	94,089 (151,422)	0.7 day	87 (140)	6.0×10^{14} (5.5×10^{14})	dirty ice?
Janus	Dollfus, 1966	94,120 (151,472)	0.7 day	137 (220)	2.2×10^{15} (2.0×10^{15})	dirty ice?
Mimas	Herschel, 1789	115,280 (185,520)	0.9 day	244 (392)	4.2×10^{16} (3.8×10^{16})	ice
Enceladus	Herschel, 1789	147,900 (238,020)	1.4 days	310 (500)	8.8×10^{16} (8.0×10^{16})	ice
Tethys	Cassini, 1684	183,090 (294,660)	1.9 days	659 (1,060)	8.4×10^{17} (7.6×10^{17})	ice
Telesto	Smith & others, 1980	183,090 (294,660)	1.9 days	21 (34)	unknown	ice?
Calypso	Pascu & others, 1980	183,090 (294,660)	1.9 days	21 (34)	unknown	ice?
Dione	Cassini, 1684	234,500 (377,400)	2.7 days	696 (1,120)	1.2×10^{18} (1.1×10^{18})	dirty ice
Helene	Laques & Lecacheux, 1980	234,500 (377,400)	2.7 days	22 (36)	unknown	dirty ice?
Rhea	Cassini, 1672	327,490 (527,040)	4.5 days	950 (1,528)	2.8×10^{18} (2.5×10^{18})	ice
Titan	Huygens, 1655	759,210 (1,221,830)	16 days	3,200 (5,150)	1.5×10^{20} (1.4×10^{20})	liquid methane, ice
Hyperion	Bond, 1848	920,310 (1,481,100)	21.3 days	218 (350)	1.9×10^{16} (1.7×10^{16})	dirty ice?
Iapetus	Cassini, 1671	2,212,900 (3,561,300)	79.3 days	892 (1,436)	2.1×10^{18} (1.9×10^{18})	ice, carbon-rich dirt
Phoebe	Pickering, 1898	8,048,000 (12,952,000)	550.5 days	143 (230)	4.4×10^{14} (4.0×10^{14})	ice, carbon-rich dirt?
Uranus						
Cordelia	Voyager 2, 1986	30,926 (49,770)	0.3 day	16 (26)	unknown	carbon-rich dirt, ice?
Ophelia	Voyager 2, 1986	33,424 (53,790)	0.4 day	19 (30)	unknown	carbon-rich dirt, ice?
Bianca	Voyager 2, 1986	36,764 (59,166)	0.4 day	26 (42)	unknown	carbon-rich dirt, ice?
Cressida	Voyager 2, 1986	38,388 (61,780)	0.5 day	39 (62)	unknown	carbon-rich dirt, ice?
Desdemona	Voyager 2, 1986	38,948 (62,680)	0.5 day	34 (54)	unknown	carbon-rich dirt, ice?
Juliet	Voyager 2, 1986	39,985 (64,350)	0.5 day	52 (84)	unknown	carbon-rich dirt, ice?
Portia	Voyager 2, 1986	41,066 (66,090)	0.5 day	67 (108)	unknown	carbon-rich dirt, ice?
Rosalind	Voyager 2, 1986	43,459 (69,940)	0.6 day	34 (54)	unknown	carbon-rich dirt, ice?
Belinda	Voyager 2, 1986	46,762 (75,256)	0.6 day	41 (66)	unknown	carbon-rich dirt, ice?
S/1986 U10	Karkoshka, 1999	47,483 (76,416)	0.6 day	25 (40)?	unknown	unknown
Puck	Voyager 2, 1986	53,444 (86,010)	0.8 day	96 (154)	unknown	carbon-rich dirt, ice?
Miranda	Kuiper, 1948	80,399 (129,390)	1.4 days	301 (484)	7.6×10^{16} (6.9×10^{16})	ice
Ariel	Lassell, 1851	118,694 (191,020)	2.5 days	720 (1,158)	1.5×10^{18} (1.4×10^{18})	ice
Umbriel	Lassell, 1851	165,471 (266,300)	4.1 days	728 (1,172)	1.3×10^{18} (1.2×10^{18})	ice
Titania	Herschel, 1787	270,862 (435,910)	8.7 days	982 (1,580)	3.9×10^{18} (3.5×10^{18})	ice
Oberon	Herschel, 1787	362,583 (583,520)	13.5 days	947 (1,524)	3.3×10^{18} (3.0×10^{18})	ice
Caliban	Gladman & others, 1997	4,455,000 (7,169,000)	579 days	37 (60)	unknown	unknown
S/1999 U1	Gladman & others, 1999	6,200,000 (10,000,000)?	unknown	12 (20)?	unknown	unknown
Sycorax	Nicholson & others, 1997	7,589,000 (12,214,000)	1,289 days	100 (160)	unknown	unknown
S/1999 U2	Gladman & others, 1999	15,500,000 (25,000,000)?	unknown	12 (20)?	unknown	unknown

NAME	DISCOVERY	DISTANCE FROM PLANET IN MILES (KM)	ORBIT TIME	DIAMETER IN MILES (KM)	MASS IN TONS (TONNES)	SURFACE COMPOSITION
Neptune						
Naiad	Voyager 2, 1989	29,967 (48,227)	0.3 day	36 (58)	unknown	carbon-rich dirt, ice?
Thalassa	Voyager 2, 1989	31,112 (50,070)	0.3 day	50 (80)	unknown	carbon-rich dirt, ice?
Despina	Voyager 2, 1989	32,638 (52,526)	0.3 day	92 (148)	unknown	carbon-rich dirt, ice?
Galatea	Voyager 2, 1989	38,496 (61,953)	0.4 day	98 (158)	unknown	carbon-rich dirt, ice?
Larissa	Reitsma & Voyager 2, 1989	45,701 (73,548)	0.6 day	129 (208)	unknown	carbon-rich dirt, ice?
Proteus	Voyager 2, 1989	73,103 (117,647)	1.1 days	271 (436)	unknown	carbon-rich dirt, ice?
Triton	Lassell, 1846	220,438 (354,760)	5.9 days	1,681 (2,706)	2.4×10^{19} (2.2×10^{19})	nitrogen & methane ice
Nereid	Kuiper, 1949	3,425,900 (5,513,400)	360.1 days	211 (340)	unknown	carbon-rich dirt, ice?
Pluto						
Charon	Christy, 1978	12,201 (19,636)	6.4 days	737 (1,186)	2.1×10^{18} (1.9×10^{18})	ice

NOTES ON MOON FACTS

NAME: 45 Eugenia and 243 Ida are asteroids with moons of their own.

ORBIT TIME: All days are Earth days.

MASS: The very large numbers measuring mass are given in scientific notation, such as 3.7×10^9. The little number after the 10 is the number of zeros that comes after the 1. Thus, 10^9 is 1,000,000,000, and 3.7×10^9 is 3,700,000,000, or 3,700 million.

• A tonne is a metric ton, equal to 1,000 kg or about 2,200 pounds.

• A question mark indicates that the value is an unconfirmed estimate.

METEOR SHOWERS

Dates may vary slightly

SHOWER	CONSTELLATION	DATE	PER HOUR	PARENT OBJECT
Quadrantids	Boötes	Jan 3	40 meteors	unknown
Lyrids	Lyra	Apr 22	15 meteors	comet Thatcher
Eta Aquarids	Aquarius	May 5	20 meteors	comet Halley
Delta Aquarids	Aquarius	July 28	20 meteors	unknown
Perseids	Perseus	Aug 12	50 meteors	comet Swift-Tuttle
Orionids	Orion	Oct 22	25 meteors	comet Halley
Taurids	Taurus	Nov 3	15 meteors	comet Encke
Leonids	Leo	Nov 17	15 meteors	comet Tempel-Tuttle
Geminids	Gemini	Dec 14	50 meteors	asteroid 3200 Phaethon
Ursids	Ursa Minor	Dec 23	20 meteors	comet Tuttle

SOLAR ECLIPSES

DATE	TYPE	BEST SEEN FROM
Mar 19, 2007	partial	east Asia, Alaska
Sept 11, 2007	partial	South America, Antarctica
Feb 7, 2008	partial	Antarctica, east Australia, New Zealand
Aug 1, 2008	total	north Canada, Greenland, Siberia, Mongolia, China
Jan 26, 2009	partial	south Africa, Antarctica, southeast Asia, Australia
July 22, 2009	total	India, Nepal, China, central Pacific Ocean
Jan 15, 2010	partial	central Africa, India, Burma, China
July 11, 2010	total	south Pacific Ocean, Easter Island, Chile, Argentina
Jan 4, 2011	partial	Europe, north Africa, central Asia
June 1, 2011	partial	east Asia, Alaska, north Canada, Iceland
July 1, 2011	partial	south Indian Ocean
Nov 25, 2011	partial	south Africa, Antarctica, Tasmania, New Zealand
May 20, 2012	partial	China, Japan, Pacific Ocean, west USA
Nov 13, 2012	total	north Australia, south Pacific Ocean
May 10, 2013	partial	north Australia, Solomon Islands, Pacific Ocean
Nov 3, 2013	total	Atlantic Ocean, central Africa
Apr 29, 2014	partial	south Indian Ocean, Australia, Antarctica
Oct 23, 2014	partial	north Pacific Ocean, North America
Mar 20, 2015	total	northeast Atlantic Ocean
Sept 13, 2015	partial	south Africa, south Indian Ocean, Antarctica
Mar 9, 2016	total	east Asia, Australia, Pacific
Aug 21, 2017	total	North America, northern South America
Feb 15, 2018	partial	Antarctica, southern South America
July 13, 2018	partial	south Australia
Aug 11, 2018	partial	north Europe, northeast Asia
Jan 6, 2019	partial	northeast Asia, north Pacific
July 2, 2019	total	south Pacific, South America
Dec 14, 2020	total	Pacific, southern South America, Antarctica
Dec 4, 2021	total	Antarctica, South Africa, south Atlantic
Apr 30, 2022	partial	southeast Pacific, southern South America
Oct 25, 2022	partial	Europe, northeast Africa, Middle East, west Asia
Apr 8, 2024	total	North America, Central America
Aug 12, 2026	total	northern North America, west Africa, Europe
Aug 2, 2027	total	Africa, Europe, Middle East, west & south Asia
July 22, 2028	total	southeast Asia, East Indies, Australia, New Zealand
Jan 14, 2029	partial	North America, Central. America

LUNAR ECLIPSES

DATE	TYPE	BEST SEEN FROM
Mar 3, 2007	total	Africa, Europe
Aug 28, 2007	total	central Pacific, west North & South America
Feb 21, 2008	total	North & South America, west Europe
Aug 16, 2008	partial	west Asia, Europe, Africa
Dec 21, 2009	partial	Asia, Indian Ocean, Africa, Europe
June 26, 2010	partial	central Pacific Ocean, west North & South America
Dec 21, 2010	total	North America, west South America
June 15, 2011	total	southwest Asia, Africa, Indian Ocean
Dec 10, 2011	total	west Pacific Ocean, east Asia, Alaska, Yukon
June 4, 2012	partial	central Pacific Ocean, west North & South America
Apr 15, 2014	total	North America, west South America, Pacific Ocean
Oct 8, 2014	total	Pacific Ocean, west North & South America
Apr 4, 2015	total	Pacific Ocean, west North & South America
Sept 28, 2015	total	west Europe & Africa, North & South America
Aug 7, 2017	partial	Europe, Africa, Asia, Australia
Jan 31, 2018	total	Asia, Australia, Pacific, west North America
July 27, 2018	total	South America, Eurpe, Africa, Asia, Australia
Jan 21, 2019	total	central Pacific, Americas, Europe, Africa
July 16, 2019	partial	South America, Europe, Africa, Asia, Australia
May 26, 2021	total	east Asia, Australia, Pacific, North & South America
Nov 19, 2021	partial	Americas, north Europe, east Asia, Australia, Pacific
May 16, 2022	total	North & South America, Europe, Africa
Nov 08, 2022	total	Asia, Australia, Pacific, North & South America
Oct 28, 2023	partial	east Americas, Europe, Africa, Asia, Australia

MANNED MISSIONS TO THE MOON

* The names of the astronauts who landed on the Moon are in italics.

NAME	CREW	LAUNCH DATE	ARRIVAL DATE	LANDING SITE	SAMPLES RETURNED
Apollo 8	Frank Borman, James Lovell, William Anders	Dec 21, 1968	Dec 24, 1968	no landing	no samples
Apollo 10	Thomas Stafford, John Young, Eugene Cernan	May 18, 1969	May 22, 1969	no landing	no samples
Apollo 11	*Neil Armstrong, Edwin Aldrin,* Michael Collins	July 16, 1969	July 20, 1969	Mare Tranquillitatis	49 pounds (22 kg)
Apollo 12	*Charles Conrad, Alan Bean,* Richard Gordon	Nov 14, 1969	Nov 19, 1969	Oceanus Procellarum	76 pounds (34 kg)
Apollo 13	James Lovell, John Swigert, Fred Haise	Apr 11, 1970	Apr 14, 1970	no landing	no samples
Apollo 14	*Alan Shepard, Edgar Mitchell,* Stuart Roosa	Jan 31, 1971	Feb 5, 1971	Fra Mauro highlands	93 pounds (42 kg)
Apollo 15	*David Scott, James Irwin,* Alfred Worden	July 26, 1971	July 30, 1971	Hadley Rille	171 pounds (77 kg)
Apollo 16	*John Young, Charles Duke,* Thomas Mattingly	Apr 16, 1972	Apr 21, 1972	Descartes highlands	213 pounds (96 kg)
Apollo 17	*Eugene Cernan, Harrison Schmitt,* Ronald Evans	Dec 7, 1972	Dec 11, 1972	Taurus-Littrow valley	247 pounds (111 kg)

IMPORTANT ROBOT MISSIONS IN THE SOLAR SYSTEM

MISSION	COUNTRY	TYPE	LAUNCH DATE	ARRIVAL DATE	ACHIEVEMENTS
Moon					
Luna 2	Soviet Union	impact	Sept 12, 1959	Sept 13, 1959	first impact
Luna 3	Soviet Union	flyby	Oct 4, 1959	Oct 7, 1959	first farside images show terrain is mostly highlands
Ranger 7	USA	impact	July 28, 1964	July 31, 1964	images surface until impact, finds many small craters
Ranger 8	USA	impact	Feb 17, 1965	Feb 20, 1965	impacts in Mare Tranquillitatis, takes more than 7,000 photos
Ranger 9	USA	impact	Mar 21, 1965	Mar 24, 1965	impacts in Alphonsus crater, finds volcanic vents
Zond 3	Soviet Union	flyby	July 18, 1965	July 20, 1965	photographs lunar farside
Luna 9	Soviet Union	lander	Jan 31, 1966	Feb 3, 1966	first soft landing, panoramic photos of surface
Luna 10	Soviet Union	orbiter	Mar 31, 1966	Apr 3, 1966	first spacecraft to orbit the Moon
Surveyor 1	USA	lander	May 30, 1966	June 2, 1966	first lander to make chemical measurements of surface
Lunar Orbiter 1	USA	orbiter	Aug 10, 1966	Aug 14, 1966	photo-survey of potential Apollo landing sites
Luna 11	Soviet Union	orbiter	Aug 24, 1966	Aug 28, 1966	photographs surface
Luna 12	Soviet Union	orbiter	Oct 22, 1966	Oct 25, 1966	photographs surface
Lunar Orbiter 2	USA	orbiter	Nov 6, 1966	Nov 10, 1966	photo-survey of potential Apollo landing sites
Luna 13	Soviet Union	lander	Dec 21, 1966	Dec 24, 1966	panoramic photos, mechanical soil probe
Lunar Orbiter 3	USA	orbiter	Feb 5, 1967	Feb 8, 1967	photo-survey of potential Apollo landing sites
Surveyor 3	USA	lander	Apr 17, 1967	Apr 20, 1967	takes more than 6,000 photos, Apollo 12 later lands at site
Lunar Orbiter 4	USA	orbiter	May 4, 1967	May 8, 1967	photo-survey of entire nearside hemisphere
Lunar Orbiter 5	USA	orbiter	Aug 1, 1967	Aug 5, 1967	photo-survey of geologically interesting areas
Surveyor 5	USA	lander	Sept 8, 1967	Sept 11, 1967	analyzes surface properties, takes more than 6,300 surface photos
Surveyor 6	USA	lander	Nov 7, 1967	Nov 10, 1967	takes almost 30,000 surface photos
Surveyor 7	USA	lander	Jan 7, 1968	Jan 10, 1968	lands near rim of Tycho crater, analyzes surface properties
Zond 5	Soviet Union	flyby	Sept 15, 1968	Sept 18, 1968	flies around Moon, returns to Earth Sept 21
Luna 16	Soviet Union	lander	Sept 12, 1970	Sept 20, 1970	collects rock sample and returns it to Earth
Zond 8	Soviet Union	flyby	Oct 20, 1970	Oct 24, 1970	flies around Moon, returns to Earth Oct 27
Luna 17	Soviet Union	rover	Nov 10, 1970	Nov 17, 1970	first robotic rover, drives 6 miles (10 km) on surface
Luna 20	Soviet Union	lander	Feb 14, 1972	Feb 21, 1972	automatic sample return
Luna 21	Soviet Union	rover	Jan 8, 1973	Jan 15, 1973	explores Posidonius crater, drives 23 miles (37 km)
Luna 22	Soviet Union	orbiter	May 29, 1974	June 2, 1974	photo-survey from orbit
Luna 24	Soviet Union	lander	Aug 9, 1976	Aug 14, 1976	lands in Mare Crisium, returns sample to Earth
Hiten (Muses-A)	Japan	flyby & orbiter	Jan 24, 1990	Mar 19, 1990	flies past Moon and releases satellite
Clementine	USA	orbiter	Jan 25, 1994	Feb 21, 1994	surveys surface mineralogy at high resolution
Lunar Prospector	USA	orbiter	Jan 7, 1998	Jan 11, 1998	surveys composition, finds ice in polar craters
Chandrayaan-1	India	orbiter	Feb, 2008	?	survey composition, look for water
Mercury					
Mariner 10	USA	flyby	Nov 3, 1973	Mar 29, 1974	first close-up images show cratered surface, detects large iron core
MESSENGER	USA	flyby & orbiter	Aug 3, 2004	Jan 2008	orbit to begin 2011, study atmosphere, surface, magnetic field
Venus					
Mariner 2	USA	flyby	Aug 27, 1962	Dec 14, 1962	first flyby finds heavy atmosphere, hot surface
Venera 4	Soviet Union	lander	June 12, 1967	Oct 18, 1967	measures atmosphere, fails on descent
Mariner 5	USA	flyby	June 14, 1967	Oct 19, 1967	improves measurements of atmospheric pressure and temperature
Venera 5	Soviet Union	lander	Jan 5, 1969	May 16, 1969	studies atmosphere

MISSION	COUNTRY	TYPE	LAUNCH DATE	ARRIVAL DATE	ACHIEVEMENTS
Venus (continued)					
Venera 6	Soviet Union	lander	Jan 10, 1969	May 17, 1969	studies atmosphere
Venera 8	Soviet Union	lander	Mar 27, 1972	July 22, 1972	sends back first data from surface
Mariner 10	USA	flyby	Nov 4, 1973	Feb 5, 1974	flies past on way to Mercury, photographs swirling clouds
Venera 9	Soviet Union	orbiter & lander	June 8, 1975	Oct 22, 1975	first images of surface show volcanic rocks
Venera 10	Soviet Union	orbiter & lander	June 14, 1975	Oct 25, 1975	photographs surface rocks and dirt
Pioneer Venus Orbiter	USA	orbiter	May 20, 1978	Dec 4, 1978	first global radar map of landscape, studies clouds
Pioneer Venus Probes	USA	entry probes	Aug 8, 1978	Dec 9, 1978	five probes sample atmosphere
Venera 12	Soviet Union	orbiter & lander	Sept 14, 1978	Dec 21, 1978	photographs surface, analyzes atmosphere
Venera 13	Soviet Union	orbiter & lander	Oct 30, 1981	Mar 1, 1982	photographs surface, analyzes atmosphere
Venera 14	Soviet Union	orbiter & lander	Nov 4, 1981	Mar 5, 1982	photographs surface, analyzes atmosphere
Venera 15	Soviet Union	orbiter	June 2, 1983	Oct 10, 1983	radar mapping of northern hemisphere
Venera 16	Soviet Union	orbiter	June 7, 1983	Oct 14, 1983	radar mapping of northern hemisphere
Vega 1	Soviet Union	lander & balloon	Dec 15, 1984	June 11, 1985	surveys atmosphere and winds with balloon
Vega 2	Soviet Union	lander & balloon	Dec 21, 1984	June 16, 1985	surveys atmosphere and winds with balloon
Magellan	USA	orbiter	May 4, 1989	Aug 10, 1990	surveys geology over most of Venus using radar
Galileo	USA	flyby	Oct 18, 1989	Feb 10, 1990	flies past on way to Jupiter, studies clouds
Cassini	USA	flyby	Oct 15, 1997	Apr 26, 1998	flies past on way to Saturn, sutdies clouds
Cassini	USA	flyby	Oct 15, 1997	June 24, 1999	second Venus flyby, studies clouds
Venus Express	European	orbiter	Nov 9, 2005	Apr 11, 2005	ongoing study of atmosphere and surface
Mars					
Mariner 4	USA	flyby	Nov 28, 1965	July 14, 1965	first close-up images show many craters, thin atmosphere
Mariner 6	USA	flyby	Feb 24, 1969	July 31, 1969	returns 75 photos, increases geological knowledge
Mars 3	Soviet Union	orbiter & lander	May 28, 1971	Dec 3, 1971	some data and few photos
Mariner 9	USA	orbiter	May 30, 1971	Nov 12, 1971	first survey of entire surface, finds water channels, big volcanoes
Mars 5	Soviet Union	orbiter	July 25, 1973	Feb 12, 1974	lasts a few days
Mars 6	Soviet Union	orbiter & lander	Aug 5, 1973	Mar 12, 1974	little data return
Viking 2	USA	orbiter & lander	Sept 9, 1975	Aug 7, 1976	geological survey from orbit, unsuccessful search for life on surface
Mars Global Surveyor	USA	orbiter	Nov 7, 1996	Sept 12, 1997	maps entire planet at high resolution
Mars Pathfinder	USA	lander & rover	Dec 2, 1996	July 4, 1997	explores geology of a once-flooded landscape
Nozomi (Planet-B)	Japan	orbiter	July 4, 1998	Dec 2003	studies upper atmosphere, magnetosphere, solar wind
Mars Climate Orbiter	USA	orbiter	Dec 11, 1998	Sept 23, 1999	crashes on arrival, no data returned
Mars Polar Lander	USA	lander	Jan 3, 1999	Dec 3, 1999	fails upon arrival, no data returned
Deep Space 2	USA	impactor	Jan 3, 1999	Dec 3, 1999	travels with Polar Lander, searches for subsurface ice
Mars Express	European	orbiter & lander	June 2, 2003	Dec 25, 2003	lander fails, ongoing studies to look for subsurface ice
MER—Spirit	USA	lander	June 5, 2003	Jan 4, 2004	ongoing exploration of the surface by Earth-operated rover
MER—Opportunity	USA	lander	June 25, 2003	Jan 25, 2004	ongoing exploration of the surface by Earth-operated rover
Asteroids					
Galileo	USA	flyby	Oct 18, 1989	Oct 29, 1991	first close-up images of an asteroid, 951 Gaspra, show craters
Galileo	USA	flyby	Oct 18, 1989	Aug 28, 1993	asteroid 243 Ida: survey of cratered surface, finds moon, Dactyl
NEAR	USA	flyby	Feb 17, 1996	June 27, 1997	asteroid 253 Mathilde: reveals big craters, low density
NEAR	USA	flyby	Feb 17, 1996	Dec 23, 1998	asteroid 433 Eros: survey of craters and features
Deep Space 1	USA	flyby	Oct 24, 1998	July 29, 1999	asteroid 9969 Braille: study of magnetic field, surface composition
NEAR	USA	orbiter	Feb 17, 1996	Feb 14, 2000	asteroid 433 Eros: first spacecraft to orbit an asteroid
Jupiter					
Pioneer 10	USA	flyby	Mar 3, 1972	Dec 3, 1973	first detailed study of a gas-giant planet
Pioneer 11	USA	flyby	Apr 6, 1973	Dec 3, 1974	studies polar regions of Jupiter, magnetic environment
Voyager 1	USA	flyby	Sept 5, 1977	Mar 5, 1979	first detailed images of planet and moons, discovers ring system
Voyager 2	USA	flyby	Aug 20, 1977	July 9, 1979	follow-up on Voyager 1's discoveries
Galileo	USA	orbiter & entry	Oct 18, 1989	Dec 7, 1995	first atmosphere probe, orbital tour of planet and moons
Saturn					
Pioneer 11	USA	flyby	Apr 6, 1973	Sept 1, 1979	first spacecraft visit, discovers new rings
Voyager 1	USA	flyby	Sept 5, 1977	Nov 12, 1980	detailed portraits of clouds, rings, and moons
Voyager 2	USA	flyby	Aug 20, 1977	Aug 25, 1981	follow-up on Voyager 1's discoveries
Cassini	USA	flyby	Oct 15, 1997	July, 2004	orbital tour of planet and moons, lander for Titan
Uranus					
Voyager 2	USA	flyby	Aug 20, 1977	Jan 24, 1986	first spacecraft visit, studies rings and moons, finds new moons
Neptune					
Voyager 2	USA	flyby	Aug 20, 1977	Aug 25, 1989	first spacecraft visit, studies storms, finds geysers on Triton
Pluto & Kuiper Belt					
New Horizons	USA	flyby	Jan 19, 2006	est July, 2014	study surfaces of Pluto, Charon and Kuiper Belt objects
Comets					
Giotto	European	flyby	July 2, 1985	Mar 14, 1986	photographs nucleus of comet Halley
Stardust	USA	flyby	Feb 7, 1999	Jan 2, 2004	sample collection & return from comet Wild 2
Deep Impact	USA	impactor	Jan 12, 2005	July 4, 2005	impact with Tempel 1, return surface samples

Constellation Facts

CONSTELLATION	MEANING	HEMISPHERE	HIGHLIGHTS
Andromeda	the Princess	Northern	spiral galaxy M31 (Andromeda), double star Gamma Andromedae, open cluster NGC 752
Antlia	the Air Pump	Southern	planetary nebula NGC 3132, spiral galaxy NGC 2997
Apus	the Bird of Paradise	Southern	double star Delta Apodis, variable star S Apodis, variable star Theta Apodis
Aquarius	the Water Carrier	equatorial	globular cluster M2, planetary nebulas NGC 7009 (Saturn) and NGC 7293 (Helix)
Aquila	the Eagle	equatorial	bright star Altair, variable stars Eta Aquilae and R Aquilae, open cluster NGC 6709
Ara	the Altar	Southern	open cluster NGC 6193, globular cluster NGC 6397
Aries	the Ram	Northern	double stars Gamma Arietis, Lambda Arietis, and Pi Arietis
Auriga	the Charioteer	Northern	bright star Capella, open clusters M36, M37, and M38, double star Omega Aurigae
Boötes	the Herdsman	Northern	bright star Arcturus, double star Mu Boötis
Caelum	the Chisel	Southern	double star Gamma Caeli, variable star R Caeli
Camelopardalis	the Giraffe	Southern	double star Beta Camelopardalis, variable star VZ Camelopardalis, star cluster NGC 1502
Cancer	the Crab	Northern	open clusters M44 (Beehive) and M67, double stars Zeta Cancri and Iota Cancri
Canes Venatici	the Hunting Dogs	Northern	spiral galaxies M51 (Whirlpool) and M94, globular cluster M3
Canis Major	the Big Dog	Southern	bright star Sirius, open clusters M41 and NGC 2362
Canis Minor	the Little Dog	equatorial	bright star Procyon
Capricornus	the Sea Goat	Southern	double stars Alpha Capricorni and Beta Capricorni, globular cluster M30
Carina	the Keel	Southern	bright star Canopus, emission nebula Eta Carinae, open clusters NGC 3532 and IC 2602
Cassiopeia	the Queen	Northern	variable star Gamma Cassiopeiae, open cluster M52
Centaurus	the Centaur	Southern	bright star Alpha Centauri, globular cluster Omega Centauri, elliptical galaxy NGC 5128
Cepheus	the King	Northern	variable stars Delta Cephei and Mu Cephei
Cetus	the Sea Monster	equatorial	variable star Mira Ceti, Seyfert galaxy M77
Chamaeleon	the Chameleon	Southern	double star Delta Chamaeleontis, planetary nebula NGC 3195
Circinus	the Drawing Compass	Southern	double star Alpha Circini
Columba	the Dove	Southern	variable star T Columbae, globular cluster NGC 1851
Coma Berenices	Berenice's Hair	Northern	globular cluster M53, spiral galaxies M64 (Black-eye) and NGC 4565
Corona Australis	the Southern Crown	Southern	double star Kappa Coronae Australis, globular cluster NGC 6541
Corona Borealis	the Northern Crown	Northern	double star Nu Coronae Borealis, variable star R Coronae Borealis
Corvus	the Crow	Southern	variable star R Corvi, galaxies NGC 4038 and NGC 4039 (Antennae galaxies)
Crater	the Cup	Southern	—
Crux	the Southern Cross	Southern	bright star Acrux, open cluster NGC 4755 (Jewel Box), dark nebula the Coalsack
Cygnus	the Swan	Northern	bright star Deneb, double star Beta Cygni, emission nebula NGC 7000 (North America)
Delphinus	the Dolphin	Northern	double star Gamma Delphini
Dorado	the Goldfish	Southern	irregular galaxy the Large Magellanic Cloud, emission nebula NGC 2070 (Tarantula)
Draco	the Dragon	Northern	double stars Psi Draconis and 39 Draconis, planetary nebula NGC 6543
Equuleus	the Little Horse	Northern	double star Gamma Equulei
Eridanus	the River	Southern	bright star Achernar, triple star Omicron 2 Eridani
Fornax	the Furnace	Southern	barred spiral galaxy NGC 1365 (Great Barred Spiral)
Gemini	the Twins	Northern	bright stars Castor and Pollux, open cluster M35, planetary nebula NGC 2392 (Clownface)
Grus	the Crane	Southern	double stars Delta Gruis and Mu Gruis
Hercules	the Strongman	Northern	variable star Alpha Herculis, globular clusters M13 (Hercules) and M92
Horologium	the Clock	Southern	variable stars R Horologii and TW Horologii
Hydra	the Sea Serpent	equatorial	double star 27 Hydrae, open cluster M48, planetary nebula NGC 3242, spiral galaxy M83
Hydrus	the Water Snake	Southern	double star Pi Hydri
Indus	the Indian	Southern	double star Theta Indi
Lacerta	the Lizard	Northern	—
Leo	the Lion	equatorial	bright star Regulus, double star Gamma Leonis, spiral galaxies M65 and M66
Leo Minor	the Little Lion	Northern	—
Lepus	the Hare	Southern	double star Gamma Leporis, globular cluster M79
Libra	the Scales	Southern	double star Alpha Librae, variable star Delta Librae
Lupus	the Wolf	Southern	open cluster NGC 5822, globular cluster NGC 5986
Lynx	the Lynx	Northern	—
Lyra	the Lyre	Northern	bright star Vega, variable star Beta Lyrae, planetary nebula M57 (Ring)
Mensa	the Table	Southern	—
Microscopium	the Microscope	Southern	double star Alpha Microscopii
Monoceros	the Unicorn	equatorial	open cluster M50, nebulas NGC 2237 (Rosette) and NGC 2264 (Cone)
Musca	the Fly	Southern	double star Theta Muscae, globular clusters NGC 4372 and NGC 4833
Norma	the Level	Southern	open clusters NGC 6067 and NGC 6087
Octans	the Octant	Southern	pole star Sigma Octantis, double star Lambda Octantis
Ophiuchus	the Serpent Carrier	equatorial	open clusters IC 4665 and NGC 6633, globular clusters M10 and M12
Orion	the Hunter	equatorial	bright stars Betelgeuse and Rigel, emission nebula M42 (Orion), dark nebula IC 434 (Horsehead)
Pavo	the Peacock	Southern	variable star Kappa Pavonis, globular cluster NGC 6752
Pegasus	the Flying Horse	Northern	double star Epsilon Pegasi, globular cluster M15
Perseus	the Hero	Northern	variable star Algol (Beta Persei), open clusters NGC 869 and NGC 884 (Double Cluster)
Phoenix	the Firebird	Southern	double and variable star Zeta Phoenicis
Pictor	the Painter's Easel	Southern	—
Pisces	the Fishes	equatorial	double star Rho and 94 Piscium, spiral galaxy M74
Piscis Austrinus	the Southern Fish	Southern	bright star Fomalhaut
Puppis	the Stern	Southern	variable star L2 Puppis, open clusters M46 and M47
Pyxis	the Compass	Southern	—

CONSTELLATION	MEANING	HEMISPHERE	HIGHLIGHTS
Reticulum	the Reticle	Southern	double star Zeta Reticuli
Sagitta	the Arrow	Northern	globular cluster M71
Sagittarius	the Archer	Southern	globular clusters M22 and M23, emission nebulas M8 (Lagoon), M17 (Omega), M20 (Trifid)
Scorpius	the Scorpion	Southern	bright star Antares, double star Beta Scorpii, open cluster M7, globular clusters M4 and M80
Sculptor	the Sculptor	Southern	spiral galaxies NGC 253 and NGC 55
Scutum	the Shield	Northern	open cluster M11 (Wild Duck)
Serpens	the Serpent	equatorial	double star Nu Serpentis, emission nebula M16 (Eagle), globular cluster M5
Sextans	the Sextant	equatorial	double star 17 and 18 Sextantis, elliptical galaxy NGC 3115 (Spindle)
Taurus	the Bull	equatorial	bright star Aldebaran, open clusters M45 (Pleiades) and Hyades, supernova remnant M1 (Crab)
Telescopium	the Telescope	Southern	double star Delta Telescopii
Triangulum	the Triangle	Northern	spiral galaxy M33 (Pinwheel)
Triangulum Australe	the Southern Triangle	Southern	variable star R Trianguli Australe, open cluster NGC 6025
Tucana	the Toucan	Southern	double star Beta Tucanae, globular cluster 47 Tucanae, irregular galaxy the Small Magellanic Cloud
Ursa Major	the Big Bear	Northern	double star Mizar and Alcor, spiral galaxies M81 and M101, peculiar galaxy M82
Ursa Minor	the Little Bear	Northern	Polaris the Pole Star, double star Gamma and 11 Ursae Minoris
Vela	the Sails	Southern	double star Gamma Velorum, open clusters IC 2391 and NGC 2547
Virgo	the Maiden	equatorial	bright star Spica, elliptical galaxies M47, M87, and M104 (Sombrero), quasar 3C 273
Volans	the Flying Fish	Southern	double star Gamma Volantis, barred spiral galaxy NGC 2442
Vulpecula	the Little Fox	Northern	planetary nebula M27 (Dumbbell)

BRIGHTEST STAR FACTS

STAR	CONSTELLATION	COLOR AND TYPE	COMPANION STARS	APPARENT MAGNITUDE	ACTUAL MAGNITUDE	DIAMETER (SUN = 1)	DISTANCE FROM EARTH	WHAT YOU NEED TO SEE IT
Sirius	Canis Major	white main sequence	1 companion	−1.44	+1.4	2.4	8.6 ly	naked eye
Canopus	Carina	white giant	0 companions	−0.72	−3.5	80	117 ly	naked eye
Alpha Centauri	Centaurus	yellow main sequence	2 companions	−0.28	+4.4	1.0	4.3 ly	naked eye
Arcturus	Boötes	red giant	0 companions	−0.05	−0.27	20	36.7 ly	naked eye
Vega	Lyra	white main sequence	0 companions	+0.03	+0.48	2.4	25.3 ly	naked eye
Capella	Auriga	yellow giant	1 companion	+0.08	−0.60	10	42 ly	naked eye
Rigel	Orion	blue-white supergiant	1 companion	+0.14	−6.8	55	800 ly	naked eye
Procyon	Canis Minor	white subgiant	1 companion	+0.40	+2.68	1.3	11.4 ly	naked eye
Betelgeuse	Orion	red supergiant	0 companions	+0.41	−5.5	800	427 ly	naked eye
Achernar	Eridanus	blue-white main sequence	0 companions	+0.45	−2.5	3.9	144 ly	naked eye

VARIABLE STAR FACTS

STAR	CONSTELLATION	TYPE	MAGNITUDE RANGE	PERIOD (DAYS)
R Canis Majoris	Canis Major	eclipsing	5.7–6.3	1.1
Algol (Beta Persei)	Perseus	eclipsing	2.1–3.4	2.9
Delta Cephei	Cepheus	Cepheid	3.5–4.4	5.4
Eta Aquilae	Aquila	Cepheid	3.5–4.3	7.2
Beta Lyrae	Lyra	eclipsing	3.4–4.3	12.9
Alpha Herculis	Hercules	semi-regular	3.0–4.0	50–130
L2 Puppis	Puppis	pulsating	2.6–6.2	141
Mira (Omicron Ceti)	Cetus	pulsating	3.4–9.3	332
R Hydrae	Hydra	pulsating	3.4–10.7	389
RX Leporis	Lepus	irregular	5.4–7.4	irreg.

NOTES ON CONSTELLATION FACTS

HEMISPHERE: This tells you where the constellation is most easily seen—in the Northern Hemisphere, the Southern Hemisphere, or around the equator. Depending on where you live, you might be able to see a constellation that is not listed for your part of the world. Refer to the star maps, pages 94–109.

NOTES ON STAR & STAR CLUSTER FACTS

COMPANIONS: This tells you whether the star is part of a double or multiple system.

APPARENT MAGNITUDE: This is how bright the planet looks in the sky. Brighter objects have smaller numbers than dimmer objects.

DISTANCE FROM EARTH: The figures for distance (and for the diameter of star clusters) are in light-years (ly).

STAR CLUSTER FACTS

CLUSTER	CONSTELLATION	TYPE	NUMBER OF STARS	APPARENT MAGNITUDE	DIAMETER	DISTANCE FROM EARTH	WHAT YOU NEED TO SEE IT
Hyades	Taurus	open	100	0.8	17 ly	150 ly	naked eye
Pleiades	Taurus	open	several hundred	1.6	13 ly	375 ly	naked eye
Beehive	Cancer	open	50	3.9	15 ly	590 ly	binoculars
Double Cluster	Perseus	open	350	4.3	61 ly	7,000 ly	telescope
47 Tucanae	Tucana	globular	460,000	4.4	125 ly	16,000 ly	telescope
Omega Centauri	Centaurus	globular	1,100,000	4.5	180 ly	17,000 ly	telescope
Jewel Box	Crux	open	50	5.2	24 ly	6,800 ly	telescope
Hercules cluster (M13)	Hercules	globular	220,000	6.4	110 ly	21,000 ly	telescope
M15	Pegasus	globular	410,000	7.0	120 ly	34,000 ly	telescope
M4	Scorpius	globular	44,000	7.1	50 ly	14,000 ly	telescope

NEBULA FACTS

NEBULA	CONSTELLATION	TYPE	APPARENT MAGNITUDE	DIAMETER	DISTANCE FROM EARTH	WHAT YOU NEED TO SEE IT
NGC 7293 (Helix nebula)	Aquarius	planetary	6.5	2 ly	600 ly	telescope
M27 (Dumbbell nebula)	Vulpecula	planetary	8.1	2 ly	815 ly	telescope
M57 (Ring nebula)	Lyra	planetary	9.0	0.4 ly	1,140 ly	telescope
IC 434 (Horsehead nebula)	Orion	dark	—	20 ly?	1,200 ly?	telescope
M42 (Orion nebula)	Orion	emission	4.0	40 ly	1,500 ly	telescope
NGC 2264 (Cone nebula)	Monoceros	dark	—	50 ly	3,000 ly	telescope
M20 (Trifid nebula)	Sagittarius	emission/reflection	8.5	40 ly	5,000 ly	telescope
M8 (Lagoon nebula)	Sagittarius	emission	5.8	130 ly	5,200 ly	telescope
M1 (Crab nebula)	Taurus	supernova remnant	8.4	13.7 ly	6,520 ly	telescope
M16 (Eagle nebula)	Serpens	emission	6.0	315 ly	7,000 ly	telescope

GALAXY FACTS

GALAXY	CONSTELLATION	TYPE	GALAXY CLUSTER	APPARENT MAGNITUDE	DIAMETER	DISTANCE FROM EARTH	WHAT YOU NEED TO SEE IT
M81	Ursa Major	spiral	Coma-Sculptor cloud	7.9	30,000 ly	4,500,000 ly	telescope
M83	Hydra	spiral	Coma-Sculptor cloud	8.2	52,000 ly	15,000,000 ly	telescope
M51 (Whirlpool)	Canes Venatici	spiral	Coma-Sculptor cloud	9.0	50,000 ly	15,000,000 ly	telescope
M101	Ursa Major	spiral	Coma-Sculptor cloud	7.9	120,000 ly	17,500,000 ly	telescope
NGC 6946	Cepheus	spiral	Coma-Sculptor cloud	8.9	78,000 ly	18,000,000 ly	telescope
NGC 5128 (Centaurus A)	Centaurus	giant elliptical	Coma-Sculptor cloud	7.0	138,000 ly	26,000,000 ly	telescope
M87	Virgo	giant elliptical	Virgo cluster	8.6	147,000 ly	55,000,000 ly	telescope
NGC 1365 (Great Barred Spiral)	Fornax	barred spiral	Fornax cluster	9.5	157,800 ly	55,000,000 ly	telescope
M104 (Sombrero)	Virgo	spiral	Virgo cluster	8.3	160,000 ly	65,000,000 ly	telescope
NGC 4038/4039 (Antennae)	Corvus	spirals	Crater cloud	10.7	220,000 ly	82,800,000 ly	telescope
NGC 1275	Perseus	Seyfert	Perseus cluster	11.6	175,000 ly	230,000,000 ly	telescope
3C 273	Virgo	quasar	unknown	12.0	unknown	1,900,000,000 ly	telescope

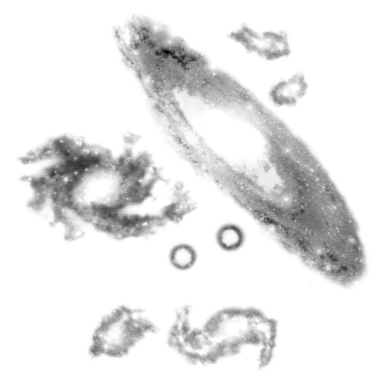

LOCAL GROUP FACTS

GALAXY	TYPE	APPARENT MAGNITUDE	DIAMETER	DISTANCE FROM EARTH
Milky Way	spiral	—	100,000 ly	—
SagDEG	elliptical	3.6	unknown	80,000 ly
Large Magellanic Cloud	irregular	0.6	34,000 ly	179,000 ly
Small Magellanic Cloud	irregular	2.8	17,000 ly	210,000 ly
Sculptor dwarf	irregular	9.1	1,400 ly	284,000 ly
Sextans I	elliptical	10.3	3,000 ly	300,000 ly
Ursa Minor dwarf	elliptical	10.0	1,000 ly	300,000 ly
Carina	elliptical	10.6	500 ly	300,000 ly
Draco dwarf	elliptical	10.9	500 ly	300,000 ly
Fornax dwarf	elliptical	8.5	3,000 ly	500,000 ly
Leo I	elliptical	11.8	1,000 ly	600,000 ly
Leo II	elliptical	12.3	500 ly	600,000 ly
NGC 6822	irregular	9.3	8,000 ly	1,700,000 ly
Wolf-Lundmark-Melotte	irregular	11.3	7,000 ly	2,000,000 ly
IC 5152	irregular	11.7	5,000 ly	2,000,000 ly
NGC 205	elliptical	8.6	10,000 ly	2,200,000 ly
NGC 147	elliptical	10.4	10,000 ly	2,200,000 ly
NGC 185	elliptical	10.1	6,000 ly	2,200,000 ly
M32	elliptical	9.0	5,000 ly	2,200,000 ly
Andromeda III	elliptical	13.5	3,000 ly	2,200,000 ly
Andromeda I	elliptical	14.4	2,000 ly	2,200,000 ly
Andromeda II	elliptical	13.0	2,000 ly	2,200,000 ly
M31 (Andromeda)	spiral	4.4	128,000 ly	2,500,000 ly
IC 1613	irregular	10.0	12,000 ly	2,500,000 ly
M33 (Pinwheel)	spiral	6.3	50,000 ly	2,600,000 ly
DDO 210	irregular	15.3	4,000 ly	3,000,000 ly
Pisces	irregular	15.5	500 ly	3,000,000 ly
IC 10	irregular	11.7	6,000 ly	4,000,000 ly
Sextans A	irregular	—	unknown	4,000,000 ly?
SagDIG	irregular	15.6	5,000 ly	4,000,000 ly
GR 8	irregular	14.6	200 ly	4,000,000 ly
Antlia	elliptical	14.8	unknown	4,100,000 ly?
Pegasus	irregular	12.4	8,000 ly	5,000,000 ly
Leo A	irregular	12.7	7,000 ly	5,000,000 ly
Tucana	elliptical	15.1	unknown	unknown

NOTES ON NEBULA, GALAXY, AND LOCAL GROUP FACTS

APPARENT MAGNITUDE: This is how bright the planet looks in the sky. Brighter objects have smaller numbers than dimmer objects.

DIAMETER/DISTANCE FROM EARTH: The figures given are in light-years (ly).

• A question mark indicates that the value is an unconfirmed estimate.

Universal Records

HOTTEST PLANET SURFACE IN OUR SOLAR SYSTEM
The surface of Venus, 880°F (470°C). At its hottest, Mercury comes pretty close: 800°F (427°C). Venus's thick atmosphere traps the Sun's heat, so midnight temperatures are as hot as those at noontime. (And the rocks are hot enough to glow dull red!)

COLDEST PLANET SURFACE IN OUR SOLAR SYSTEM
Pluto when farthest from the Sun. The actual temperature at that point has not yet been measured because Pluto has not made a full orbit since it was discovered in 1930. Pluto will reach the farthest point in its orbit in February 2114. At present, Pluto's surface temperature is –387°F (–233°C)—and it is slowly falling!

BIGGEST CRATER IN OUR SOLAR SYSTEM
South Pole-Aitken Basin on the Moon, roughly 1,600 miles (2,500 km) in diameter. This ancient impact scar is so heavily marked with smaller craters that it was not discovered until the Clementine probe visited the Moon in 1994. Scientists used data from Clementine to carefully map the Moon's surface. This mapping revealed the basin, a broad depression in the lunar farside that is more than 7 miles (12 km) deep.

TALLEST MOUNTAIN IN OUR SOLAR SYSTEM
Olympus Mons on Mars, rising 15 miles (24 km) above its base. The second tallest is Maxwell Montes on Venus, which rises 7 miles (11 km) above the planet's average surface. Earth's officially tallest peak is Mount Everest, 5.5 miles (8.8 km) above sea level. However, Hawaii's Mauna Kea can also claim to be the tallest, since it rises about 5.6 miles (9 km) above the ocean floor it stands on.

BIGGEST CANYON IN OUR SOLAR SYSTEM
Valles Marineris on Mars, roughly 2,500 miles (4,000 km) long, with a maximum width of about 370 miles (600 km) and a maximum depth of 5 miles (8 km). If it were in the United States, this canyon could extend from San Francisco on the west coast to the Appalachian Mountains in Virginia near the east coast. In Europe, it would stretch from Paris, France, to Russia's Ural Mountains.

BIGGEST MOON IN OUR SOLAR SYSTEM
Jupiter's Ganymede, 3,273 miles (5,268 km) in diameter. If Ganymede orbited the Sun instead of Jupiter, it would easily qualify as a planet. It is larger than either Mercury or Pluto.

BIGGEST PLANET IN OUR SOLAR SYSTEM
Jupiter, with 317.8 times the mass of Earth, and about 11 times its diameter. Jupiter contains more mass than all the rest of the planets, moons, comets, and asteroids put together.

BIGGEST KNOWN PLANET
An unnamed planet orbiting the star HD 114762. This planet appears to have 11 times the mass of Jupiter, but some astronomers think it may actually be a brown dwarf, an object that is like a small, dim, cool star. If it is a brown dwarf, then the most massive planet would be HAT-P-2b, with 8 times Jupiter's mass, that orbits an F-type star. (This Universal Record is very likely to change as research continues.)

GREATEST METEOR SHOWER
The Leonids on November 13, 1833, with up to 200,000 meteors per hour. Onlookers said that the meteors "fell like snowflakes," and many uneducated people thought the world was about to come to an end. The remarkable display helped astronomers realize that meteors were entering Earth's atmosphere from outer space, and were not just an Earth-based event like rain.

BIGGEST METEORITE
Hoba meteorite in Namibia, weighing 65 tons (60 tonnes)—about as heavy as nine elephants! Discovered in 1920, this iron meteorite almost 10 feet (3 m) long still lies in the ground where it landed. It was originally even larger—the discolored soil surrounding it shows that part of the meteorite has weathered away.

BIGGEST ASTEROID
1 Ceres, 567 miles (913 km) in diameter. This largest of all asteroids was also the first one to be found—and its discovery came on the first day of the 19th century: January 1, 1801. The discoverer of Ceres was Giuseppe Piazzi (1746–1826) and the place was the Palermo Observatory in Sicily.

CLOSEST COMET TO EARTH
Comet Lexell in 1770, at a distance of 1.4 million miles (2.2 million km) from Earth—less than six times the distance to the Moon. Despite coming so close, this comet never developed much of a tail and its head looked no bigger than five times the size of the Moon in our night sky.

LONGEST COMET TAIL
Comet Hyakutake in January 1996, at 354 million miles (570 million km) long. This tail was long enough to reach from Earth to the Sun four times. This comet is known as the "Great Comet of 1996."

BRIGHTEST STAR IN OUR NIGHT SKY
Sirius, –1.46 magnitude. Sirius is actually a double star, and its dim companion was the first white dwarf star to be discovered.

BROADEST STAR
Betelgeuse in Orion, about 800 times the Sun's diameter. If it replaced the Sun in our Solar System, this bloated red supergiant star would reach past the orbit of Jupiter.

MOST MASSIVE STAR
Eta Carinae, about 150 times as massive as the Sun. Astronomers are not certain if Eta Carinae is really one star or two.

LEAST MASSIVE STAR
Gliese 105C, about 10 percent as massive as the Sun. This is about as small as a star can be and still be a true star (an object that fuses hydrogen into helium).

NEAREST STAR
Proxima Centauri, third member of the Alpha Centauri system. This cool red dwarf star lies about 4.2 light-years away, about 0.1 light-year closer to us than the other two stars in the system.

GLOBULAR STAR CLUSTER WITH THE MOST STARS
Omega Centauri, with 1.1 million stars. This globular cluster measures about 180 light-years in diameter.

MOST MASSIVE GALAXY
Giant elliptical M87 in the constellation of Virgo, with at least 800 billion Suns worth of mass. M87 is a member of the Virgo cluster of galaxies.

LEAST MASSIVE GALAXY
The Pegasus II dwarf elliptical, about 10 million solar masses. Smaller galaxies may exist, but because they are not very luminous, astronomers cannot detect them unless they also lie close to us.

NEAREST GALAXY
Canis Major dwarf irregular, 42,000 light-years from the center of the Milky Way. This galaxy is the current record holder, but surveys find new dwarf elliptical galaxies every year or so, and an even closer galaxy may yet be found.

MOST DISTANT OBJECT VISIBLE TO THE NAKED EYE
Andromeda galaxy (M31), 2.5 million light-years away. When you look at this galaxy, you are seeing light that left the galaxy when the most recent great Ice Ages were beginning on Earth.

MOST DISTANT OBJECT DETECTED
An unnamed galaxy in Ursa Major, 12.6 billion light-years away. This galaxy may not hold the record for very long. Astronomers working with giant telescopes on Earth and the Hubble Space Telescope find a new and more distant record-holder once or twice a year.

TIMELINE OF ASTRONOMY

30,000 BC Lunar phases scratched on bone—the oldest astronomical record?

4000 BC Sumerians of Mesopotamia make the first records of Leo, Taurus, and Scorpius, the oldest constellations still used today.

600 BC Greek philosopher Thales probably knows the cause of solar and lunar eclipses.

525 BC Greek philosopher Pythagoras recognizes that Earth is round.

350 BC Greek philosopher Aristotle provides a scientific explanation of why Earth is round.

325 BC Greek mathematician Eudoxus explains celestial motions in terms of several crystal spheres with Earth at their center.

300 BC Greek astronomer Aristarchus proposes a Sun-centered model for the universe. But his ideas are ignored until Copernicus's time, almost 2,000 years later.

200 BC Greek astronomer Eratosthenes measures the circumference of Earth, getting a result close to the modern one.

150 BC Greek astronomer Hipparchus creates system of magnitudes to measure star brightness, discovers a slow wobble in Earth's axis (precession), and compiles the first star catalog.

AD 150 Greek astronomer Claudius Ptolemy publishes the *Almagest*, a detailed summing-up of all the ancient world's astronomical knowledge. It dominates the subject for more than 1,000 years.

AD 165 Chinese astronomers make the first accurately dated observations, recording sunspots on the face of the Sun.

AD 635 A Chinese scholar records the rule that a comet's tail always points away from the Sun.

1543 Nicolaus Copernicus publishes his book *On the Revolutions of the Celestial Spheres*, proposing a Sun-centered solar system.

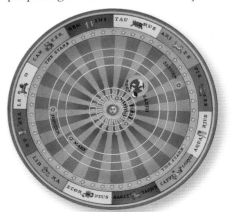

1572 Tycho Brahe sees a supernova in Cassiopeia and determines that it lies beyond the Moon. This discovery conflicts with ancient ideas of the heavens being unchangeable, and it encourages Tycho to make a whole new set of accurate observations.

1576 Tycho builds his Uraniborg observatory on an island in the Baltic Sea and begins compiling the world's most accurate observations of the motions of stars and planets.

1600 Tycho Brahe hires Johannes Kepler as his mathematical assistant to work on the observations.

1608 Hans Lippershey in the Netherlands invents the telescope.

1609 Using Tycho Brahe's observations, Kepler determines that Mars's orbit is elliptical, a key advance over ancient astronomy, which had insisted on circular orbits. Galileo Galilei hears of the telescope and, following the reported description, builds his own. He is the first person to use the telescope for astronomy.

1610 Galileo publishes his telescope discoveries of moons orbiting Jupiter, craters on the Moon, and stars in the Milky Way. He starts promoting a Copernican model of the solar system.

1616 The Roman Catholic Church bans Copernican ideas as "false and absurd."

1619 Kepler discovers a simple mathematical relationship between the length of a planet's year and its distance from the Sun.

1633 Galileo is put under house arrest by the Church for promoting Copernican ideas.

1665 Isaac Newton starts developing mathematical physics.

1687 Newton publishes his book *The Mathematical Principles of Natural Philosophy*, which links astronomy with physics and puts both on firm mathematical ground.

1727 James Bradley discovers the aberration of starlight, an apparent shift in the positon of a star caused by the motion of Earth. It is the first physical proof that Earth moves around the Sun.

1758 Comet Halley returns as forecast by Edmond Halley, the first predicted return of a comet.

1781 William Herschel discovers seventh planet, Uranus. This is the first planet to be discovered since prehistoric times.

1833 A spectacular Leonid meteor shower shows astronomers that meteors come from space and do not originate in the atmosphere.

1835 The Roman Catholic Church removes books by Copernicus and Galileo from its list of banned works.

1838 Friedrich Bessel measures the parallax of 61 Cygni, the first direct measurement of a star's distance.

1846 Johann Galle and Heinrich d'Arrest find the eighth planet, Neptune, following predictions made by Urbain Leverrier (and, independently, by John C. Adams).

1860s The spectroscope begins to show astronomers what stars and nebulas are made of.

1880s Photography becomes an important tool for astronomy because it can detect things in the sky that people cannot see and it provides a permanent record.

1905 Albert Einstein's special theory of relativity is published.

1908 Ejnar Hertzsprung divides the population of stars into two groups, giants and dwarfs. It is the first step in learning how stars change as they age.

1910 The return of comet Halley creates the world's first media event.

1912 Henrietta Leavitt discovers that Cepheid variable stars with long periods of variation are systematically brighter than those with shorter periods.
Vesto Slipher discovers that most "spiral nebulas" are flying away from Earth, the first detection of an expanding universe.

1916 Einstein publishes his general theory of relativity, which predicts that the universe is expanding.

1917 100-inch (2.5-m) Hooker reflector telescope completed at Mount Wilson, California, USA.

1919 Einstein's general theory of relativity is confirmed by observations of a total solar eclipse seen from Brazil and West Africa.

1923 Edwin Hubble uses Cepheid variables to show that "spiral nebulas" are galaxies lying outside the Milky Way.

1929 Hubble presents observational evidence for an expanding universe and provides the first estimates of its age and rate of expansion.

1930 Clyde Tombaugh discovers the ninth planet, Pluto.

1931 Karl Jansky builds a rotating aerial and discovers radio waves coming from space. These radio waves had been predicted in the 1880s but were not found because astronomers had no way to detect them.

1937 Grote Reber discovers radio waves coming from the center of the Milky Way, using a radio telescope built in his own backyard.

1938 Hans Bethe publishes a theory explaining how the Sun and other stars shine because of nuclear reactions.

1942 John Hey and colleagues discover radio noise coming from the Sun.

1946 Hey and colleagues identify the most powerful radio source in the sky, the radio galaxy Cygnus A.

1948 George Gamow, Ralph Alpher, and Robert Herman describe how chemical elements were formed in the Big Bang.
200-inch (5-m) Hale Telescope is completed at Palomar Mountain, California, USA.
Jan Oort proposes that comets come from a vast cloud orbiting far beyond Pluto.

1952 Walter Baade announces that galaxies are twice as far away as astronomers had previously assumed.

1957 Launch of Sputnik 1 satellite by the Soviet Union (now Russia) starts the Space Age.

1959 First photographs of the Moon's farside returned by Soviet probe, Luna 3.

1961 Yuri Gagarin from the Soviet Union is the first person to fly in space.

1962 Mariner 2 spacecraft flies past Venus, first probe to visit another planet, discovers dense atmosphere and verifies hot surface.
Orbiting Solar Observatory, the first astronomical satellite, is launched.

1963 Maarten Schmidt discovers that quasars are objects with big redshifts and must lie very far away.

1965 Arno Penzias and Robert Wilson discover the cosmic background radiation—the faded glow of the Big Bang explosion in which the universe began.
Mariner 4 spacecraft is the first to fly past Mars. It discovers lots of craters.

1967 Jocelyn Bell-Burnell discovers pulsars, which are soon identified as neutron stars, one of the objects that massive stars can finish as.

1969 Apollo 11 astronauts Neil Armstrong and Edwin Aldrin make the first manned landing on the Moon.

1971 Mariner 9 is the first spacecraft to orbit another planet, Mars. Finds evidence of past water.

1973 Pioneer 10 makes first flyby of Jupiter and detects powerful radiation belts.

1974 Mariner 10 makes first two of three flybys of Mercury (third in 1975). Finds evidence of massive iron core and giant impacts.

1975 Venera 9 takes the first photos from the surface of Venus.

1976 Viking 1 and 2 land on Mars. They find no signs of life.

1977 Charles Kowal finds Chiron, the first comet discovered in the outer solar system.
Uranus's rings are discovered by astronomers aboard the Kuiper Airborne Observatory.

1978 James Christy discovers Charon, Pluto's moon.

1979 Voyager 1 and 2 spacecraft fly past Jupiter. Make detailed survey of planet and moons and find its rings.
Pioneer 11 makes first flyby of Saturn.

1980 Alan Guth proposes a period of extremely fast expansion in the early history of the universe, which he calls cosmic inflation.
Voyager 1 spacecraft makes first detailed study of Saturn system.
Very Large Array radio telescope starts working in New Mexico, USA.

1983 Infrared Astronomical Satellite (IRAS) completes the first full survey of the infrared sky.

1985/6 Comet Halley's return is met by a fleet of space probes.

1986 Voyager 2 makes first flyby of Uranus.

1987 Supernova 1987A appears in the Large Magellanic Cloud.

1989 Voyager 2 spacecraft makes first flyby of Neptune. Captures details of the planet and its moons—and its rings, suspected to exist since 1981.
Margaret Geller and John Huchra announce evidence for walls and voids in the distribution of galaxies in the universe.

1990 Hubble Space Telescope is launched.

1991 Galileo spacecraft on the way to Jupiter makes first asteroid flyby, passing 951 Gaspra.
Compton Gamma-Ray Observatory begins survey of universe at high-energy wavelengths, seeking cause of mysterious bursts of high energy.

1992 COBE satellite observatory confirms predictions of Big Bang theory.

1994 Comet Shoemaker-Levy 9 crashes into Jupiter.

1995 Discovery of first planet to orbit ordinary star other than the Sun, orbiting 51 Pegasi.
Galileo spacecraft sends probe into Jupiter's atmosphere, begins tour of Jupiter's moons.

1996 Black hole confirmed at center of Milky Way galaxy.

1997 Mars Pathfinder lands on Mars with Sojourner Rover.

1999 Chandra X-Ray Observatory is launched to look for X-rays from distant objects.

2000 The NEAR-Shoemaker spacecraft makes first landing on an asteroid, Eros.

2001 Mars Odyssey arrives at Mars and begins mapping the surface and atmosphere.

2004 The Mars Exploration Rovers, Spirit and Opportunity arrive at Mars.

2006 Pluto is officially demoted from a planet to a dwarf planet because, unlike the other eight planets, it has failed to clear its close area and its orbit of other objects.

2007 Evidence of water steam is found in the atmosphere of a planet near another star like our Sun. The planet, HD 189733b is roughly the size of Jupiter and sits in the constellation Vulpecula.

Glossary

A

active galaxy ~ A galaxy that emits a lot of radiation, perhaps from gas falling into a central black hole.

antenna ~ A device used to collect radio waves from the universe. Many antennas are made of an open mesh of aluminum or steel.

asteroid ~ A small rocky or metallic object orbiting the Sun, sometimes called a minor planet. Most asteroids orbit in the main asteroid belt between Mars and Jupiter.

astronomical unit (AU) ~ The average distance between Earth and the Sun, about 93 million miles (150 million km).

astronomy ~ The scientific study of the universe, including the solar system, stars, and galaxies.

atmosphere ~ A layer of gas surrounding a planet, moon, or star.

aurora ~ A colorful glow in Earth's upper atmosphere caused by the impact of high-energy particles from the Sun. Sometimes called the aurora borealis (or Northern Lights) and the aurora australis (or Southern Lights).

axis (as in rotation axis) ~ The imaginary line through the center of a planet, moon, star, or galaxy around which it rotates.

B

belt ~ A band of dark clouds on a gas-giant planet. Also, a region of the Solar System, such as the asteroid belt between Mars and Jupiter.

Big Bang ~ The extremely hot explosion that produced all the matter in the universe about 13.7 billion years ago, according to the best current theory of the universe's origin.

Big Crunch ~ One possible future fate for the universe. According to this theory, at some far distant time, gravity would stop the current expansion of the universe and then pull all matter back together into a single, highly compressed black hole.

billion ~ A thousand million. In numerals, it is written as 1,000,000,000.

binoculars ~ Two low-power telescopes yoked together. Binoculars make a good "first telescope" for beginners.

black hole ~ A massive, infinitely dense object whose gravity is so strong that no light or other radiation can escape from it. Black holes can be large or small, depending on how much mass they contain.

brightness ~ The intensity of light (or other radiation) emitted by an object. On Earth we see the object's apparent brightness, which depends on how bright it really is and how far away it lies. Astronomers also calculate an actual (or absolute) brightness based on how bright an object would be at a standard distance of 32.6 light-years.

brown dwarf ~ A star-like object not quite massive enough to start hydrogen fusion reactions and shine like a true star. A brown dwarf has less than about 10 percent of the Sun's mass.

C

canyon ~ A long channel in the surface of a planet or moon caused by geological faulting or by erosion.

capture ~ The process in which the gravity of a planet or moon attracts and holds onto another body. Astronomers think Neptune captured its moon Triton early in the planet's history.

celestial object ~ Any natural object that appears in our sky. Planets, moons, asteroids, comets, stars, and galaxies are all celestial objects.

celestial poles ~ The imaginary points among the northern and southern stars where Earth's rotation axis, if extended, would touch the sky.

cluster ~ A group of stars or galaxies that is held together by their gravity.

coma ~ The gaseous atmosphere that surrounds the icy nucleus of a comet. It forms as the comet's ices evaporate in the warmth of sunlight and can be thousands of miles wide.

comet ~ A small body made of ices and dust that orbits the Sun on an elongated path. When near the Sun, its ices grow warm, and the comet develops a large coma and streams off long tails of dust and gas.

command module ~ The main part of the Apollo spacecraft that carried the crew. It did not descend to the Moon's surface.

constellation ~ One of the 88 officially recognized patterns of stars that divide up the entire night sky. Most constellations that we use today came from the star myths and legends of ancient civilizations.

continent ~ The largest kind of landmass on Earth, and perhaps on other planets as well.

convection ~ A heat-driven process in which hot material moves up in an atmosphere, in a star, or even in a planet whose rocks are softened by heat. Water boiling in a pot moves by convection.

convective zone ~ A region in an atmosphere, a star, or a planet where convection occurs.

Copernican model ~ The model of the Solar System that places the Sun at the center with the planets in orbit around it. It is named for Nicolaus Copernicus (1472–1543), the Polish astronomer and churchman who described it in his book *On the Revolutions of the Celestial Spheres*.

core ~ The central part of an object. Earth's core contains nickel and iron. The Sun gets its energy from nuclear fusion reactions in its core. The Milky Way galaxy may have a black hole in its core.

corona ~ The high-temperature outer atmosphere of the Sun. It is visible from Earth only during a total solar eclipse.

cosmic background radiation ~ A very low-temperature radiation coming from all parts of the sky. It is the fading glow of the Big Bang explosion.

cosmos ~ The universe—which is to say everything, including you!

crater ~ A dish- or bowl-shaped depression in the surface of a planet, moon, or asteroid. Most are geological scars caused by the high-speed impact of a meteorite.

crescent Moon ~ The narrow curved phase of the Moon that appears between New Moon and First Quarter, or between Last Quarter and New Moon.

crust ~ The outer layer of a rocky planet, moon, or asteroid. We live on Earth's crust.

D

dark nebula ~ A cloud of interstellar dust that blocks the light of more distant stars. The Horsehead nebula in Orion is a dark nebula.

day (rotation time and solar day) ~ A planet or moon's sidereal day is its rotation time, the time it takes to make one full spin on its axis. Its solar day lasts from one noon to the next.

debris ~ The remains of something that has been destroyed or broken. The material thrown out by the impact of a meteorite is called debris. Debris can also refer to any material drifting through space.

deep space ~ A term generally used to include everything beyond the Solar System.

disk (of a galaxy) ~ The broad region of a spiral galaxy that surrounds the nucleus. The Sun lies in the disk of the Milky Way.

Doppler shift ~ A change in the color of light produced by a planet, star, or galaxy as it moves toward or away from us.

double star ~ Two stars linked by gravity and orbiting each other.

E

earthshine ~ Sunlight reflecting from Earth that gently lights the part of the Moon that is not in direct sunlight. Earthshine produces what some people call "the old Moon in the new Moon's arms." For someone standing on the Moon, earthshine is exactly like moonlight is for us on Earth.

eclipse ~ When one celestial body passes in front of another, dimming its light. Solar eclipses occur when the Moon lies between Earth and the Sun, and lunar eclipses occur when Earth lies between the Sun and Moon.

eclipsing binary ~ A double star that appears to dim and brighten regularly. When one star moves behind the other and is eclipsed, its light is cut off and the combined light we see dims. When the star comes out again, the combined light brightens.

electromagnetic spectrum ~ The full range of radiation in waves produced by celestial bodies. It runs from very long-wavelength radio waves through visible wavelengths to high-energy gamma rays.

ellipse ~ The oval path followed by celestial objects in orbit. Planets and comets travel through space in ellipses.

elliptical galaxy ~ A ball- or oval-shaped galaxy that lacks a disk with spiral arms and is made up of older reddish stars. Elliptical galaxies include the most massive galaxies as well as the least massive. For example, M87 is a giant elliptical galaxy, while the Sculptor dwarf is a tiny dwarf elliptical galaxy.

emission nebula ~ An interstellar cloud of gas (mainly hydrogen) that glows from the radiation of nearby hot stars. The North America nebula in Cygnus is a famous emission nebula.

entry probe ~ A robot spacecraft designed to enter the atmosphere of a planet or moon and collect information as it falls. Some entry probes survive to land on the surface, but most are destroyed by increasing heat and pressure, as the Galileo mission's entry probe was at Jupiter in 1995.

equator ~ The imaginary line on the globe of a planet, moon, or star that lies halfway between its two poles.

equinox ~ The moment when the Sun appears to stand directly above a planet's equator. This is the date when day and night are equally long at any point on the planet.

extraterrestrial ~ Anything that comes from outside planet Earth.

F

fireball ~ A meteor that is bright enough to cast a shadow.

First Quarter ~ The lunar phase when the Moon looks half-lit in the evening sky and has traveled the first quarter of its orbit around Earth.

flyby ~ A spacecraft visit to a planet or moon in which the probe does not land or orbit. This is usually the first stage of investigation, followed by an orbiter and then a lander craft.

Full Moon ~ The lunar phase when the Moon's disk is fully lit by the Sun.

G

galaxy ~ A collection of millions or billions of stars plus lots of gas and dust, held together by gravity. There are spiral, elliptical, and irregular types of galaxies.

Galilean moon ~ Any of the four largest moons of Jupiter: Io, Europa, Ganymede, or Callisto.

The name honors Galileo Galilei (1564–1642), an Italian astronomer who discovered the moons in 1610.

gamma rays ~ The electromagnetic radiation with the shortest waves and highest energy. Gamma rays come from the most violent astronomical processes, such as active galaxies, supernovas, and black holes.

gas giant ~ A large planet composed mainly of hydrogen. In the Solar System, Jupiter, Saturn, Uranus, and Neptune are gas-giant planets.

geyser ~ A jet of gas or hot liquid that erupts from the ground. Geysers on Earth send up streams of boiling water, but geysers on Neptune's moon Triton erupt warm nitrogen gas.

gibbous Moon ~ The partly rounded lunar phase that appears between First Quarter and Full Moon, and between Full Moon and Last Quarter.

globular star cluster ~ A spherical cluster bound by gravity that may contain up to a million stars. The Milky Way contains more than a hundred known globular clusters.

granule ~ A bubble of hot gas at the Sun's surface. The smallest granules are about 300 miles (500 km) in diameter.

gravitational lens ~ A galaxy (or other massive object) between Earth and a more distant object. The massive object's gravity bends the light from the distant object and creates distorted or multiple images of it.

gravity ~ The force that attracts one object to another. Gravity holds galaxies together and it holds planets, moons, and spacecraft in orbit. It also holds you on the ground.

greenhouse effect ~ The warming of a planet's surface by trapped solar heat. Sunlight passes through the atmosphere and heats the surface. But since the warmth can't easily escape through the atmosphere, the surface grows hotter.

H

hemisphere (northern and southern) ~ One half of a planetary globe. Earth is divided into the Northern and Southern hemispheres by the equator.

Hertzsprung-Russell diagram ~ A graph that shows the brightness and temperature for all stars.

horizon ~ The distant line where the ground and sky meet.

I

infrared radiation ~ Invisible radiation that travels in slightly longer waves than visible light does. We feel infrared radiation as heat when we are near a fire or radiator.

interferometry ~ A technique for linking two or more telescopes together so they work to give a much sharper picture of astronomical objects.

interstellar matter ~ Any material drifting through space between the stars. Some interstellar matter is dust, some is gas. Eventually much of this gas and dust will end up making new stars.

irregular galaxy ~ A small galaxy that has no obvious shape or structure, such as the Small Magellanic Cloud. Most irregular galaxies have lots of gas and dust.

K

Kuiper Belt ~ A region beyond the orbit of Neptune where multitudes of icy comets orbit the Sun.

L

lander ~ Any spacecraft that sets down on another planet or moon. Lander missions, which may carry rovers to explore areas away from the lander, usually follow flyby and orbiter missions.

Last Quarter ~ The lunar phase when the Moon looks half-lit in the morning sky and is about to begin the last quarter of its orbit around Earth.

lava ~ Molten rock that has erupted from the interior of a planet or moon through a volcano or a crack in the surface.

light-year ~ The distance that light travels in one year. One light-year equals about 6 trillion miles (10 trillion km).

Local Group ~ A cluster of about 35 galaxies to which the Milky Way galaxy belongs. Other Local Group members include the Large and Small Magellanic Clouds and the Andromeda (M31) and Pinwheel (M33) galaxies.

long-period comet ~ Any comet with an orbit lasting longer than 200 years.

lunar module ~ The part of the Apollo spacecraft that carried two astronauts to the Moon's surface.

M

magma ~ Molten rock that remains underground. If it erupts, it is called lava.

magnetic field ~ A region of space where an object exerts a detectable magnetic force.

magnetic poles ~ The two opposite points on a spinning planet, moon, or star where magnetic fields pass from the surface into space.

magnitude ~ The unit for measuring the brightness of celestial objects. Brighter objects are given smaller magnitude numbers than dimmer objects— a star of magnitude 1 is brighter than a star of magnitude 6, for example. Very bright objects are given negative magnitude numbers—the Sun shines at magnitude –26.8. Apparent magnitude describes how bright a star looks in Earth's night sky. Actual (or absolute) magnitude is the brightness the star would have if it was placed at a distance of 32.6 light-years from Earth.

main sequence ~ The strip on the Hertzsprung-Russell diagram that includes the Sun and most other stars. On the diagram, it runs from upper left (high temperature, high brightness) to lower right (low temperature, low brightness).

mantle ~ The layer inside a planet or moon that is below the crust, but above the core. It may be entirely rocky or a mixture of ice and rock.

mare (plural maria) ~ (Pronounced MAH-ray and MAH-ree-ah.) One of the smooth dark patches on the Moon. The maria are old lava flows. Early astronomers thought the patches were the beds of dried-up oceans, so they named them *mare,* the Latin word for "sea."

meteor ~ The bright streak of light produced by a bit of space debris burning up as it enters the atmosphere at high speed. Meteors are also called shooting stars.

meteorite ~ A piece of solid debris that lands on the surface of a planet or moon. It may be stony or metallic or a mixture of the two. Most are pieces broken off from asteroids.

meteoroid ~ Any small debris traveling through space. Larger meteoroids are usually pieces of shattered asteroids. Smaller meteoroids are mostly dust particles shed by comets.

meteor shower ~ A large number of meteors that appear to come from one small area of sky. A meteor shower happens when Earth runs into the debris thrown off by a comet. Meteor showers are named for the constellation from which they appear to come. The Perseids, for example, which are most active around August 12, appear to come from the constellation of Perseus and are debris from comet Swift-Tuttle.

Milky Way ~ The galaxy that contains our Solar System and all the stars you can see in the night sky with the naked eye. Also, the softly glowing band of light, made from faint stars, that arcs across the night sky.

moon ~ A natural object orbiting a planet. Also called a satellite.

multiple star ~ Three or more stars that are linked by gravity and orbit one another. The star nearest the Sun is the multiple system of Alpha Centauri, which has three stars: Alpha Centauri A and B, plus Proxima Centauri.

N

naked eye ~ What you can see with just your ordinary vision, without using a telescope or binoculars.

near-Earth asteroid ~ Any asteroid that comes close to Earth. Astronomers think that thousands of asteroids may have near-Earth orbits.

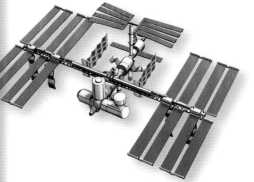

nebula ~ A cloud of interstellar gas and dust that may be bright or dark. Nebulas are the birthplaces of stars.

neutron star ~ The highly dense remnant of a star that has blown up in a supernova. Neutron stars are about the size of a city and spin rapidly. When we detect a neutron star, it is called a pulsar.

New Moon ~ The lunar phase when the Moon passes between Earth and the Sun and is not lit up in the sky. Many people also call a crescent Moon low in the evening sky a "new Moon," although by that time several days have passed since the true moment of New Moon.

night vision ~ Changes that occur in your eyes to help you see more in the dark. The changes take about 15 minutes, and will be cancelled if you glance at a bright light for even an instant.

nova ~ A white dwarf star in a double-star system that brightens suddenly by several magnitudes. The outburst happens when gas pulled from the companion star falls onto the white dwarf and explodes in a nuclear reaction.

nuclear reaction ~ A process in which a star fuses simple elements into more complex ones, releasing huge amounts of energy.

nucleus ~ The core of a comet or galaxy. In a comet, the nucleus is the lump of ice and dust that forms its central part. In a galaxy, the nucleus is the collection of stars and gas that lie at its center.

O

Oort Cloud ~ A swarm of trillions of comets believed to extend from the Kuiper Belt out roughly halfway to the nearest star, or about 2 light-years.

open star cluster ~ A group of several hundred to a thousand stars bound by gravity and moving through space together.

optical telescope ~ Any telescope that collects visible light.

orbit ~ The path of an object, such as Earth, as it moves around another object, such as the Sun. Also, to move around another object under the control of its gravity, as in "Mars orbits the Sun."

orbiter ~ A spacecraft that orbits a planet or moon. Generally, an orbiter is the second stage of exploration—flyby probes go first, then orbiters provide more detailed views, then landers explore the surface.

P

phase ~ The changes in the appearance of an object, such as the Moon, as we see more or less of it lit by the Sun.

photosphere ~ The visible surface of the Sun or any other star.

planet ~ A large object, such as Mars or Jupiter, that orbits a star, such as the Sun. Planets shine by reflecting sunlight— they do not produce their own light as a star does.

planetary nebula ~ A cloud of gas puffed off by a dying star. It has no relation to planets, but is called a planetary nebula because it appears pale and round in a telescope, roughly like the planet Uranus or Neptune.

planetesimal ~ A small body that formed in the early stages of the Solar System's evolution. Planetesimals were the building blocks of planets. They were mostly rock or mostly ice.

plate tectonics ~ A theory that explains changes in Earth's crust by the movement of about two dozen stiff crustal plates. These collide and separate slowly, driven by the motion of molten rock in Earth's mantle.

poles ~ Two opposite points on the surface of a spinning planet, moon, or star. The axis of the planet, moon, or star passes through the poles.

probe ~ An unmanned spacecraft sent from Earth to explore an object in the Solar System. Its data are sent back to Earth as radio signals.

prominence ~ On the Sun, a cloud of cooler gas lying above its surface. Prominences are held up by the Sun's powerful magnetic field.

proto-Sun ~ The body that formed at the center of the solar nebula and later became the Sun.

Ptolemaic model ~ The ancient world's vision of the universe, as described in a work by Greek astronomer Claudius Ptolemy around AD 150. In the Ptolemaic model, Earth lies in the center, while the Sun, planets, and stars all move around it. This model was accepted for nearly 1,500 years, but was replaced by the Copernican model.

P

pulsar ~ A neutron star that sends out beams of radio waves as it spins. These produce regularly timed pulses of radio signals in radio telescopes on Earth.

pulsating variable ~ A star that changes in brightness as it swells and shrinks every few days, weeks, or months.

Q

quasar ~ Short for quasi-stellar radio source, quasars are believed to be the active cores of very distant and very luminous galaxies. Probably powered by matter falling into black holes, quasars emit incredible amounts of energy.

R

radar astronomy ~ The study of solar system objects by bouncing radio waves off their surfaces with a radio telescope.

radiation ~ Energy that is carried through space as waves or particles. Also, the process that carries energy through space.

radiative zone ~ The middle zone of the Sun (and other stars) where energy travels by radiation. Below it is the core, above it is the convective zone.

radio energy ~ Invisible radiation that travels in longer waves than infrared and visible light do.

radio galaxy ~ A type of active galaxy that is a strong source of radio energy.

radio telescope ~ A telescope designed to collect radio waves.

ray ~ A bright streak of shattered rock that surrounds a fresh impact crater. The Moon's longest rays extend from the crater Tycho.

red giant ~ A large, cool star that is in a late stage of its life. Red giants are often pulsating variable stars.

red supergiant ~ The red giant stage in the life of a very large and massive star.

reflection nebula ~ A cloud of interstellar dust that shines by reflecting the light of nearby stars.

reflector ~ A telescope that collects light and forms an image using a mirror.

refractor ~ A telescope that collects light and forms an image using a lens.

relativity theory ~ A theory by Albert Einstein (1879–1955) that explains properties of the universe, such as mass, space, time, and motion, as they are seen by different observers moving relative to each other.

rings ~ Small particles that fill an orbit around a planet. Rings are believed to be the remains of broken-up moons.

rocky planet ~ One of the four small planets (Mercury, Venus, Earth, and Mars) that is made mostly of rock. Sometimes called a terrestrial planet.

rotation ~ The spin of a planet, moon, or star on its axis.

rover ~ An unmanned spacecraft that can move around on the surface of a planet or moon. Also, a four-wheeled "car" driven by Apollo astronauts on the Moon.

S

satellite ~ Any object that orbits a larger object. A moon is the natural satellite of a planet, while a spacecraft orbiting a planet is an artificial satellite.

satellite galaxy ~ A small galaxy that orbits a larger one. The Large Magellanic Cloud is a satellite of the Milky Way galaxy.

satellite observatory ~ A telescope placed in orbit around Earth or the Sun to make observations without the interference of Earth's atmosphere.

season ~ Regular changes in the weather on a planet, caused by the tilt of its rotation axis. As the planet moves around the Sun, this tilt means that the amount of solar energy falling on any particular region varies.

service module ~ The part of the Apollo spacecraft that provided the fuel, rocket engine, and living supplies for the command module and the astronauts.

Seyfert galaxy ~ A kind of active galaxy with unusual, often violent core activity. Discovered by American astronomer Carl Seyfert in 1942.

short-period comet ~ Any comet with an orbit lasting less than 200 years.

sidereal day ~ A planet's rotation time, that is, the time it takes to spin once on its axis. Earth's sidereal day lasts 23 hours 56 minutes.

skylore ~ Myths and legends about stars and constellations.

solar day ~ The time from one noon to the next. Earth's solar day lasts 24 hours.

solar flare ~ A powerful explosion from a small region on the Sun. Often an aurora will appear in Earth's night sky a day or two later when the particles ejected by the solar flare reach Earth.

solar nebula ~ The swirling cloud of gas and dust that condensed to form the Sun and planets.

Solar System ~ Originally, this referred only to our Sun and the planets, moons, comets, and asteroids that orbit it. The term is now also used more generally for other stars and their families of planets.

solar wind ~ A high-speed stream of charged particles flowing from the Sun in all directions.

solstice ~ The time in the year when a planet's pole tilts most directly toward (or away from) the Sun, and the Sun reaches its highest (or lowest) position in the sky at noon. The solstice marks the beginning of summer and winter.

space ~ Everything above Earth's atmosphere.

space shuttle ~ A reusable NASA spacecraft that carries people and cargo into orbit around Earth. NASA's space shuttle fleet consists of three craft: Discovery, Atlantis, and Endeavour.

space station ~ A large satellite that orbits Earth and can be occupied by people for long periods of time.

space telescope ~ In general, any telescope placed in space. The Hubble Space Telescope, named for American astronomer Edwin Hubble (1889–1953), was launched by NASA in 1990 and has made many discoveries, studying everything from lunar craters to the farthest galaxies.

spectrograph ~ An instrument that breaks the light from a celestial object into its component colors for analysis.

spectrum ~ The rainbow of color from an object such as the Sun or a star. It is produced by breaking the light into its component colors using a spectrograph.

spiral arm ~ The curving arm of a spiral galaxy. Spiral arms are rich in stars and gas. The Sun lies in a spiral arm of the Milky Way galaxy.

spiral galaxy ~ A large galaxy with several starry arms reaching out from a dense core, like a pinwheel. Some spiral galaxies have a roughly oblong-shaped center that resembles a broad bar. These are called barred spiral galaxies.

star ~ A large ball of hydrogen gas that produces light and heat by means of nuclear reactions in its core. The Sun is a star.

star cloud ~ A patch of Milky Way where the stars lie so close together that they look like a glowing cloud.

stellar association ~ A group of up to a hundred young stars that formed together and are now scattered across hundreds of light-years. The bright stars of the constellation Perseus belong to several associations.

supercluster ~ A loose collection of several clusters of galaxies, all bound by gravity. The Local Supercluster contains the Local Group, the Virgo cluster, and other galaxy clusters.

supernova ~ The explosion of a massive star in which it blows off its outer atmosphere, temporarily equalling an entire galaxy in brightness. Supernovas occur when a giant star runs out of fuel, or when a star collects too much gas from its companion star.

supernova remnant ~ An expanding cloud of gas that has been thrown into space by a supernova explosion.

T

telescope ~ Any instrument that collects light or other forms of radiation so astronomers can study celestial objects better.

tide ~ The distortion of one body by the gravity of another that is nearby. The Moon raises tides in Earth's oceans, and the Sun does also. When the solar and lunar tides combine, the effect is stronger and is called a spring tide.

tonne ~ A metric ton, equal to 1,000 kg or about 2,200 pounds.

trillion ~ A thousand billion, or a million million. In numerals, it is written as 1,000,000,000,000.

Trojan asteroids ~ Two groups of asteroids that orbit the Sun in the same orbit as Jupiter. One group travels ahead of Jupiter, the other behind.

U–Z

ultraviolet radiation ~ Invisible radiation that travels in slightly shorter waves than visible light does. The Sun's ultraviolet radiation causes sunburn.

universe ~ Everything that exists—all the galaxies, black holes, stars, nebulas, moons, planets, comets, asteroids, meteoroids, and dust scattered through space. This includes you!

variable star ~ Any star whose brightness appears to change over periods ranging from minutes to years. A variable can be an eclipsing binary or a pulsating variable.

visible light ~ Radiation that the human eye can see.

wavelength ~ The distance between two successive waves of energy passing through space.

white dwarf ~ A small, very hot star near the end of its life. It is essentially the leftover core of a red giant star.

X-rays ~ Invisible radiation that travels in shorter waves than ultraviolet and visible light do. X-rays are emitted by very hot objects and energetic events, such as exploding stars and colliding galaxies.

year ~ The time it takes a planet to orbit the Sun. Earth's year lasts 365.25 days.

zodiac ~ A band of 12 constellations that the Sun appears to move through during the year. The zodiac constellations are: Pisces the Fishes, Aries the Ram, Taurus the Bull, Gemini the Twins, Cancer the Crab, Leo the Lion, Virgo the Maiden, Libra the Scales, Scorpius the Scorpion, Sagittarius the Archer, Capricornus the Sea Goat, and Aquarius the Water Carrier.

zone ~ A band of bright clouds in the atmosphere of a gas-giant planet.

Index

A

Achernar 105, 107, 117
active galaxies 84, 85
Adams, John Couch 30, 58
Adonis 51
Aldebaran 104, 106
Aldrin, Buzz 24
Algol 70, 100
Alpha Centauri 10, 64, 65, 68, 103, 109, 117
Altair 99, 100, 101, 102, 104
Andromeda 94, 100
Andromeda galaxy (M31) 12, 13, 66, 70, 82, 83, 94, 98, 100, 119
Antares 109
Antennae galaxies 80
Apollo (asteroid) 51
Apollo program (US) 24, 42, 114
    Apollo 8: 24
    Apollo 11: 24
    Apollo 15: 42
    journey to Moon 24–25
Aquarius the Water Carrier 101, 104
Aquila the Eagle 99, 101, 102, 104
Arcturus 96, 97, 102, 108, 117
Arecibo Radio Telescope 20
Ariel 57, 112
Aristarchus 16
Armstrong, Neil 24
asteroids 8, 28, 30, 46, 50–51
    collision with Earth 50
    distance from Sun 28
    fact file 110, 111, 119
    gravity 51
    orbits 50
    Trojan asteroids 50, 51
astronomers, early 14
astronomical unit (AU) 8, 9, 110
astronomy 8
    ancient 14–15
    timeline 120–1
astrophysicists 18
Auriga the Charioteer 95, 100, 106
aurora 40
axis, of planet 29, 30, 40

B

barred spiral galaxies 80, 81, 108
Beehive cluster 97, 106
Beta Centauri 103, 109
Betelgeuse 64, 68, 71, 78, 91, 95, 106, 117, 119
Big Bang 12, 86, 87
Big Crunch 86, 87
Big Dipper 76, 93, 94, 96, 98
    shape over time 90
black holes 12, 18, 72, 73, 78, 84–85
    galactic 84
    gravity 84
    stellar 84
Blue Planet 38
Boötes the Herdsman 96, 97, 102, 108
Brahe, Tycho 16, 17, 120
Bunsen, Robert 18

C

calendars 14
Callisto 52, 53, 112
Caloris Basin 34
Cancer the Crab 97, 106
Canis Major, the Big Dog 95, 106, 109
Canis Minor, the Little Dog 95, 97, 106, 108
Canopus 105, 106, 107, 109, 117
Capella 95, 100, 106, 117
Carina the Keel 107, 109
Cartwheel galaxy 80
Cassini division 54, 55
Cassini spacecraft (orbiter) 9, 26, 27, 54
Cassiopeia the Queen 94, 96, 98, 100
Castor 95, 96, 106
cataclysmic variable 70
Centaurus A (NGC 5128), radio galaxy 84
Centaurus the Centaur 103, 107, 109
Cepheid variables 70, 120
Cepheus the King 94, 98, 100
Ceres 50, 119
Cetus the Sea Monster 94, 101, 104
Chandra X-Ray Observatory 22, 121
Charon 26, 60, 61, 113
Christy, James 60
Coalsack nebula 103
Columba the Dove 107
coma, of comet 62
Coma cluster (galaxies) 13, 22
comet Encke 62, 63
comet Hale-Bopp 62, 63
comet Halley 18, 62, 63, 120, 121
comet Hyakutake 8, 119
comet Lexell 119
comet Shoemaker-Levy 9: 52, 62, 121
comet Wild 2 27, 62
comets 8, 28, 30, 46, 62–63, 92, 121
    fact file 110, 111
    long-period 62
    orbits 28
    short-period 62
    structure 62, 63
    sungrazers 119
    see also individual names, "comet Encke," etc.
Compton Gamma-Ray Observatory 22, 23
Cone nebula 67
constellations 14, 88, 90–91
    apparent movement 92
    fact file 116–117
    Greek letters for stars 90
    see also individual names
Copernicus, Nicolaus 16, 120
corona, of Sun 32
Corona Australis, the Southern Crown 103
Corona Borealis, the Northern Crown 102
COROT space telescope 74
Cosmic Background Explorer (COBE) 86
cosmologists 12, 13
cosmos 12, 13
Crab nebula (M1) 72, 106
Crux, the Southern Cross 93, 103, 107, 109
Crux-Centaurus arm, of Milky Way 79
Cygnus arm, of Milky Way 79
Cygnus the Swan 98, 99, 102

D

Dactyl 50
d'Arrest, Heinrich 58
deep space 64–65, 86
Deimos 48, 112
Delphinus the Dolphin 102
Deneb 99, 100, 102
diamond-ring effect 44
Dog Star see Sirius
Doppler, Christian 19
Doppler shift 19, 74
double-star supernova 72
Draco the Dragon 96, 98
Draco dwarf galaxy 83
Dumbbell nebula (M27) 99
dwarf elliptical galaxies 80, 81, 82, 119

E

Eagle nebula 66, 67, 78, 102
Earth 30, 38–39
    atmosphere 39
    craters 46
    day/night 29, 40, 41
    distance from Sun 8, 9, 28
    equator 41
    erosion 38
    fact file 110
    life 38, 39
    magnetic field 40
    oceans 39
    precession 120
    seasons 40–41
    shape 16
    speed in orbit 8
    volcanoes 38
earthshine 44
eclipses
    lunar 14, 44, 88, 113
    solar 14, 32, 44, 113
eclipsing binary 70
Einstein, Albert 18, 120
Einstein Cross 84, 85
electromagnetic spectrum 22–23
ellipses 28
elliptical galaxies 12, 64, 80, 81, 82, 108
    dwarf 80, 81, 82, 119
Enceladus 55, 112
equinox 40
Eridanus the River 105, 107
Eros 50, 51
Eta Carinae 70, 107, 119
Europa 52, 53, 112

F

fireballs 46
Fomalhaut 101, 104
Fornax cluster, of galaxies 82
Fornax dwarf galaxy 82, 83
Fornax the Furnace 105

G

Gagarin, Yuri 24, 121
galactic black holes 84, 85
galaxies 10, 86, 118
    active 84, 85
    ancient 86
    Andromeda (M31) 12, 13, 66, 70, 82, 83, 94, 98, 100, 119
    barred spirals 80, 81, 108
    classification 81
    clusters 65, 80
    colliding 12, 80
    Coma cluster 13, 22
    Draco dwarf 83
    dwarf ellipticals 80, 81, 82, 119
    elliptical 12, 64, 80, 82, 108
    Fornax cluster 82
    Fornax dwarf 82, 83
    gravity 84
    groups 64, 65
    IC 1613: 82
    irregular 12, 64, 80, 81, 82
    Large Magellanic Cloud 83
        see also separate entry
    Leo I: 83
    Leo II: 83
    Local Group 82–83
        see also separate entry
    M32: 82
    M65: 97
    M66: 97
    M81: 98
    M83: 108
    M87: 12, 80, 81, 83, 108, 119
    NGC 147: 82
    NGC 185: 82
    NGC 205: 82, 83
    NGC 6822: 82

galaxies (continued)
    nomenclature 90
    Pegasus II: 119
    Pinwheel (M33) 13, 19, 82, 101
    Sculptor dwarf 82, 83
    Seyfert 84
    Small Magellanic Cloud 83
        see also separate entry
    Sombrero 13
    spiral 11, 12, 19, 64, 65, 80, 81, 82, 96
    Ursa Minor dwarf 83
    Virgo cluster 82, 83, 97, 108
    X-ray image 22
Galileo Galilei 16, 17, 52, 54, 78, 120
Galileo orbiter 27, 50, 52
Galle, Johann 58
Ganymede 52, 53, 60, 112, 119
Gaspra 50
Gemini the Twins 91, 95, 96, 106
Giotto space probe 62, 63
gravity 55, 66, 82, 86
    gas giants' effect on Pluto 31
    Jupiter's effect on asteroids 50
    Moon's effect on Earth tides 44
    Newton's theory 16
    between planets and star 28, 74
Great Barred Spiral (NGC 1365) 80, 81, 105
Great Dark Spot 58
Great Observatories 22
Great Red Spot 52, 53
Great Square of Pegasus 101, 104
Grus the Crane 105

H

Hale Telescope (Mt Palomar) 20, 121
Halley, Edmond 18, 63
Halley's comet 18, 62, 63, 120, 121
    nucleus 63
Hayabusa (space probe) 50, 51
Helix nebula 67
Hercules 96, 102
Hercules cluster (M13) 96
Herschel crater 55
Herschel, William 18, 30, 56, 120
Hertzsprung, Ejnar 120
Hertzsprung-Russell diagram 69
Hidalgo 51
Hipparchus 16, 120
Hoba meteorite 46, 119
Horsehead nebula 65, 66
Hourglass nebula 22
Hubble, Edwin 18, 19, 70, 81, 82, 121
Hubble Space Telescope (HST) 22, 56, 86, 121
Huygens probe 9, 54
Hyades 76, 95, 101, 106
Hydra the Sea Serpent 97, 108

I

Iapetus 55, 112
icy planetesimals 60
Ida 50
InfraRed Astronomy Satellite (IRAS) 79, 121
Infrared Space Observatory 13
interferometry 20
International Space Station 24, 25
Io 52, 112
    volcanoes 28
Irwin, James 42
Itokawa 51

J

Jewel Box 64-65, 109
Jupiter 30, 30–31, 52–53
    atmosphere 27
    distance from Sun 28
    fact file 110, 112
    gaseous 52
    gravity 50

Jupiter (continued)
Great Red Spot 52, 53
mass 30, 119
moons 16, 52, 112
rings 52, 54
winds 52

K

Keck Telescopes (Hawaii) 20–21
Kepler, Johannes 16, 120
Kepler space telescope 74
Kirchoff, Robert 18
Kuiper Belt 60, 62

L

Lagoon nebula (M8) 64, 99
Large Magellanic Cloud 11, 80, 82, 83, 105, 107
Leda 52, 112
Leo I/II galaxies 83
Leo the Lion 90, 97, 106, 108
Leonid meteor shower 119, 120
Lepus the Hare 95
Leverrier, Urbain 30, 58
Libra the Scales 102
light
bent 84, 85
speed of 10
light-years 10, 64
Little Dipper *see* Ursa Minor
Local Group 12, 13, 82–83, 101
Andromeda galaxy 82, 101
fact file 118
Milky Way 82, 101
Local Supercluster 12, 82
Luna 16 43
lunar eclipse *see* eclipses, lunar
Lunar Prospector 29, 42, 43
Lupus the Wolf 103
Lyra the Lyre 96, 100, 102

M

Maat Mons volcano 36
Magellan, Ferdinand 104
Magellan spacecraft 36, 37
Magellanic Clouds 11, 80, 82, 104,105,107
magnitude 16, 71, 92, 118
Mariner 10 34, 35
Mars 9, 24, 26, 30, 48–49
boulder Yogi 27
distance from Sun 28
fact file 110, 112
moons 8, 48, 112
Olympus Mons 48, 119
orbit 28
polar ice cap 48
red rocks 28
travel time 25
Valles Marineris 48, 119
Mars Pathfinder mission 26, 29, 48
Mars Polar Lander 49
massive-star supernova 72–73
Mathilde 50
Mercury 14, 30, 34–35
craters 34
distance from Sun 28
fact file 110
scarps 34
Messenger spacecraft 34
Messier, Charles 90
Meteor Crater, Arizona 46
meteor showers 47, 88, 113
Leonids 119, 120
meteor storm 46
meteorites 42, 46, 47, 119
iron 46
Mars, ALH 84001: 46
stony 46
stony-iron 46
meteoroids 46, 47
meteors 46

Milky Way 78–79, 88, 98, 99
black hole 78, 79
bulge 78, 79, 102
Milky Way (continued)
disk 78
dust clouds 79
galactic halo 78, 79
infrared image 79
Local Group member 13, 82
side views 77, 78
spiral galaxy 10, 11, 12, 78, 80
structure 80
using binoculars 103, 109
Mimas 55, 112
minor planets *see* asteroids
Mir space station 24, 25
Mira 70, 101, 104
Miranda 56, 57, 112
Monoceros the Unicorn 106
Moon 10, 42–43, 60
craters 8, 42
day/night 44
distance from Earth 9, 16
effect on tides 44
fact file 112
farside hemisphere 42
formation 42 3
gravity 42
lunar ice 42
manned missions 114
maria 42
nearside hemisphere 42, 43
orbit 44
phases 14, 44–45
rock samples 24, 25, 43
waxing/waning 45
Moon buggy 25
Moon goddess 15
Moon landings 24
moons (planetary satellites) 8, 16, 28, 30, 48, 52, 54, 55, 56, 58, 60, 112, 113

N

Naiad 58
National Aeronautics and Space Administration (NASA) 22
neap tides 44
Near-Earth Asteroid Rendezvous (NEAR) 50, 51
nebulas 10, 18, 64, 66–67, 68, 118
emission nebula 66
NGC 6543: 10
kinds of 90
planetary 66, 67, 69
reflection nebula 66
see also individual names
Neptune 26, 28, 30, 31, 58–59
distance from Sun 29
fact file 111, 113
Great Dark Spot 58
moon orbits 59
moons 58, 113
orbit 58
ring arcs 59
rings 54, 58 9
Scooter 58
storms 58
Nereid 59, 113
neutron stars 72, 73, 121
New General Catalogue 90
New Horizons mission 26, 60, 61
Newton, Isaac 16, 17, 18, 120
North America nebula 100
Northern Cross *see* Cygnus the Swan
Northern Lights 40
Nova Cygni 1975 71
novas 70, 71
see also supernovas

O

Oberon 57, 112
Olympus Mons 48, 119

Omega Centauri 76, 78, 79
Oort Cloud 60, 62, 121
Ophiuchus the Serpent Carrier 99
Opportunity (rover) 9
Orbiting Solar Observatory 22, 121
orbits 18
elliptical 28
Orion arm, of Milky Way 78, 79
Orion the Hunter 71, 90, 91, 95, 101, 104, 105, 106
Orion nebula (M42) 66, 78, 95

P

Pan 54, 112
parallax 10
Parsons, William 96
Pathfinder mission 26, 29, 48
Pavo the Peacock 105
Pegasus the Horse 94, 101
Great Square of Pegasus 101, 104
Pegasus II galaxy 119
Perseus arm, of Milky Way 78, 79
Perseus the Hero 76, 94, 100
Phobos 48, 112
Phoenix the Firebird 105
photography, time-lapse 88, 92
photosphere 32
Pinwheel galaxy (M33) 13, 19, 82, 101
Pioneer spacecraft 36
Pioneer 11: 54
Pisces the Fishes 101, 104
Piscis Austrinus, the Southern Fish 101, 104
planetary rings 8, 9, 28, 52, 54–55, 56, 58–59, 121
planetesimals 31
icy 60
planets 14, 18, 28, 64, 92
birth 30
distance from Sun 28–29
effect of gravity on orbits 16
features 111
gas giants 27, 30, 31, 52, 54, 56, 58
minor *see* asteroids
moons *see* moons (planetary satellites)
with naked eye 88
orbits 28–29
in other systems 28, 74–75
rings *see* planetary rings
rocky 30, 34, 36, 38, 48
rotation 29, 30
to scale 30–31
where to look 92
year 29
plate tectonics 38, 39
Pleiades 76–77, 78, 82, 88, 95, 104, 106
Plough *see* Big Dipper
Pluto 26, 30, 31, 60–61
day/month 61
distance from Sun 29
eccentric orbit 60
fact file 111, 119
icy planetesimal 60
moons *see* Charon
orbit 28
Polaris 93, 94, 96, 98, 100
Pole Star (northern) *see* Polaris
Pollux 95, 96, 106
probes *see* space probes
Procyon 95, 97, 106, 108, 117
prominences 32, 33
proto-planets 31
proto-Sun 30
Proxima Centauri 68, 119
Ptolemy, Claudius 16, 90, 120
pulsars 72, 73, 121
pulsating variables 70, 71
Pup 68

Q

quasars 20, 84, 121

R

radiation 22
radio telescopes 20, 78
Arecibo 20
Very Large Array 11, 21
Red Planet 48
Regulus 97, 106, 108
relativity theory 18, 120
Rigel 71, 90, 91, 95, 106, 107, 117
Ring nebula (M57) 100
Ringed Planet 54
rockets 24, 26
Saturn 5: 25
ROSAT space telescope 22, 65
Rosette nebula 10
rover craft 26, 27, 48

S

Sagittarius the Archer 99, 102, 103
Sagittarius arm, of Milky Way 78, 79
satellites (Soviet) 24
Saturn 27, 30, 31, 54–55
Cassini division 54
distance from Sun 28
fact file 111, 112
mass 54
moons 8, 54, 55, 112
radio image 21
ring system 8, 9, 28, 54–55
winds 54
Scooter 58
Scorpius the Scorpion 90, 99, 103, 109
Sculptor dwarf galaxy 82, 83
Serpens the Serpent 99, 102
Seven Sisters *see* Pleiades
Seyfert galaxy NGC 1275: 84
Shoemaker-Levy 9: 52, 62
shooting stars *see* meteors
sidereal day 29
Sirius 15, 68, 71, 95, 106, 109, 117, 119
Small Magellanic Cloud 11, 80, 81, 82, 83, 103, 105, 107
Sojourner (rover) 26, 27, 48
solar eclipse *see* eclipses, solar
solar flares 32
Solar and Heliospheric Observatory 33
solar nebula 30
Solar System 8, 9, 10, 28–29
birth 30–31
robot missions 114–115
solar systems, elsewhere 74–75
solar wind 40
solstice 40
Sombrero galaxy 13
Southern Lights 40
space debris 46–47
space flights
Apollo program (US) 24
first satellite 24
manned missions to Moon 114
space observatories 22
space probes 26, 36, 52, 114–115
airbag landings 26–27
entry probe 27
space shuttles 24
launch 25
space stations 24
International 24, 25
Mir (Russian) 24, 25
spacewalking 25
spectroscope 18–19
spectrum 18, 19
speed of light 10
Spica 97, 108
spiral galaxies 11, 12, 19, 64, 65, 80, 81, 82, 96
barred 80, 81, 108
Spirit (rover) 9
Spitzer Space Telescope 22, 23
SPOT satellite 39

spring tides 44
star atlas 88
star catalog 16, 120
star chart, Indian 91
star clusters 64, 76–77, 117
47 Tucanae 103
associations 76
galaxies 64
globular 64, 76, 77, 78, 119
M22: 11
kinds of 90
open 64, 76, 77, 78
star maps
how to use 92–93
key to symbols 92–93
northern hemisphere 94–101
autumn 101
spring 96–97
summer 98–99
winter 94–95
southern hemisphere 102–109
autumn 108–109
spring 104–105
summer 106–107
winter 102–103
star trails 92
Stardust probe 27, 62
stargazing 88–89
binoculars 88
compass directions 92
Earth's rotation 92
finding north/south 93
flashlight 88
latitude 93
light pollution 88
naked eye 88
naked-eye planets 88, 92
star atlas 88
telescopes 88
stars 10, 18, 32, 64, 65, 68–69
aging 66, 70
birth 66, 68, 72, 80, 86
brightest 117
brown dwarfs 68
distance 91
double-star systems 68, 70, 72, 74
Hertzsprung-Russell diagram 69

stars (continued)
life cycle 68–69
magnitude 16, 71, 92, 118
main sequence 68
movement 90
neutron 72, 73, 121
nuclear fusion 68
red giants 32, 64, 68, 69, 70, 72, 76, 77
red supergiants 64, 69, 72
triple-star system 68
variable 70–71, 117
white dwarfs 32, 68, 69, 70, 72, 76, 77
wobbling 74–75
stellar associations 76
stellar black holes 84
Stonehenge 15
Summer Triangle 99, 100
Sun 8, 10, 14, 28, 31, 32–33, 68
effect on Earth 40–41
fact file 110
nuclear fusion 32
part of open cluster 76
position in galaxy 78
sound waves 32
sunspot cycle 32
Sun god 15
sunlight 40
sunspots 32, 33, 120
cycle 32
supernovas 70, 72–73
double-star supernova 72
massive-star supernova 72–73
supernova 1987A: 72, 107
supernova remnant 72, 73

T

Tarantula nebula 109
Taurus the Bull 90, 91, 95, 101, 104, 106
telescopes 8, 13, 18, 88
first invention 16, 17
Galileo's 17
giant 64, 96
Hale Telescope 20, 121

telescopes (continued)
Herschel's 18, 20
Keck Telescopes 20–21
lenses 21
mirrors 20, 21
Newton's 17
optical 20
radio see radio telescopes
reflectors 17, 20, 21
refractors 20, 21
steady mount 88
Sun filters 32
tracking 20
Vatican Telescope 20
Very Large Telescope (Chile) 13
X-ray 22
tides, on Earth 44
Titan 27, 54, 55, 112
Titania 56, 57, 112
Tombaugh, Clyde 30, 60
Triangulum the Triangle 101
Trifid nebula (M20) 102
Triton 58, 59, 60, 113
Trojan asteroids 50, 51
Tucana the Toucan 105

U

Ulysses spacecraft 33
Umbriel 57, 112
universe 12, 70, 82, 86–87
Copernican model 16–17
dark matter 86
Earth-centered model 14–15, 16
expanding 18, 19, 86, 87
mass 86
structure 86
Uranus 18, 26, 30, 31, 56–57
distance from Sun 28
fact file 111, 112
moons 56, 112
rings 54, 56, 121
seasons 56
Ursa Major, the Big Bear 94, 96, 98
Ursa Minor, the Little Bear 94, 96, 98, 100
Ursa Minor dwarf galaxy 83

V

Valles Marineris 48, 119
variable stars 70–71, 117, 120
cataclysmic variable 70
eclipsing binary 70
pulsating variable 70, 71
Vatican Telescope 20
Vega 96, 99, 100, 102, 117
Venera landers (Soviet) 27, 36, 37
Venus 14, 30, 36–37
Alpha Regio hemisphere 36
Aphrodite Terra hemisphere 37
distance from Sun 28
fact file 110
greenhouse effect 36, 119
lava flows 36
Maat Mons volcano 36
phases 16
sulfuric acid clouds 36
Very Large Array radio telescope 11, 21, 121
Very Large Telescope (Chile) 13
Viking 2 lander 9
Virgo cluster, of galaxies 82, 83, 97, 108
Virgo the Maiden 97, 108
Voyager 1: 9, 27, 52, 54
Voyager 2: 27, 29, 54, 56, 57, 58, 59

W

web sites, useful 92
Whirlpool galaxy (M51) 80, 81, 96

Y

year, length 14, 29

Z

zodiac 14

Acknowledgments

Weldon Owen would like to thank the following people for their assistance in the production of this book: Helen Bateman, Mike Croll, Michael Hann, Veronica Hilton, John Mapps, Stuart McVicar, Cliff Watt, Kelly Booth, Andreas Schueller, Erin Zaunbrecher. Eclipse predictions by Fred Espenak, NASA's GSFC.

Photographic credits: AAO = Anglo-Australian Observatory, AF = Akira Fujii, ESO = European Southern Observatory, NOAO = National Optical Astronomy Observatories, ROE = Royal Observatory, Edinburgh, SPL = Science Photo Library, STScI = Space Telescope Science Institute, TPL = The Photo Library, Sydney, TS =Tom Stack & Associates
t=top, b=bottom, c=center, l=left, r=right
3, Oliver Strewe/Weldon Owen; 8t Superstock; c TPL/Rev.Ronald Royer/SPL;
b TPL/NASA/DVR/SPL; 9 TPL; 10bl AAO/ROE; br TPL/STScI/SPL; 11tr TPL/Kim Gordon/SPL; 12bl TPL/NASA/SPL; br The Observatories of the Carnegie Institute of Washington; 13tl NOAO; cr ESO; 14 The Bridgeman Art Library/British Museum, London; 15tl William Austral/MacQuitty/Camera Press; tr The Granger Collection; c TPL/Paul Thompson; 18c ASP/Mt Wilson and Las Campanas Observatories; 19tl Malin/IAC/RGO; tr TPL/Hale Observatories; 20tl Richard J. Wainscoat; tr Corbis/Roger Ressemeyer; 21bl TPL/David Nunuk/SPL; br TPL/NASA/SPL; 22l TPL/Max Planck Institute/SPL; r STScI/NASA 25 t TPL/NASA/SPL; cl Novosti, London; cr TPL/NASA/SPL; b TPL/NASA/SPL; 27 TPL/NASA/SPL; 32tr Tony & Daphne Hallas/Astrophoto; cl TPL/SPL; cr TPL/SPL 33 bl TPL/Geoff Tomkinson/SPL; 34 TS/JPL/TSADO; 36cl NASA; cr TPL/SPL/David P. Anderson/NASA; 38tl Auscape/Maurice & Katia Krafft; tr TPL/Ted Mead; 39c NASA; b TPL/SPL/NASA; 40c A; b NASA; 42cl TPL/SPL/BMDO/NRL/LLNL; cr NASA; 44tr TPL/Fred Espenak/SPL; cr TPL/John Sanford/SPL; br AF; 46tr TPL/John Sanford/SP; cr TPL/David Nunuk/SPL; 48cl TPL/USGS/SPL; cr TPL/NASA/SPL; 50t NASA; cr NASA; cl John Hopkins University Applied Physics Laboratory; b TPL/NASA/SPL; 52t TPL/NASA/SPL; cl NASA; cr NASA; b TPL/NASA/SPL;

56 NASA/JPL; 58 NASA; 60 TPL/STScI; 62 TPL/John Chumack; 63bl TPL/SPL; br TPL/European Space Agency/SPL; 64bl NASA/STScI; br NASA/STScI; 64-65 NASA/STScI; 65tc NASA/STScI; bl AAO/David Malin; br TPL/Fred Espenak/SPL; 66t TPL/ROE; c AAO/David Malin; b TPL/STScI/NASA; 67tr TPL/I.M House; c TPL/STScI/NASA; bl AAO/David Malin; br AAO/David Malin; 68br TPL/Lick Observatory; 70bl NASA/STScI; 71br AF; 72cl AAO/ROE; cr NASA/STScI; 76t AF; 78t NASA/STScI; tc NASA/STScI; c TPL/Tony Hallas/SPL; bc AF; b AAO/David Malin; 79bl TPL/NASA/SPL; br TPL/Fred Espenak/SPL; 80t AAO/David Malin; c NASA/STScI; 82 AAO/ROE; 83tl TPL/NASA/SPL; tc AAO/ROE; tr TPL/SPL; 84t NASA/Chandra X-Ray Observatory/MFSC; ct NASA/STScI; cb TPL/SPL/AAO/ David Malin; b TPL/Max Planck Institute/SPL; 86c NASA/STScI; 87c TPL/NASA/SPL; 88t David Miller; c Jerry Schad; bl Oliver Strewe/Weldon Owen; br AF; 90-91 The Granger Collection, New York; 91t Alan Dyer; c British Library, London; 92bl TPL/Pekka Parviainen/SPL; 94t AF; c AF; 95t A; c TPL/SPL; 96t TPL/Kim Gordon; c NOAO; 97 AF; 98cl TPL/Celestial Image Pict/SPL; cr Bill and Sally Fletcher; 99t TPL/SPL; cr TPL/Kim Gordon/SPL; 100tc TPL/Kim Gordon/SPL; bc TPL/Tony Hallas/SPL; 101t TS/Bill and Sally Fletcher; c TPL/John Sanford; 102cl TPL/SPL; cr TPL/SPL; 103c AAO/David Malin, cr TPL/Fred Espenak/SPL; 104 AF; 105t AAO/David Malin; c AF; 106t TPL/Tony Hallas/SPL; c TPL/J. Hester & P. Scowen/SPL; 107cl TPL/SPL; cr AAO/ROE; 108t AAO/David Malin; c TPL/NOAO/SPL; 109c TPL/SPL; t AAO/David Malin; 121 TPL/NASA/SPL.

Illustration credits: Wildlife Art Ltd.
18-25, 120cr, 121br, 121cr, 124bl, **Tom Connell**; 1(constellations), 14-17, 94-109, 116cr, 117tr, 120cl, 120bl, 120c, 123tr, 125bl **Luigi Gallante**; 68-73, 78-83, 117bl, 118cl, 121tr, **Lee Gibbons**; 1c, 3, 8-13, 26-65, 66-67 (digital manipulation), 74-78, 84-87, 90-93, 112cr, 113-115, 117br, 118tr, 119tr, 120r, 121tl, 121cl, 121c, 121bc, 122, 123b, 124br, 124tr, 125tr, **David A. Hardy**; all Projects & Amazing Facts, 119bl, 120tl, 12tr, **Sandra Pond**; 38bc, 38br, 39bl, 39br, 88-89, **Jonathon Potter**.